THE GRANULARITY OF
GROWTH

HOW TO IDENTIFY THE SOURCES OF GROWTH AND DRIVE ENDURING COMPANY PERFORMANCE

PATRICK VIGUERIE, SVEN SMIT, AND MEHRDAD BAGHAI

WILEY

John Wiley & Sons, Inc.

For general information on our other products and services or for technical support, please contact our Customer Care Department within the United States at (800) 762-2974, outside the United States at (317) 572-3993 or fax (317) 572-4002.

Wiley also publishes its books in a variety of electronic formats. Some content that appears in print may not be available in electronic books. For more information about Wiley products, visit our web site at www.wiley.com.

ISBN 978-0-470-27020-2

Printed in the United States of America

10 9 8 7 6 5

To

Susie, Shaun, Alex, and Sam Viguerie

Bibi and Veerle Smit and Jan Ferdel Smit, an ideas man

Roya and Naysan Baghai

Contents

Special thanks

We owe a great deal of gratitude to our partner Angus Dawson, who for all intents and purposes has been the fourth author of this book. He has been instrumental in the development and refinement of our thinking, especially on the architecture for growth. As McKinsey's growth service line leader in Asia, he has also ensured a more global orientation to our work. In addition, he has led the writing of *The Granularity of Growth: Asia*, a companion volume that explores the particular opportunities and challenges of growth in this most dynamic and fast-changing region.

We have also been lucky to have truly gifted team leaders who have superbly managed our many working teams. Carrie Thompson and Martijn Allessie were our first thought partners and the leaders who led our teams through the murkiest days of the research. Ralph Wiechers subsequently picked up the team leadership role and drove the advancement and refinement of our thinking brilliantly.

Quite simply, there would be no book without the four of them.

Acknowledgements

This book is the product of a collaboration among many people. Our clients, colleagues, friends, and families have all made major contributions to our thinking and we would like to recognize and thank them for their support.

First, and most important, we want to thank our clients who have encouraged us to develop our ideas. Achieving and sustaining growth in multi-billion-dollar corporations is a serious leadership and management challenge. Our ideas have benefited enormously from our work with clients who have taken on this challenge.

We thank those who, as reviewers, braved early drafts of this book to give us feedback and encouragement. In particular, we appreciate the frank and constructive voices of Charles Conn, Costas Markides, Anita McGahan, David Redhill, and Phil Rosenzweig in helping us to reshape our thinking.

We acknowledge the support of our partners who have supported our multi-year research effort. Beyond funding, our colleagues have contributed enormously to the ideas we put forward on their behalf and to their application in real corporate environments. Without their intellectual challenges and the ability to test our ideas, no book would have been possible. We would also like to note the leadership of Ian Davis, Lenny Mendonca, Scott Beardsley, Gordon Orr, and Peter Bisson, who have been advocates and sponsors of our work inside and outside McKinsey.

While scores of other partners have contributed to McKinsey's work on growth, we would like to mention specifically Claudio Feser, Will Garrett, Carlo Germano, Asmuss Komm, Robert Palter, Stefano Proverbio, Occo Roelofsen, and Stefano Visalli. We also acknowledge the original contributions made by our former partners Steve Coley and David White to our early thinking on growth.

Our teams conducted painstaking, detailed analysis and case research that not only formed the analytical basis for our idea development but also provided extraordinarily valuable documentation of case studies. At one time or another, all of the following made significant contributions to our work:

Kevin Cheng, Abhijeet Dwivedi, Olga Hallax, Giovanni Iachello, Robert Mulcare, Carlos Ocampo, Amee Patel, Sejal Patel, Mary Rachide, Gajan Retnasaba, Namit Sharma, Christian Sønderstrup, Teun van der Kamp, and Robert Weston. We are also indebted to the hard work of the entire team at McKinsey Knowledge Center in India: Megha Agarwal, Ankit Ahuja, Ripsy Bakshi, Vineeta Chopra, Chintan Dhebar, Sumit Dora, Himanshu Jain, Amit Jeffrey, Dipty Joshi, Vipin Karnani, Rohit Malhotra, Amit Marwah, Devesh Mittal, Bhawna Prakash, Mudit Sahai, Abhishek Sharma, Amit H. Sharma, Ashish Sharma, Sidhartha Sharma, Richa Suri, and Sakshi Trikha.

We also want to make a special acknowledgement to Ivan Hutnik and Jill Willder who, through many tireless hours, helped us to synthesize our thinking and express our thoughts more clearly and succinctly. They have been an invaluable source of intellectual challenge, and, indeed, have played a real role in the refinement and articulation of our ideas.

Pom Somkabcharti and Martin Liu of Cyan Books have worked with us during this entire research and writing effort. Pom in particular has been an enduring source of encouragement, emotional support, creative magic, and hands-on work to drive our publishing effort. Both have believed in our project from the outset and been tireless advocates for its success. We are truly indebted to them. We would also like to thank Pamela van Giessen and her team at Wiley for all their hard work to make our North American edition a success.

And, of course, none of this would have been possible without the professional assistance of Nichole Brien, Marije Kamerling, Vicki Lunceford, and Emma Peachey who helped us through the many iterations of the manuscript. We are thankful for their professionalism and constant support.

Finally, we note the influence that McKinsey legend Marvin Bower has had on our thinking. We remember him best by a remark he made at a partners' conference:

> "For the future, my great ambition—and I'm assured it's being carried out—is that we produce a firm that is going to continue indefinitely into the future. There aren't many organizations of that sort."

Preface

After a brief spell out of the management limelight, growth has once again taken center stage. Following the collapse of the internet bubble, it disappeared from view for a while as companies scrambled to rebalance their businesses by focusing on execution. But now it's back, and with a vengeance.

Of course, growth never really went away as a management concern. Without growth, companies can't hope to deliver the continuous increase in revenues and returns that shareholders are looking for. As CEOs are only too aware, such expectations aren't easy to meet and involve much more than simply steering the performance of the business. The markets take competence and effective delivery for granted, and discount them; what they want to see is performance beyond the current trajectory. But where will this growth come from?

The nature of the challenge

The purpose of this book is to answer that question by exploring the particular challenges faced by large corporations in driving and sustaining growth.

The first of these is a basic numbers problem: the bigger you are, the harder it is to drive the next quantum of growth. Take the median Fortune Global 500 company with roughly US$25 billion in revenue. To sustain growth at just the rate of global GDP growth (say, roughly 6.2 percent), it needs to find about US$1.6 billion in incremental revenue every year. As Procter & Gamble's CEO said recently, his company's growth challenge is to add a business the size of its entire UK operation or a brand the size of Tide *every single year!*[1]

The second challenge facing large companies has to do with longevity: the longer you've been in business and the larger you are, the more likely it is that your business is maturing. As it does so, it will almost inevitably encounter the problems of aging: innovation starts to slow and returns gradually decline. What's more, the sheer size of a mature organization can produce inertia. As the organization becomes ever more attuned to its operating metrics, it can easily lose touch with evolving customer needs, new competitors, and new business models.

Although this book focuses on growth in large companies, many of its insights apply to smaller companies too. Its central theme is a call for senior executives to develop a broad yet fine-grained vision about where their companies' growth will come from, and then to design strategies and organizations that reflect the texture of the markets in which they compete. We aim to provide a sound analytic and conceptual foundation, rich in practical insights, for CEOs and management teams wrestling with their growth strategy.

A definition of terms

But first, a question: what exactly do we mean by "growth"? Some business commentators define growth narrowly, focusing exclusively on organic growth or confining the discussion to new business building. In this book we define growth more broadly, as an increase in top-line revenues obtained either organically or through acquisition, either within or outside the core business.

We have chosen this broader definition for several reasons. As we will demonstrate, revenue and its development trajectory provide, over time, a good (though not perfect) indication of a company's role, influence, leadership, and standing in its markets. In the long term, sustained positive revenue growth is highly correlated with superior profits and value creation.[2] That said, the decision to grow is by no means a trivial undertaking, and it isn't the right course for every corporation. Growth poses multiple challenges, and whether a company should pursue it will depend largely on the economic and market conditions facing its businesses.

And what exactly do we mean by "granularity," and why have we made it the central theme of this book? Granularity is not a term traditionally used in business. It is, however, used frequently in scientific and engineering circles to refer to the size of the components within a larger system. A description of a system is more granular (or "fine-grained") if the description involves a larger number of components. For example, planet Earth could be described in terms of continents, countries, states and provinces, cities, towns, and villages, in order of increasing granularity.

Over time, we've become convinced that there is a problem with the broad-brush way that many companies describe their business opportunities. Large companies in particular suffer from the tyranny of the average view: "China is where the action is." "Pharmaceuticals is a high-growth industry." "Aging will generate increased demand for healthcare." The list goes on. Popular though these generalizations are, they are of very little help to executives looking for meaningful opportunities for growth.

In this book, we argue that real winning plays can emerge only from a much finer understanding of market segments, their needs, and the capabilities required to serve them well. To uncover pockets of opportunity, executives need to dig down to deeper levels of their businesses and organizations—something that many of them have been unwilling or unable to do. Companies may well have worked out how to manage their operations in minute detail, yet they still handle strategic choices at a high level. The challenge is to find a way to make these choices at a more granular level without losing focus or drowning in a sea of complexity.

Understanding growth better

Growth has long been a focus for McKinsey & Company. Ten years ago, we invested in a special research initiative to study the challenges of sustaining growth in large companies. The results of that study were published in a book, *The Alchemy of Growth,*[3] which revealed the importance of simultaneously managing the short-term performance imperative of the market and building a pipeline of growth initiatives for the future. The "three horizons" model used to illustrate this concept has since been widely adopted. It argues that companies that wish to sustain profitable growth should adopt a balanced set of initiatives across three horizons at once: extending and defending the profitability of the core business (horizon 1), building new engines of growth (horizon 2), and creating viable options for future growth (horizon 3).

In the years that have followed, we have advised many large companies on their growth efforts and launched another major research initiative. We have carried out extensive studies of growth in large companies by using proprietary databases to profile the performance of hundreds of the world's most important corporations, a process that has yielded valuable new insights.

First, our new methods for breaking growth down into its constituent elements produce a much richer description of the growth opportunities facing a company and, hence, provide an even stronger basis for formulating a growth direction. This has enabled us to enhance our three horizons model, which now incorporates a far more robust and granular understanding of the sources of revenue growth.

Second, over the past decade we have observed the spectacular growth of specially designed growth companies. Private-equity firms and special-purpose acquisition companies now own more than 6 percent of the entire global economy. Their success can't be explained solely by their strategies; their efficacy is in no small measure due to their unique organization design and management processes, or what we call "architecture."

Third, the internet boom and bust, as well as the accelerating growth of China and India, have acted as a reminder that growth leaders in supply-constrained markets may face unfamiliar challenges. With this new world come new and very different growth opportunities.[4]

The Granularity of Growth provides a rigorous analytical foundation for understanding growth and an architecture for managing it. While complementary to *The Alchemy of Growth,* it is, nonetheless, a very different book, written in a different context to address a different set of challenges.

How this book is organized

In the Introduction, we make the case for growth. We look at large companies' track record in driving top-line growth and generating shareholder returns over two economic cycles and show that growth is a superior predictor of future shareholder returns and increases a company's chance of survival by a factor of five.

The main body of the book is written in three parts, each devoted to a big step on the path to growth: first deciding on your *ambition* for growth, then choosing a *direction* for growth, and, finally, designing an *architecture* for growth. Together these three parts describe the journey you make in defining your growth strategy and creating the organization you need to carry it out. Let's take a quick look at the themes covered in each part.

Part I: Your growth ambition

Our research revealed a striking fact: nearly 80 percent of the growth differences between large companies have to do with choices about *where to compete*, that is, which market segments to participate in and how much M&A activity to pursue. Just as markets are granular, so too are pockets of potential growth—which means you need to make your "where to compete" choices at a granular level.

To help with these choices, you can benchmark your growth performance against that of your peers using a methodology that is as robust as those used to analyze and compare costs and execution. It involves breaking down your revenue growth performance into three elements: portfolio momentum, inorganic activity, and organic share gain.

Part II: Your growth direction

Shaping the growth trajectory of a large company is a long-term proposition. It's not about pushing and shoving the front line to reach the next level of performance, but about giving your units the resources they need to deliver growth—or, alternatively, deciding to look for that growth elsewhere. Instead of beating up people for missing a target, not running fast enough, or not working hard enough, you either scale up to provide a unit with more talent, capital, and resources, or scale down to release it from a battle it can never win.

Companies seeking to scale up should be aware of the opportunities for inorganic growth. Another surprising insight generated by our research was the magnitude of the contribution made by M&A to top-line growth: it accounts for 30 percent of the revenue growth at an average large company.

To help you make the transition from a granular analysis to an overall growth direction, we offer a new tool, the growth map, that provides a rigorous basis for deciding on growth initiatives in the short, medium, and long term.

Part III: Your growth architecture

Most organizations would probably describe themselves as designed to drive the performance of their current businesses; fewer would claim that they are also designed for growth. To grow successfully, you need not only a clear direction but also a design that enables you to make granular choices at scale. At the lowest level, your organization needs to reflect the texture of the market and the set of opportunities it presents. At the highest level, your organization needs to take advantage of its scale in a way that reinforces both the strategies of the individual units and the direction of the overall portfolio.

We believe that the leaders of large institutions need to avoid taking an averaged view of all their businesses; instead, they should manage them with greater focus at a more detailed level, while continuing to take advantage of their scale. The approach we describe will help you do just that without drowning in a sea of reports or getting lost in a fog of complexity.

■ ■ ■

We hope this book will reveal why growth is so important, what enables certain companies to grow so spectacularly, how they are able to take both a broad and a granular view of their markets, why they are careful to ensure that their growth comes from multiple sources, and how they choose the markets in which they compete.

This book is primarily about corporate strategy and growth in large companies. It deals less with strategy at the business-unit level.[5] We are trying to shape your thinking about the three choices we've mentioned: deciding what growth ambition would be appropriate for your corporation, setting your growth direction, and developing the architecture to enable you to manage growth effectively.

By the end of the book we should have gone some way toward demystifying the secrets of growth and revealing what it is that makes a few companies so very successful at achieving it. We hope this will help you make your own personal choices on whether and how to lead the growth journey.

NOTES

[1] A. G. Lafley, Procter & Gamble 2004 annual report.

[2] The metric we use in this book for shareholder value creation is total return to shareholders (TRS), which reflects both movements in stock prices and value created through the distribution of dividends.

[3] M. Baghai, S. Coley, and D. White, *The Alchemy of Growth* (Orion Business, London, 1999).

[4] We explore some of these challenges in depth in the companion volume to this book, *The Granularity of Growth: Asia* (Cyan, London, 2007).

[5] We don't offer ideas about how to introduce new products or cross-sell to existing customers. Nor do we discuss the kinds of advantage that a particular business should or shouldn't seek to exploit. That territory is extensively mapped by other management books.

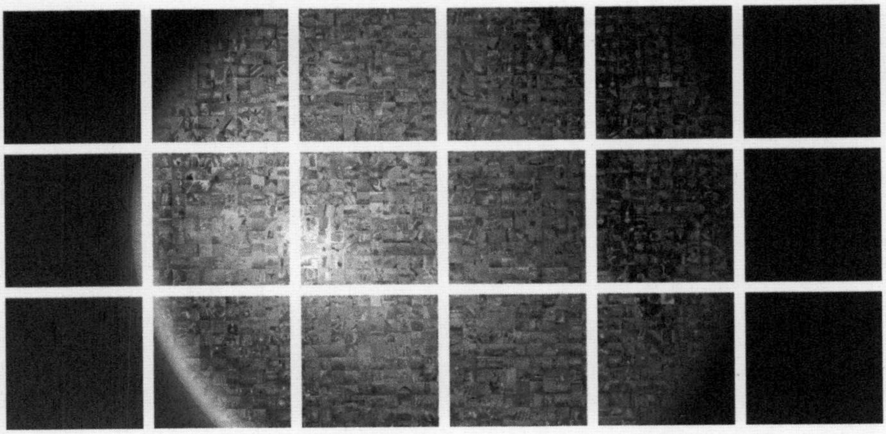

Introduction: Grow or go

"Should I stay or should I go?"
The Clash, 1982

- Over the long term, growth really matters to performance . . .

- . . . and to survival too: we found that companies delivering growth rates below GDP during one economic cycle were five times more likely to disappear before the next

- It *is* possible for a large company to sustain above-average growth and value creation over two economic cycles

- Many companies that were challenged during one cycle managed to recover during the next

- The most difficult thing is to sustain performance in the absence of growth

W E BEGIN BY focusing on a simple question: can the largest of large companies as defined by revenue hope to sustain growth over significant periods of time?

Let's start our look at growth by going back in time and identifying the 100 largest companies in the United States in 1984.[1] We chose to look at the United States because it offers the richest stock of data on some of the biggest companies in the world, and the eighties because they are recent enough to yield meaningful performance data, yet distant enough to give us a view that spans two distinct business cycles: 1984–94 and 1994–2004. We prefer to use business cycles rather than decades or arbitrary periods of time; although different industries face different circumstances, we can be sure that the companies we're analyzing are at least on a similar footing in terms of broad economic context if we observe them through two cycles. We'll examine two indicators of performance over this period: revenue growth and shareholder value creation, as measured by total return to shareholders (TRS).

The first step is to look at company performance during the first economic cycle. We grouped our sample by value creation and by revenue growth in the two-by-two matrix illustrated in Figure I.1, using the S&P 500 market index and US GDP as the breakpoints.

Using the market index to split the sample by value creation makes it easy to answer the practical question, "Would a shareholder rather have invested in this company or in an index fund?"

Using GDP to split the sample by revenue growth provides a point of reference to the wider economy. By measuring whether a company is gaining or losing in relation to the economy as a whole, we can understand the nature of the challenges it may face: for example, a company that grows more slowly than GDP may face a price/cost squeeze.

A company's performance during the first cycle from 1984 to 1994 determines where it fits in the matrix. The upper-right quadrant contains those companies that have outperformed in both revenue growth and TRS (the "growth giants"). The lower-right quadrant contains those companies that have lagged in revenue growth but outperformed in value creation (the "performers"). The lower-left quadrant contains those companies that have lagged in both dimensions (the "challenged"). Finally, the upper-left quadrant contains those companies that have outperformed in revenue growth but lagged in value creation (the "unrewarded").

I.1 The growth performance matrix
Share of sample by category based on 1984–94 performance

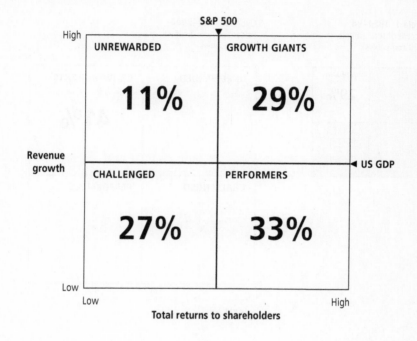

Let's look at each of these quadrants in turn.

Perseverance among the growth giants
At the end of the first business cycle in 1994, 29 percent of the companies in our sample qualified as growth giants. They outperformed both the economy and the stock market in terms of revenue and value creation. The median growth giant delivered shareholder returns with a compound annual growth rate (CAGR) of about 18 percent and revenue growth with a CAGR of 9 percent. Any investor would naturally be thrilled with this performance.

Even more impressively, if we jump to 2004 and the end of the second economic cycle, two in five of these companies (41 percent, to be precise) persisted in their performance (Figure I.2). That is, they outperformed the economy and the market index in both revenue growth and value creation for another complete cycle.

I.2 The growth giants
How they fared in the second cycle

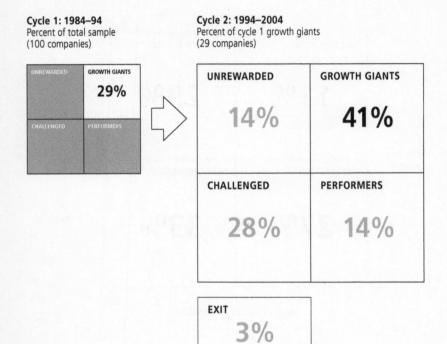

Cycle 1: 1984–94
Percent of total sample
(100 companies)

Cycle 2: 1994–2004
Percent of cycle 1 growth giants
(29 companies)

Decline among the performers
Our next group of companies, the performers, managed to reward their shareholders at growth-giant levels for the first economic cycle even though their revenue base grew more slowly than the wider economy. However, their fortunes took a turn for the worse during the second cycle (Figure I.3). Only 9 percent or three companies out of the 33—Southern Company, Consolidated Edison, and ITT—managed to sustain the combination of continued value creation with low revenue growth through to 2004.

So what happened to the rest? Just over a third exited, most through acquisition, their boards having decided that being bought was a better deal for shareholders than continuing to operate independently. This meant that the exit rate of the performers was *12 times* that of the growth giants. Nine companies (27 percent) continued to grow slowly and were unable to continue reward-ing their shareholders in line with the broader market; they became

1.3 The performers
How they fared in the second cycle

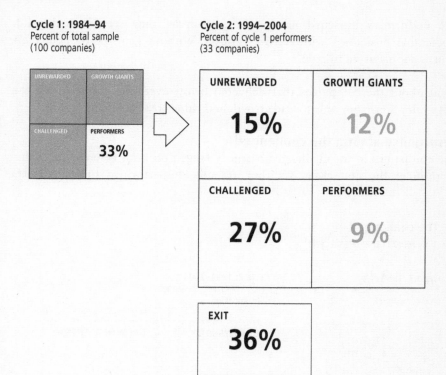

Cycle 1: 1984–94
Percent of total sample
(100 companies)

Cycle 2: 1994–2004
Percent of cycle 1 performers
(33 companies)

UNREWARDED	GROWTH GIANTS
15%	12%
CHALLENGED	PERFORMERS
27%	9%

EXIT
36%

Numbers do not always add up to 100% because of rounding

"challenged" (with below-average growth and below-average shareholder value) in the next economic cycle.

Another 27 percent managed to boost their revenue growth rates. Among these, four companies (Burlington Northern Santa Fe, Exxon Mobil, ConocoPhillips, and Chevron) managed to become growth giants in the next cycle by consolidating their position through M&A. The remaining five companies found revenue growth but failed to deliver commensurate shareholder value during the cycle, and joined the "unrewarded" category.

What this means is that being a performer is a tough act to sustain over the long term. Although a large company can drive value for a time by enhancing its operating performance, it will eventually hit a wall if it fails to deliver revenue growth, and will either see its returns decline or find itself an acquisition target.

The performers intrigued us. In the first cycle, they seemed rock-solid: predictable businesses with outsize returns. Without growth, though, their returns soon started to fade.

What about the companies that delivered below-average returns during the first cycle? Were they able to find growth and value creation during the next?

Resurgence among the challenged

The companies in the challenged category lagged on both revenue and value creation in the first cycle, yet they actually outperformed the performers

I.4 The challenged
How they fared in the second cycle

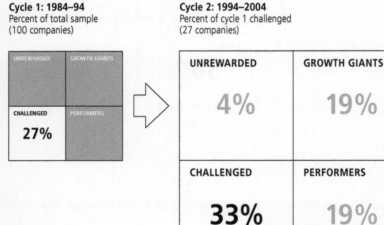

Cycle 1: 1984–94
Percent of total sample
(100 companies)

UNREWARDED	GROWTH GIANTS
CHALLENGED 27%	PERFORMERS

Cycle 2: 1994–2004
Percent of cycle 1 challenged
(27 companies)

UNREWARDED 4%	GROWTH GIANTS 19%
CHALLENGED **33%**	PERFORMERS 19%

EXIT 26%

Numbers do not always add up to 100% because of rounding

during the second cycle (Figure I.4). Thirty-eight percent of the challenged recovered and generated above-average shareholder returns in the second cycle, compared with only 21 percent of performers. This suggests that a performance crisis may be a better catalyst for growth than the complacency induced by achieving acceptable returns despite slow growth. As the Dutch saying goes, "Under pressure, everything becomes fluid."

Uncertainty among the unrewarded

Now for the fourth group. The unrewarded companies grew faster than the US economy, but underperformed in terms of shareholder returns. More than a third of them (four companies) went on to achieve superior TRS performance during the second cycle (Figure I.5). Another third slipped into the challenged category; 18 percent were acquired; and, notably, just

I.5 The unrewarded
How they fared in the second cycle

Cycle 1: 1984–94
Percent of total sample
(100 companies)

Cycle 2: 1994–2004
Percent of cycle 1 unrewarded
(11 companies)

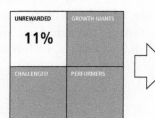

UNREWARDED	GROWTH GIANTS
9%	**18%**

CHALLENGED	PERFORMERS
36%	**18%**

EXIT
18%

Numbers do not always add up to 100% because of rounding

9 percent remained in the unrewarded category. Although it's hard to draw strong conclusions from only 11 performance trajectories, they do indicate that unrewarded companies tend not to stay that way but get shifted into other groups over time.

Growth, survival, and value creation

What broad insights can we draw from this look at long-term performance?

First, growth really does matter, and not just to a company's performance, but to its very survival. Strikingly, a company that grew more slowly than GDP for the first economic cycle was *five times more likely* to disappear as a going concern before the end of the next cycle than a company that expanded more rapidly. This is particularly interesting in light of the fact that the survival rates of high-TRS and low-TRS companies are quite similar. Clearly, growth and not TRS is the differentiator here.

Moreover, companies with above-average revenue growth during the first cycle, whether or not it was accompanied by superior value creation, were more likely to exhibit above-average TRS during the next cycle. Two-fifths of the first-cycle growth giants sustained their performance in both revenue and value creation through the second cycle, and more than half (55 percent) continued creating value at a high rate. Interestingly, both the challenged and unrewarded companies had a better chance of surviving and achieving high TRS during the second cycle than the performers did. It was the performers that faced the worst odds (Figure I.6).

I.6 Performers slump in second cycle

Share of companies that outperformed market in TRS in cycle 2 (1994–2004), percent

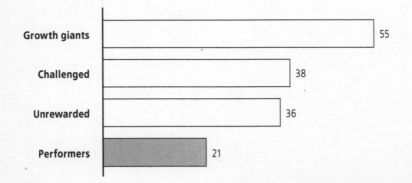

Growth giants	55
Challenged	38
Unrewarded	36
Performers	21

Why is this the case? Although surprising at first sight, the plight of the performers stands to reason when you think about it: during the first cycle many of these companies competed in industry sectors that were growing slowly (or "lacking a tailwind," as we put it). These sectors consolidated during the next cycle.

Most of the performers that were not acquired continue to struggle with low revenue and earnings growth. Because of the nature of the segments in which they participate, they aren't in a position to capture enough gains solely by reducing costs or restructuring to compensate for the lack of top-line growth. Growth could come only if they were to embark on an acquisition program or change their business mix. In terms of our two-by-two matrix, there was a big shift to the left in the second cycle as expectations for future value creation in the form of TRS declined.

You might ask if this phenomenon is confined to the United States. The answer is no; we see similar patterns elsewhere.

In Europe, too, sustained revenue growth is the key to long-term value creation. Companies that are growing slowly have underperformed the market over a ten- to twenty-year timeframe. Slow growers are less likely to be acquired, partly because most of the region's M&A has taken place in the sectors where the action is, such as pharmaceuticals. Another reason, perhaps, is that the consolidation of companies across individual countries has yet to happen in full force. Over time, we can expect it to increase, particularly given the fragmentation of sectors by country. As private equity becomes ever more important it could accelerate this trend, especially at the point of exit.

In Asia, performance and growth are linked in much the same way. Where we can obtain reliable data extending back over two business cycles, we have performed the same analysis on the largest companies in major markets such as Japan, Australia, Taiwan, India, Malaysia, Indonesia, Hong Kong, and Korea. In nearly all of them, as in the US, very few companies manage to outperform the market across two business cycles without growing faster than GDP. The main difference, with the exception of Australia and, increasingly, Japan, is that Asia's M&A markets are less developed so that the penalty for underperformance is less likely to be exit via acquisition.

Time to go?

Companies that don't increase their top line eventually hit a "TRS wall" and often become targets for acquisition. Even the largest companies may well find themselves grappling with fundamental "grow or go" decisions.

This is not to say that companies should make staying independent their overriding objective. The value of selling is often underestimated. Exit through acquisition can be the right strategy, and often creates great value for shareholders. Our analysis of challenged companies shows that of those that chose to sell, the ones that did best were those that delivered shareholder returns comparable to those of performers and growth giants, and sold out early rather than late.

Among US "local exchange" telecom operators in the period after divestiture,[2] two of the companies that chose to sell, namely Ameritech and BellSouth, have outperformed the companies that survived to see 2007, namely the "new AT&T" (the renamed SBC Communications) and Verizon (which began life as Bell Atlantic). It's interesting to note that Ameritech, one of the first to sell, did best of all for its shareholders by selling in 1999, taking advantage of market timing as investor enthusiasm for all things telecom pushed valuations to unprecedented heights. The overall picture is somewhat more complex than it may appear, however. The new AT&T has enjoyed an exceptional 34 percent TRS in the past year and has assembled a set of assets through M&A over the years that give it a broad leadership position in the US telecom industry.

Selling may or may not be the right thing to do, but companies would be well advised to bear it in mind as a viable option for at least part of their portfolio. After studying the relationship between growth and value creation in great detail, we have come to the conclusion that companies face a stark choice: they must either grow or go.

- Our analysis of the sources of TRS highlights revenue growth, operating margins, distributions of cash to shareholders, and changes in expectations of returns as the key determinants of long-term value creation.

- There are **two ways to grow**: fast growth with stable or improving operating margins, or moderate growth with improving operating margins.

- In the absence of growth, there are **two ways to go and still create value**: by returning significant amounts of capital or exiting through acquisition.

- Over the long term, any other course of action is likely to produce below-average returns.

For those of you who would like to understand the case for growth in greater depth, we have included two appendices that explain the analysis in more detail.

Finally, we should note that growth does not necessarily come at the expense of increased risk. High-growth companies don't exhibit higher beta or volatility than low-growth companies.[3] Indeed, in a dynamic global marketplace, standing still is likely to be the riskier strategy in the long term.

NOTES

[1] The sample was derived from the top 100 companies by market capitalization and the top 100 by revenue. Seventy-five of the companies in our sample belonged to both lists; the rest came in roughly equal numbers from each one.

[2] On 1 January 1984, AT&T's local operations were split into seven independent regional Bell operating companies or "baby Bells": v, Bell Atlantic, BellSouth, NYNEX, Pacific Telesis, Southwestern Bell, and US West.

[3] To shed some light on this question, we analyzed the relationship between growth and market risk. We calculated the average beta (the sensitivity of a single stock or entire portfolio to broad market movements) for the four categories of companies in our database, as well as the share-price volatility. We found no significant difference overall between lower- and higher-growth companies in terms of beta or volatility.

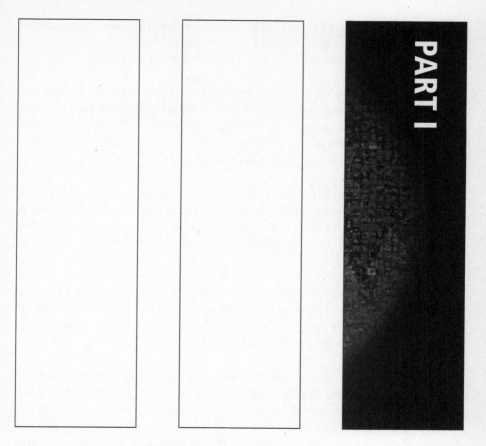

PART I

Your growth ambition

THE "GROW OR GO" DYNAMICS we have just outlined represent an unforgiving environment for large companies. The odds of sustaining performance and growth over the long term are indeed long ones.

The first part of this book addresses the fundamental questions you face as a leader when you are defining your company's ambition for long-term growth: Should we concentrate on growing the businesses we have? Build an institution that is capable of driving growth well into the future? Consolidate our industry? Diversify? Sell our company in the next few years?

Your answer will naturally shape your company's agenda in many ways: your investment priorities and spending levels; your target markets; your decision to diversify or focus your business portfolio; your hiring; your organization structure; your use of leadership time; and your use of M&A, to name just a few.

Growth is a tricky topic, so it's important that your company should have a view on the best way to think about it. We all know intuitively that growth is good. It creates healthy companies, opens up opportunities, excites talent, and rewards shareholders. But do we know how to achieve it?

Previous attempts to explore how companies can grow have depended largely on anecdotal evidence. Pankaj Ghemawat, a professor of strategy at IESE and Harvard Business School, notes that "It's hard to assess the empirical validity of growth books because none of them focus on presenting data."[1] We have done our utmost to buck this trend; indeed, if anything, you may conclude that we may have provided too much evidence to support our claims. But we have tried to organize the book in such a way that readers who want a full account of our analysis can find it, while others who prefer to take in our main conclusions quickly can do so too.

What we will show in this book is that performance is *granular,* by which we mean **driven by growth in the sub-segments and categories of industries** in which a company competes as well as by the **revenues that it acquires through M&A activity.** We will also show that these drivers are generally **much more important than market-share gains** in determining how fast you grow.

This seemingly counterintuitive finding has important implications. A typical management team needs to change the way it thinks about company resources, not least its own time. It needs to pay more attention to which businesses the company is in, and particularly the sub-segments in which it competes.

There are four chapters in this part of the book, each intended to guide you as you think about your company's growth ambition.

- In chapter 1, "A granular world," we show that when you are searching for growth, analyses of industries and megatrends are usually pitched at too high a level to offer you any help. In order to identify growth opportunities, you need to get well below the industry level. We define five levels of granularity and show where the most valuable insights are to be found.

- In chapter 2, "Understanding your company's performance," we show that choices about where to compete account for nearly 80 percent of the differences in top-line growth among companies. We introduce a methodology for breaking down the sources of revenue growth into the three core components of portfolio momentum, market-share gain, and M&A—what we call the growth "cylinders." We then examine how companies perform in terms of each one.

- In chapter 3, "Firing on multiple cylinders," we demonstrate that most companies need to fire on more than one of these growth cylinders over time if they are to achieve excellent growth performance. We look at the relationships between growth cylinders, revenues, and shareholder returns, and compare the impact of different growth cylinder strategies at several companies. This enables us to formulate guidelines for defining exceptional, great, good, and poor growth performance.

- In chapter 4, "A granular company," we combine the concept of firing on multiple cylinders with the idea of granularity to create a powerful tool, the growth MRI. Its purpose is to enable you to analyze your growth performance at the right level of detail.

NOTE

[1] P. Ghemawat in "The growth boosters," *Harvard Business Review,* July 2004, pp. 35–40, a review of three books: Chris Zook's *Beyond the Core,* Ram Charan's *Profitable Growth is Everyone's Business,* and Adrian Slywotzky and Richard Wise's *How to Grow When Markets Don't.*

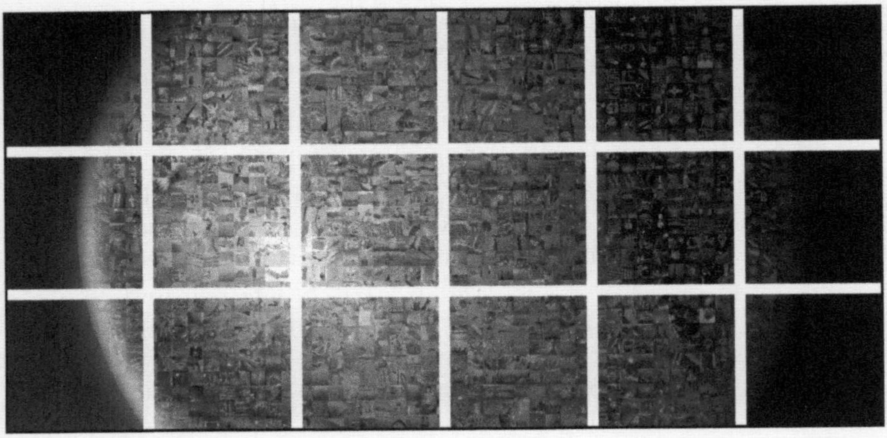

1

A granular world

"It's a small world after all"
Song at a Disneyland ride

- Companies should base their growth strategies on granular views of their markets

- There's no such thing as a growth industry; most so-called growth industries have mature segments, and most mature industries have granular growth pockets

- Once you adopt a granular perspective, "megatrends" such as aging vary enormously from market to market

PEOPLE TEND TO TALK about growth in sweeping terms. Terms such as "growth industry" and "mature industry"—while catchy and convenient —are loaded, imprecise, and often downright wrong. One of the most important empirical findings from our research is that there's no such thing as a growth industry. The real definition of a growth market exists at a level much deeper than industry. Most so-called "growth" industries have sub-industries or segments that aren't growing, and most "mature" industries and geographies have at least a few sub-industries or segments that are growing rapidly.

The histogram in Figure 1.1 illustrates this well. In Europe, telecommunications is generally regarded as a mature industry. Yet telecom companies show wide variations in their portfolio growth rates because there are broad differences in the growth of their underlying markets.

Wireless grows more quickly than wireline does, for example, and even within wireless and wireline there are significant variations. Wireless is growing more slowly in western Europe than in eastern Europe. Within wireline, broadband internet is experiencing rapid growth and voice is declining. In addition, the degree of exposure to fast-growing markets outside Europe varies from company to company. So within the European telecom industry as a whole, different companies have made different portfolio choices that have given them different levels of exposure to growth segments and countries.

1.1 Variations within a "mature" industry
Spread of market growth rates* for 10 telcos with EU HQs, 1999–2005

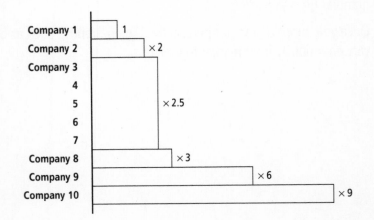

* Expressed as multiples of company 1

1.2 Growth giants have a clear edge

Average outperformance by growth giants of overall industry CAGR, 1999–2005

Industry	Market growth outperformance* Percentage points
High-tech	5.8
Retail and wholesale	2.5
Healthcare	2.3
Electric power and natural gas	2.2
Media and entertainment	2.2
Financial institutions	1.7
Consumer goods	1.6

* Includes changes in market growth due to portfolio shifts

The same variability is evident in apparently high-growth sectors too. If we take a representative set of large high-tech companies, for instance, and calculate the weighted average growth rate of the market segments that each company participates in, we find that the results range from –6 to 34 percent. Clearly, what looks like a growth industry to some looks mature to others.

If we revisit the set of growth giants we described in the Introduction, we can see that even when they don't operate in what we would consider to be growth industries or markets, they *still* outperform their industry peers. Figure 1.2 shows how well the growth giants do in some of the industries where we have the largest samples: high-tech, retail and wholesale, healthcare, media and entertainment, consumer goods, financial institutions, and electric power and natural gas (EPNG). In every case, the growth giants outclass their competitors in market growth: in EPNG, for instance, they have an edge of 2.2 percentage points over the industry as a whole.

So what does this tell us? One message is that there is hope for companies seeking to grow in seemingly mature industries. They don't have to abandon their entire business in search of a new one with a better growth rate, even if they could. Instead, they need to look deeper into their current industry and businesses in order to identify pockets of potential growth, and then focus their time and resources on these faster-growing and more profitable segments.

This is where granularity comes in.

Why granularity matters

Granularity isn't a term traditionally used in business. We've borrowed it from the world of science and engineering, where it is used to refer to the size of the components within a larger system. If we take what we might call a non-granular (or "coarse-grained") view of the system, what we might see is the system as a whole or perhaps the larger sub-systems within it. In a granular (or "fine-grained") view of the system, on the other hand, we might see some of the individual small components that go to make it up.

To make this more concrete, imagine we are looking at Google Earth. It shows a sequence of pictures from a satellite camera as it zooms in on the Earth from space. The first image we see is the whole planet. As the magnification increases and the field of view narrows, a continent comes into focus. Next we see the outline of an individual country, then a city, and finally a street or building. Before our eyes, the image of the Earth is progressively becoming more and more granular.

So why have we decided to apply the idea of granularity to business, and specifically to growth?

As we mentioned in the Preface, we want to get away from the broad-brush terms in which business opportunities are often described. Using the idea of granularity helps us cut through generalizations about industries ("Pharmaceuticals is a high-growth industry") and markets ("China is where the action is") to reveal a much more nuanced view of the world.

Second, we believe that if the texture of markets is granular, then so too should be the way that companies operate. This poses a challenge for corporations that structure their organizations and activities in an aggregated way. We are not arguing against scale. Rather, we are arguing that scale should not come at the expense of granularity.

For us, then, granularity conveys two important and related ideas: first, a fine-grained understanding of markets and growth opportunities and, second, a sharply focused, precise, and detailed way to manage discrete initiatives and activities across the corporation. We believe that applying both these ideas greatly increases a company's chance of success in identifying and pursuing growth opportunities. Our aim in this book is to show you how you can "de-average" *both* your view of your markets and your organization *and* the way in which you make choices and allocate resources—all while seeing both the forest and the trees.

In this chapter, we look at the granularity of markets. We come back to what this implies for your company's organization in part III.

Levels of granularity

A company formulating its growth strategy needs to develop insights into trends, future growth rates, and market structures at much greater depth than the aggregate industry level. Insights into sub-industries, segments, categories, and micro-markets are the building blocks of portfolio choices. They are indispensable for companies seeking to make the right decisions about where to compete.

All of which poses a practical question: when you make these decisions, what level should you be looking at to get the insights you need? How deep should you go? We'll now introduce a framework to help you find the answer.

To find out how granular strategic decisions need to be with respect to particular markets, we carried out a systematic analysis of how market selection correlates with company growth. There is already a well-developed academic literature on the relationship between industry choice and profitability.[1] We have applied a similar methodology to look at how industry choice affects top-line growth, while making a few key changes to the analysis.

What we set out to test is the extent to which industry growth rates are correlated with company-specific organic growth rates. First, we took the sample of companies we described in the Introduction and stripped out M&A from each company's reported top-line revenue. We did this to control for the fact that different companies in the same industry use M&A in very different ways and see very different effects on their top-line growth rates. Since buyers and sellers are usually both from the same industry, the decision to be a buyer (or a seller) is specific to the company, and not a function of the industry growth rate.

Removing inorganic growth from the equation is only the first step. It is even more important to make sure that the correlation tests are performed at the right level of granularity. The only way to establish the impact of the decisions executives make about market selection and portfolio commitments is to examine the level at which these decisions are actually made—a level far deeper than that of industry.

Let's start by looking at the six levels of granularity that we have identified, as illustrated in Figure 1.3.

1.3 Levels of granularity

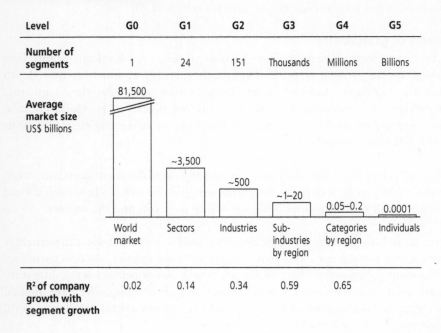

Level	G0	G1	G2	G3	G4	G5
Number of segments	1	24	151	Thousands	Millions	Billions

Average market size US$ billions

	World market	Sectors	Industries	Sub-industries by region	Categories by region	Individuals
	81,500	~3,500	~500	~1–20	0.05–0.2	0.0001

| R^2 of company growth with segment growth | 0.02 | 0.14 | 0.34 | 0.59 | 0.65 | |

Granularity level G0

The Earth—or, in our context, the global marketplace—is the highest level of aggregation with the least granularity: the ultimate segment of one. The world economy is growing by roughly 6.2 percent a year in nominal terms. By 2005, its total output had reached $81.5 trillion. This is the global pie.

Granularity level G1

If we want to investigate why some companies grow at a rate that is faster or slower than about 6 percent, the first step is to divide up the economy. The Global Industry Classification Standard (GICS) carves it up into 24 broad industry groups ranging from telecommunications services to energy to biotech. These sectors have an average market size of $3.5 trillion. If you plot sector growth and company growth, as we have done in Figure 1.4, no obvious correlation can be seen.

Each point on the graph represents a company, and each vertical set of points represents a sector. The vertical spread for any set of points thus shows the variation in company growth rates within that sector.

1.4 Sector growth or company growth?

Scatter of sector and company growth, CAGR based on US$, 1999–2005, percent

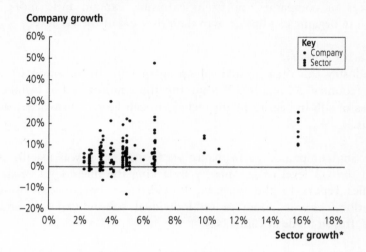

* Using Global Industry Classification Standard (GICS) developed by Morgan Stanley Capital International
Sample: Granular growth decomposition database

In fact, at this level of aggregation, the growth of sectors explains only about 14 percent of total company organic growth. This is because the growth rate of different *sectors* runs in the range of 2 to 16 percent, whereas the spread of growth at individual *companies* is much broader, ranging from –13 to 48 percent. This reinforces our point that talk of growth industries is meaningless.

Granularity level G2

Frankly, decisions at the G1 level (such as whether to be in telecommunications, energy, or biotech) are not within the ambit of most companies, so we need not dwell on them here. To get to a deeper level of granularity, we can break down the 24 groups into 151 industries by using other readily available GICS statistics. For instance, the "food, beverages, and tobacco" group breaks down into the component industries "food," "beverages," and "tobacco." The resulting G2 segments have an average size of roughly $500 billion— much more granular than the G1 sectors, but still fairly large.

We found that a typical large company in our database has at least two significant G2 industries in its portfolio, by which we mean that the industry concerned contributes at least 10 percent or more than $1 billion to the company's revenue.

This level of granularity is not yet fine enough, though, to give us the information we need to start making portfolio decisions. At the G2 level, differences in companies' portfolio exposure explain little more of the variation in organic top-line growth than they did at the G1 level.

Granularity level G3

Each industry can then be divided up again both by sub-industry and by market (country or region). Within the food industry, for instance, two examples of sub-industries might include frozen foods or savories, oils, and dressings.

In analyzing companies' performance we found that it was usually possible to reach the G3 level of granularity by taking the finest level of data that companies report to the markets. Provided we have access to enough information, we can zoom in on individual sub-industries in individual markets: frozen foods in China, say.

At this G3 level, the world market contains thousands of segments ranging in size from $1 billion to $20 billion. Our analysis shows that the growth rates of these segments explain over 60 percent of a typical company's organic top-line growth. In other words, at the G3 level, market selection becomes more important than a company's ability to beat the market, and portfolio composition is the chief factor determining why some companies grow and others don't.

Granularity level G4

Sometimes it is possible to use proprietary databases and internal company data to dig deeper than the level at which companies normally report. The definition of the G4 level of granularity varies slightly from industry to industry, but, in essence, it's the level of categories within sub-industries (such as ice cream within frozen foods) or customer segments within a broad product or service category (such as weight-conscious snackers). The G4 level is important: it represents the minimum level of granularity at which companies need to operate when setting growth priorities and making decisions about resource allocation.

At the G4 level of granularity, the world economy contains millions of growth pockets that range in value from $50 million to $200 million. In our analysis, we found that the selection of G4 segments often did even more to explain a company's organic growth than the selection of G3 segments did. The G4 level of information goes well beyond that routinely available to the stock markets. It is the level at which the real resource allocation decisions should be made.

Granularity level G5

This is a view of the world at the level of individual customers and transactions —the ultimate segment of one, numbering many billions. Although some companies have developed systems that permit highly personalized interactions with individual customers, few, if any, are able to allocate resources at this level of granularity. For most companies, most of the time, G5 will be a level too far.

Now let's apply the levels of granularity to a specific case: the aging megatrend. We start with a health warning.

Handle megatrends with caution

The term "megatrend" is often used to describe major global forces that are expected to have wide-ranging impact. As we write, megatrends are a hot topic and many people claim it's vital to ensure your company is addressing them. However, most discussions of megatrends take place at a very broad and superficial level. That may be fine for financial commentators on TV or casual dinner-party chat, but it's not much use if you happen to be the CEO of a large company trying to make decisions about where to compete or how to allocate resources.

To exploit a megatrend successfully, you need to tap into insights that are far more specific. Take the example of aging, often cited as a megatrend that will generate demand. It is frequently held responsible for the growth of the healthcare industry, for instance. Many people believe it will transform other industries such as financial services and retail over the next ten to twenty years.

Let's analyze this megatrend at progressive levels of granularity. This should help us answer the question: would I choose to exploit the aging megatrend, and if so, where and how?

G0 and G1. At the **global** level, the impact of aging remains small in comparison with other forces, such as rising GDP per capita or population changes (Figure 1.5). Overall, we estimate that aging will reduce global GDP by 0.1 percent a year. If we then look at a single country—Italy, say—we see that aging has less impact here than on the world as a whole: it reduces Italian GDP by just 0.03 percent a year.

1.5 Factors affecting industry value

Importance of factors in predicting global added value,* 1980–2004, percent

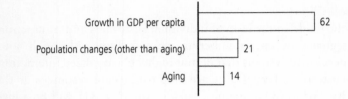

Growth in GDP per capita	62
Population changes (other than aging)	21
Aging	14

* Relative importance of the three factors βx*σx / σy, total correlation with industries >96%
Source: Global Insight; McKinsey analysis

G2. If we now look at the **industry** level, it's clear that the impact of aging varies by industry. Our analysis of the impact of aging on Italian markets reveals an interesting picture (Figure 1.6).[2] Healthcare, housing, and energy are likely to derive the greatest benefit from an aging population, with demand increasing by a compound annual growth rate of between 0.2 and 0.3 percent between now and 2020. Conversely, apparel, furniture, and cars are all likely to suffer a drop in demand of more than 0.1 percent a year, while games, toys, and sports will be hit hardest, with an annual decline of 0.4 percent.

G3. At the **sub-industry** level, we again find that the impact of aging varies. Take the Italian healthcare industry, which is expected to grow as a result of aging. Although the various sub-industries all reflect this upward trend, the degree of impact varies: for instance, "pharmacy" is expected to grow faster, at about 7 percent a year, than "health-related goods and services," at only 3 percent.

G4. To begin to spot real differences in the relative impact of aging on growth, we need to get down to the G4 category level. Within pharmaceuticals, for instance, aging is likely to have a positive effect on some drug categories (such as anti-hypertensives and calcium antagonists) and a negative effect on others (such as beta-blocking agents).

You get the idea: setting your growth direction requires you to move freely between the different levels of granularity while keeping your overall destination in view. Companies often describe their growth direction to the market at a G2 or G3 level, but specific granular strategies need to be put into action at the G4 and G5 level.

■ ■ ■

1.6 Scrutinizing a "megatrend"

The impact of aging in Italy, CAGR projections, 2005–20, percent

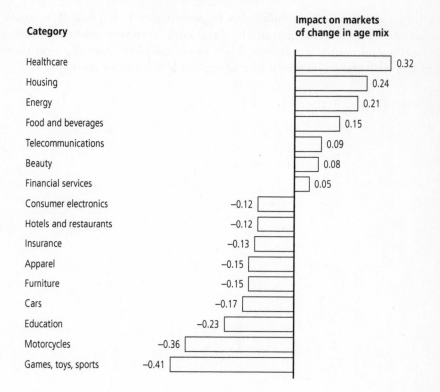

Category	Impact on markets of change in age mix
Healthcare	0.32
Housing	0.24
Energy	0.21
Food and beverages	0.15
Telecommunications	0.09
Beauty	0.08
Financial services	0.05
Consumer electronics	−0.12
Hotels and restaurants	−0.12
Insurance	−0.13
Apparel	−0.15
Furniture	−0.15
Cars	−0.17
Education	−0.23
Motorcycles	−0.36
Games, toys, sports	−0.41

Source: ISTAT; OECD; Banca d'Italia; Global Insight; McKinsey analysis

In this chapter, we've seen that companies searching for growth will find little help in analyses of industries and megatrends, which are usually pitched at too high a level to offer any real insight. In order to identify growth opportunities, you need to dig down well below the industry level. Applying the idea of granularity to your own company and markets will help you to determine the level at which the most valuable and actionable insights are to be found.

The notion of granularity adds an interesting twist to the diversification debate. Because so much of the action is at the G4 level, it's hard to argue that only investors can and should diversify by themselves. Investors can diversify at G2 level, and sometimes at G3, but not at G4. That is management's responsibility.

But how can management fulfill this responsibility? Is it possible to make decisions at this level of granularity in a large company without creating intolerable and counterproductive levels of complexity? Over the next three chapters, we'll show you that it is, and explain how you can do it.

NOTES

1 R. Schmalensee, "Do markets differ much?" *American Economic Review*, 1985, volume 75, number 3, pp. 341–51; R. P. Rumelt, "How much does industry matter?" *Strategic Management Journal*, 1991, volume 12, number 3, pp. 167–85; A. M. McGahan and M. E. Porter, "How much does industry matter, really?" *Strategic Management Journal*, 1997, volume 18, pp. 15–30.

2 Our analysis breaks down the forecast of retail consumption by category into demographic factors (change in age mix and net change in population) and other factors including rising GDP per capita. It assumes that non-consumption components of GDP such as investment, taxation, and social support are constant at 2003 percentages. Future savings behavior is extrapolated from trends over the past four years. Demographic forecasts factor in organic effects such as life expectancy, births, and deaths as well as net immigration. The study examines how organic age-mix variation changed consumption preferences across ages between 1990 and 2005. It cross-checks the estimates with actual 2005 consumption and applies observed preferences to consumption forecasts by sector through 2020. Immigrants are assumed to be less wealthy than the native population.

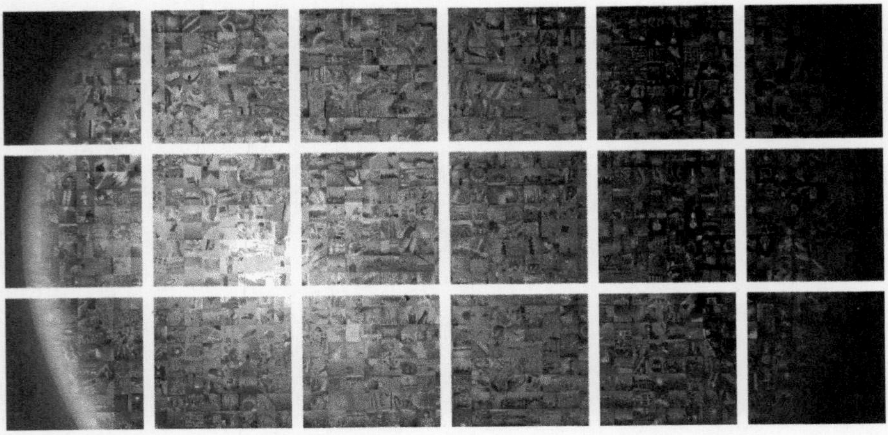

2

Understanding your company's performance

*"Not everything that can be counted counts,
and not everything that counts can be counted."*
Albert Einstein

- To understand growth, you need to disaggregate it into three components (or "cylinders," as we call them): portfolio momentum, M&A, and share gain

- Portfolio momentum and M&A account for almost 80 percent of what differentiates large-company growth performance; organic share gain accounts for just over 20 percent

- The average large company gets 6.6 percent growth from portfolio momentum, 3.1 percent from M&A, and 0.4 percent from share gain

- You can benchmark growth performance as robustly as you can benchmark cost performance

IN OUR EXPERIENCE, CEOs have a fairly deep understanding of the profit and cost performance of their own company and of their competitors. However, their ability to describe, explain, and compare revenues in terms of their company's past or future growth is often much more limited. When we ask them to compare their company's performance with that of peers, we frequently hear detailed statistics on profit performance, activity indicators, and cost benchmarks. Where growth is concerned, they sometimes mention relative market shares.

What we seldom hear, though, are apples-to-apples comparisons of top-line growth trajectories or explanations of how their company's growth performance compares with that of rivals. Why is this? The simple answer is that making these comparisons is far from easy.

Getting to the sources of growth

The growth performance of Telefónica, Spain's highly successful telecom company, illustrates this well. The company has achieved strong growth in the global telecom market over the past six years, with top-line growth of 9 percent a year. The company has made a fair number of deals, notably a series of acquisitions in South America and, more recently, the purchase of Český Telecom and O$_2$.

When we ask executives from other telecom companies to explain Telefónica's growth, they often point to its activities in South America. Although this region has clearly contributed to Telefónica's overall growth, as a deeper analysis of its performance between 1999 and 2005 reveals, it is not the only growth driver (Figure 2.1). In particular, Telefónica did very well in Spain.

So why aren't the underlying drivers of Telefónica's growth better understood? The problem is that even when we are looking at a single company there is no easy way to make a like-for-like comparison of top-line growth performance over a period of years. To benchmark growth properly, we would have to dig deeply into segment-level data in company annual reports to establish the real sources of revenue growth. We are not the first to say this; indeed, some commentators have gone so far as to propose a new form of reporting—a "sources of revenue" statement—that tracks customer revenue back to five sources.[1]

2.1 Where Telefónica grew

€ billion, 1999–2005

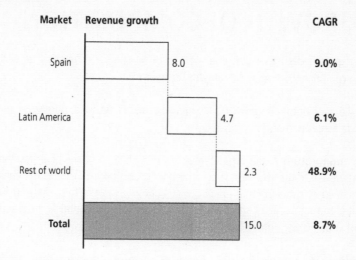

Market	Revenue growth		CAGR
Spain		8.0	9.0%
Latin America		4.7	6.1%
Rest of world		2.3	48.9%
Total		15.0	8.7%

Source: Dealogic; Hoovers; company reports; McKinsey analysis

For a proper comparison to be made, overall growth performance needs to be broken down into organic growth and inorganic M&A-driven growth, as the two are quite different in nature. In turn, organic growth needs to be broken down into its two components: the momentum of the portfolio a company starts with (by which we mean the growth rate of the underlying market segments) and the company's relative market-share performance (the difference between *company* growth rates and relevant *segment* growth rates). For the aggregate numbers to be accurate, these breakdowns need to be done at the segment level.

We believe that the only way to reach a full understanding of your own current and past growth and draw accurate comparisons with competitors' performance is to break growth down into these three components of portfolio momentum, share gain, and M&A—or growth "cylinders," as we call them. This is what we have done in a new form of analysis that we call granular growth decomposition, or simply "decomp" (see the box "Introducing granular growth decomposition").

INTRODUCING GRANULAR GROWTH DECOMPOSITION

A granular growth decomposition is a method of splitting a company's growth into three main components that we call growth "cylinders":

M&A is the net inorganic growth a company achieves when it purchases or sells revenues via acquisition or divestment.

Portfolio momentum is the organic revenue growth a company achieves through the market growth of the segments represented in its portfolio. It includes the impact of acquisitions and divestments that affect the company's exposure to underlying market growth after the first year of the transaction.[2] Portfolio momentum is, in a sense, a measure of strategic performance.

Share gain is the organic growth a company achieves through gaining or losing market share from its competitors. We define market share by the company's weighted average share of the segments in which it competes.

One other factor needs to be taken into account in the decomp: the **effects of currency fluctuation**. These can significantly distort growth measurements and, hence, perceptions of performance. A translation from one currency to another can allow companies to benefit from currency appreciation in overseas markets. Over the past few years, for instance, US companies with sales reported in Europe have benefited from the appreciation of the euro. Although we generally include currency effects in the portfolio momentum category, we sometimes highlight them separately.

McKinsey & Company has set up a dedicated team of analysts in India to perform granular growth decompositions on a large scale in order to compare companies with their peers. As each company decomp is completed, it is added to a database that provides a reference class for large-company growth performance. As far as we know, this is the only such database in the world.

At the time of writing, we have carried out granular growth decompositions for about 500 large companies, and we are adding more to our database all the time to improve our coverage while still maintaining a balanced representation of industry sectors.

Peer comparisons

To see how the granular growth decomposition can be used to gain insights into a company's growth, let's consider a hypothetical case.

Company A grew by 4.3 percent a year between 1999 and 2005. To understand where this growth came from, we need to break it down into the three cylinders, as illustrated in the left-hand column in Figure 2.2. This reveals that most of company A's growth is driven by portfolio momentum. The M&A cylinder, which represents net inorganic growth over the period, shows a negative result, meaning that the company divested more businesses than it acquired. As for share gain, this made a positive contribution to company A's overall growth, albeit a modest one. So the granular growth decomposition has shown us that company A's business segments are in growing markets and are gaining market share.

Understanding one company's performance by unraveling its real sources of growth is interesting, but drawing comparisons between peers or benchmarking

2.2 Contrasting growth trajectories

Revenue CAGR breakdown based on local currency, 1999–2005, percent

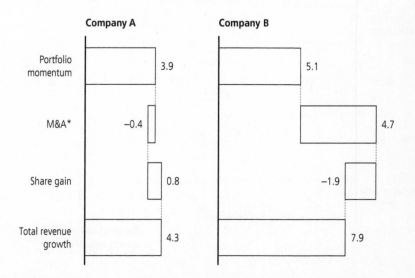

* Including arithmetic CAGR effect resulting from changes in revenue base due to inorganic activity and share gain/loss
Source: Global Insight; company reports; SDC; Dealogic; Hoovers; analyst reports; McKinsey analysis

a company against its industry can yield more valuable insights. Consider a second hypothetical company. Company B competes in the same markets as company A, and is similar in size. Its growth performance is shown in the right-hand column of Figure 2.2.

At first glance, company B appears to be outperforming company A: in terms of top-line growth, it has delivered a compound annual growth rate of 7.9 percent, as against company A's 4.3 percent. But a closer look reveals a more complex picture. Company B is actually *losing* market share. The strong contribution made by the M&A cylinder to its revenue growth—4.7 percent— is perhaps masking issues with execution elsewhere in the business. Look again at company A; in the same markets and over the same time period, it managed to gain market share. Now that we are comparing apples with apples, we are able to draw a much more accurate comparison of the two companies' individual strengths and weaknesses.

2.3 Comparing telecom players

Revenue CAGR breakdown based on local currency, 1999–2005, percent

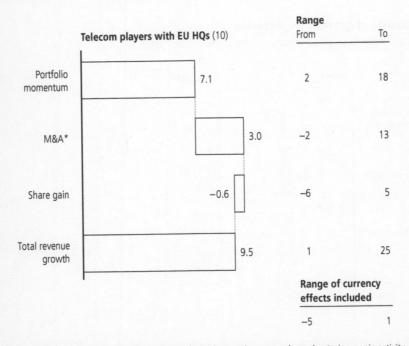

	Range	
Telecom players with EU HQs (10)	From	To
Portfolio momentum	7.1	2	18
M&A*	3.0	−2	13
Share gain	−0.6	−6	5
Total revenue growth	9.5	1	25

Range of currency effects included

| −5 | 1 |

* Including arithmetic CAGR effect resulting from changes in revenue base due to inorganic activity and share gain/loss

Source: Global Insight; company reports; SDC; Dealogic; Hoovers; analyst reports; McKinsey analysis

Now that we've seen how the granular growth decomposition works in a hypothetical case, let's see how it applies to the real world. Our team of analysts worked for more than two months to make a detailed comparison between ten telecom companies with headquarters in Europe over the period 1999 to 2005. The results of the analysis are fascinating: they partly confirm our intuitive understanding, but hold surprises too.

As Figure 2.3 reveals, the telecom companies' collective growth was driven by portfolio momentum and M&A. As a group, the companies did not gain market share; on the contrary, they lost it to attackers. But these averages conceal quite startling differences in the performance of individual players. Take inorganic growth: the top performer managed to notch up a CAGR of 13 percent, while its weakest peer turned in a negative CAGR of –2 percent. Similarly, companies varied widely in terms of portfolio momentum (a range of 2 to 18 percent) and share gain (from –6 to 5 percent).

Growth for the average large company

These numbers are all very well, you might think, but what do they tell us? Let's now look at the companies in our granular growth database to see if

2.4 Where large companies got their growth
Average revenue CAGR breakdown, 1999–2006, percentage points

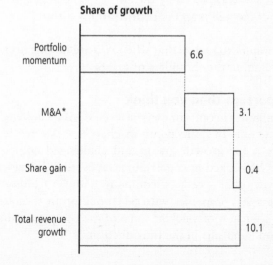

Share of growth

Portfolio momentum   6.6

M&A*   3.1

Share gain   0.4

Total revenue growth   10.1

Sample: 416 companies in granular growth decomposition database

we can reach any useful conclusions about where companies tend to get most of their growth. To find out, we took our database of 416 companies and broke down their average performance over the period 1999–2006 into the three cylinders of growth.[3] We found some of the results surprising—and so did many of the executives with whom we shared them.

The average large company grew at 10.1 percent per year over the period (Figure 2.4). Portfolio momentum accounted for 6.6 percent of this growth, M&A for 3.1 percent, and share gain for 0.4 percent. This means that virtually *all* the growth for an average company could be explained by the underlying growth rates in its market segments, coupled with its own M&A activity. We'll take each of these cylinders in turn.

Portfolio momentum: Thank your predecessor

Portfolio momentum accounts for 6.6 percent of a typical large company's 10.1 percent compound annual growth rate. In other words, almost two-thirds — 65 percent—of a large company's growth is inherited: it derives from the performance of the existing portfolio. With CEO tenures being as short as they are, what this means is that when a company reports its results, much of its growth performance has been determined by decisions taken by the previous management. The former CEO of Shell, Lo van Wachem, acknowledged as much where he told management trainees in a masterclass:

> "The actual revenue I realize today is grossly dependent on the energy reserves acquired and explored by the two CEOs before me, and CEOs two generations after me will reap the benefits of my effort."

It is a lesson in humility to realize that when you are talking about growth, you may well be standing on the shoulders of giants.

M&A: More important than you think

Across all the companies in our sample, the level of M&A activity is surprisingly high. We'll look at this in more depth in chapter 6; suffice to say here that M&A is important for growth giants and challenged companies alike. As Figure 2.4 shows, M&A activity contributes on average 3.1 percent per year in revenue growth. In other words, a company with $10 billion in revenue is acquiring, on average, companies with $310 million in revenue that year. To understand why, we can look back at some of the companies that are featured in our "grow or go" analysis in the Introduction.

Take Schlumberger and General Dynamics, both of which made the transition from the challenged category in the first business cycle (1984–94) to the growth giant category in the second (1994–2004). General Dynamics made the leap by divesting heavily in the early 1990s as the defense market deteriorated, and then going into acquisition mode once the market offered better prospects. Schlumberger also worked its way up by actively trading its portfolio. On the one hand, it strengthened its operations in the fast-growing market of oilfield products and services by making a series of acquisitions, including Camco's drilling products and services and Baker Hughes' seismic services. On the other hand, it divested businesses that didn't fit with its growth goals, such as metering, chip-testing, and IT services outside the oil industry.

If we now turn to the companies that managed to retain their growth giant status through two business cycles, we find that many of them did so by making extensive use of M&A. Some, such as GE, are renowned for the effectiveness of their M&A machine; others, such as Pfizer, are leading the consolidation of their industry. Between 1994 and 2004, when the compound annual growth rate of the pharmaceutical industry was running at 9 percent, Pfizer made several key acquisitions, buying Warner-Lambert (at that time about two-thirds its size in terms of sales) for $112 billion in 2000, and Pharmacia in 2003—a purchase that made it the world's largest research-based pharmaceutical company.

Market share: Seldom a growth driver
One important finding that came from our analysis was that market share, as defined by a company's weighted average share of the segments in which it competes, typically appears to play only a minor role in driving growth. It contributed just 0.4 percent per year to the average company's growth trajectory. This is interesting news given that gaining share organically through superior execution is precisely what many management teams dedicate their efforts, planning, and tactics to achieving—sometimes to the exclusion of all else.

This poses a couple of questions. First, isn't it only to be expected that the average company neither gains nor loses market share, since market share is a zero-sum game? Digging deep into our database, we find there are share gainers and losers, but few companies exhibit significant and sustained share gain, and those that do tend to have compelling business-model advantages. We'll say more about this in chapter 7, which is entirely devoted to share gain. Remember, too, that we calculate share gain at the segment level, so if a given company gains share in some segments and loses it in others, the net effect will be that the two cancel each other out. We'll explore this further as well.

Second, if *large* companies aren't losing share, what about the population of smaller companies that are often thought to be growing more quickly and gaining share from incumbents? It turns out that their fate differs from country to country. Our analysis suggests that in the US, the average large company does lose a bit of market share over time, whereas its European counterpart gains a bit. Although we haven't analyzed this in detail, we believe that it may have something to do with the greater dynamism of the US market for early-stage companies. If new entrants aren't capturing significant market share from incumbents, perhaps they are growing by creating or redefining categories, markets, and businesses instead.

So what conclusions can we draw from all this?

Location, location, location
Ask any real-estate agent the secret of buying the right house and there's a good chance they'll tell you "Location, location, location." How a house was built, what it looks like, how old it is, and how much it will cost you to transform it into the home of your dreams are not nearly so important as where it is. Location is paramount. Everything else can be fixed.

Is that true for companies too? Do the industries, sectors, and segments in which they compete matter far more than any other factor in determining their growth performance?

To answer this question we need to go back to the decomp database, this time to understand what drives the *differences* among the growth rates of different companies. Using a multivariate regression, we looked at the contribution of the three growth elements to differences in company growth. As Figure 2.5 reveals, 79 percent of what differentiates leading companies from the rest in terms of growth performance is explained by portfolio momentum and M&A —factors determined by *where a company chooses to compete*. Just as in real estate, then, location matters.

In terms of the individual cylinders, **portfolio momentum** or market growth explains 46 percent of the difference in growth performance between large companies, highlighting the importance of market selection in driving growth.

2.5 Performance differentiation by growth component*
Percent

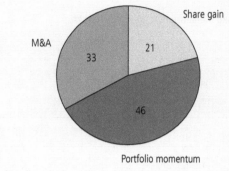

* Based on multivariate regression
Sample: 416 companies in granular growth decomposition database

M&A is responsible for 33 percent of the performance difference. That is, active acquirers grow a lot faster than companies that rely on organic growth. (We discuss whether this creates value in chapter 6.)

Share gain explains on average only about 21 percent of differential growth performance,[4] so it's hard to escape the conclusion that the effort companies put into hard work and smart execution doesn't get them very far relative to competitors.

Put another way, a company's choice of where to compete is *almost four times more important* than outperforming within its market.

At this point you may be wondering whether the relative unimportance of market share in explaining differences in growth performance applies only to certain market sectors. To find out, we compared a cross-section of industries.

Not surprisingly, the eight sectors we examined show some variation (Figure 2.6). However, the overall message remains the same: market share outperformance doesn't play a significant part in the growth differences between leading companies and average performers. In most sectors it is responsible for less than a quarter of the differential. The only major exception is the high-tech sector, at 36 percent. Here, the disruptive nature of the market and the brevity of product life cycles facilitate new entry, so allowing young upstarts to challenge the market share of established players a bit more frequently than in other sectors.

2.6 Differentiation by growth cylinder and for selected sectors
Percent (number of companies)

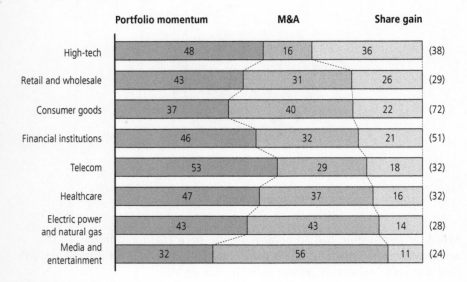

	Portfolio momentum	M&A	Share gain	
High-tech	48	16	36	(38)
Retail and wholesale	43	31	26	(29)
Consumer goods	37	40	22	(72)
Financial institutions	46	32	21	(51)
Telecom	53	29	18	(32)
Healthcare	47	37	16	(32)
Electric power and natural gas	43	43	14	(28)
Media and entertainment	32	56	11	(24)

Numbers do not always add up to 100% because of rounding
Sample: Granular growth decomposition database

Tailwinds or headwinds?
To explore further the part played by favorable markets—or what we call "tailwinds"—in differentiating growth performance, let's now return to the four categories we looked at in the Introduction and apply them to a set of companies from our growth decomposition database (Figure 2.7).[5]

The companies with **growth giant** performance are helped by favorable tailwinds and substantial M&A, which together drive their performance. On average, a growth giant with revenue growth of 16.8 percent receives 10 percent from portfolio momentum and 5 percent from M&A. The remaining 1.8 percent growth comes from market-share gains.

Unrewarded companies also benefit from tailwinds. On average, they receive just over half (6.7 percent) of their total annual growth of 12.9 percent from market momentum, and slightly less (5.3 percent) from M&A. Growth in market share contributes just 0.9 percent.

The **performers** are in the doldrums. In fact, their portfolio momentum is below the GDP growth rate and is in some cases even negative.

2.7 Decomposition by quadrant

Average revenue CAGR breakdown, 1999–2005, percent

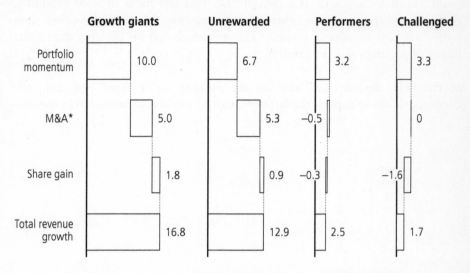

	Growth giants	Unrewarded	Performers	Challenged
Portfolio momentum	10.0	6.7	3.2	3.3
M&A*	5.0	5.3	−0.5	0
Share gain	1.8	0.9	−0.3	−1.6
Total revenue growth	16.8	12.9	2.5	1.7

* Including arithmetic CAGR effect resulting from changes in revenue base due to inorganic activity and share gain/loss
Numbers do not always add up to totals because of rounding
Sample: Granular growth decomposition database

The **challenged** companies, far from receiving favorable tailwinds, are in fact being buffeted by multiple headwinds in the markets where they operate. At 3.3 percent, their portfolio momentum is below GDP. In addition, these companies are losing market share at the rate of 1.6 percent a year.

What lessons can we draw from this? One obvious observation is that growth giants deliver, on average, more growth both overall and in each one of their cylinders—portfolio momentum, M&A, and share gain—than any other group, performers included.

■ ■ ■

It's abundantly clear from this analysis that a company's granular growth performance depends heavily on the markets in which it operates. So the next time a company announces stellar performance, it's worth taking a closer look to see how much of its growth came from better steering, and how much from a favorable tailwind. What is driving performance: execution or strategic choices?

In much the same way, it's a good idea to ask questions about your own company's performance. Do you know your numbers on growth, and your peers', both by segment and overall? Do you use them in your planning, performance appraisals, and external presentations? Are your plans consistent with your real sources of growth? Or are they based on possibly unrealistic hopes of gaining market share?

In the next chapter, we draw on the insights we've developed from the decompositions to explore the different ways in which companies have grown.

NOTES

1 M. Treacy and J. Sims, "Take command of your growth," *Harvard Business Review*, April 2004, pp. 1–9. The five sources of growth they identify are continuing sales to established customers (base retention); sales won from the competition (share gain); new sales in an expanding market (market positioning); moves into adjacent markets where core capabilities can be leveraged; and entirely new lines of business unrelated to the core.

2 Market growth within the first year after the transaction is counted as M&A for the purposes of our model; after the first year, it is classified as portfolio momentum.

3 Our granular decomposition database consisted at this point of 416 companies. We had data for the period 1999–2006 for most of them (almost 70 percent); the rest either start with 2000 data or end before 2006. Many of the analyses in this book were carried out with this full database sample of 416 companies, although some are based on an earlier version with 207 companies. We performed checks on both versions of the database to ensure the samples were representative.

4 The previous analysis showed that market share gain didn't make a significant contribution to the growth rate of the average company. This present analysis shows that it plays a more important role in explaining the differences between companies, although it is still less significant than either portfolio momentum or M&A.

5 We took a set of US-based companies from our growth decomposition database and used their revenue and value-creation performance between 1999 and 2005 to classify them according to the four performance categories in chapter 1. (Comparable segment-level data was not available for all the companies in the sample.)

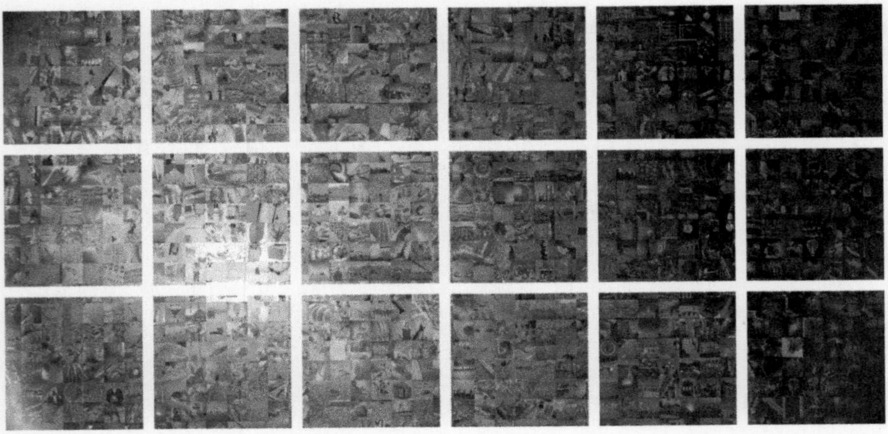

3

Firing on multiple cylinders

"Two out of three ain't bad."
Meatloaf, "Bat Out of Hell"

- Average performance on all cylinders does *not* lead to distinctive overall growth performance

- Good growth performance is associated with distinctive performance on at least one growth cylinder

- Great or exceptional growth performance is associated with distinctive performance on two or three cylinders

- Poor performance on one cylinder can be offset by distinctive performance on others

IN THE LAST CHAPTER, we showed that "where to compete" choices really do matter and established that all top-line growth can be broken down into three growth cylinders: portfolio momentum, M&A, and market-share gain. Now it's time to shift to a higher gear.

Building on the methodology we've introduced, we'll get behind the broad averages and derive some helpful rules for defining exceptional, great, good, and poor growth performance. Viewing the three growth cylinders more actively, as factors that companies can influence, we'll then examine the role that each has played in driving growth and value.

To do so, we'll again use detailed growth and value-creation histories of companies from our granular growth decomposition database. By analyzing growth cylinders across this fairly large sample, we should be able to identify correlations between their "firing patterns," revenue, and value creation.

The caveat here is timing. Given the depth at which we need to parse these companies' annual reports, our analysis is confined to the period 1999 to 2006 in which we can compare detailed segment performance year over year.[1] Although we aren't able to see the long-term picture, we do get clear insights into those six years and can compare growth results with short- to medium-term TRS trajectories. For anyone who is interested in more detail, other analysis we conducted shows that growth and TRS are less strongly correlated over shorter periods than in the longer term—which means that our findings should be borne out even more strongly over an extended time frame.

Defining cylinder firing

Now for a few notes on terminology. When we describe a company as "firing" on a particular cylinder, we mean that it is attaining a growth rate in the *top quartile* of the sample for that cylinder over a given time period. To give you a sense of what this involves for the companies in our granular growth decomposition database, we should explain that:

- A company would need to achieve average annual growth of **8.5 percent** or more from **portfolio momentum** over the period measured to qualify as firing on that cylinder.

- Similarly, to fire on the **M&A** cylinder, a company would need to grow its revenues inorganically by an average of at least **4.5 percent** a year.

- And to count as firing on the **share-gain** cylinder, it would need to grow the top line by at least **2.3 percent** a year from organic gains in market share.

Naturally, these benchmarks refer to current threshold performance and will vary by industry and time period. We make regular industry and peer comparisons to ensure they are kept accurate and up to date.

To extend our cylinder-firing terminology, here are a few more definitions:

- "Super-firing" is defined as achieving a *top-decile* performance in any cylinder.

- "Misfiring" is the opposite of firing: it's what happens when a company's cylinder performance puts it in the *bottom quartile* of the sample.

- "Neutral" is when a cylinder is neither firing nor misfiring; in other words, the company's performance falls into the middle of the sample, in the second or third quartile.

The idea of firing is important in two respects. First, we believe it can help you articulate your company's growth ambition more precisely, as an intention to fire on certain cylinders over a certain period of time. Second, it's a compelling way to benchmark your company's track record on growth, and that of your competitors.

We recognize, of course, that the engine analogy can't be pushed too far. A *car* with only three cylinders is unlikely to win any races, whereas a *company* that fires on all three growth cylinders is truly exceptional.

If we classify companies by the way they fire or misfire on their three cylinders, we can derive four categories of performance: exceptional, great, good, and poor. Let's look at each of these in turn (Figure 3.1).

Exceptional performance

Only a handful of companies fire on all three cylinders and thus qualify as exceptional. Oil refiner Valero is one of them. Propelled by strong tailwinds from rising oil prices and the tightening of refining capacity, it has recently enjoyed an extraordinary run. Between 1999 and 2005, it achieved top-line growth of 47 percent a year, with portfolio momentum

3.1 Cylinder firing patterns

End of year 1999 to end of year 2005, average CAGR, percent (number of companies)

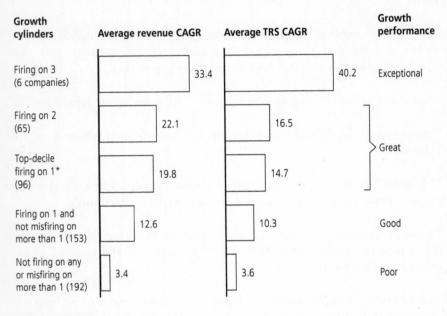

* Overlaps with other groups
Sample: 416 companies in granular growth decomposition database

contributing 27 percent, market-share gains 7 percent, and acquisitions 13 percent. Its TRS over this period ran at 49 percent a year.

Three-cylinder companies are such a rare breed—there were just six of them in our sample—that we can't draw statistically significant conclusions from them. Suffice to say that they chalked up average compound annual growth rates of 33.4 percent in revenue and 40.2 percent in TRS.

Great performance

There are two groups of companies that exemplify *great* cylinder-firing performance. First we come to the companies that fire on two cylinders, which made up almost a sixth of our sample. These companies grew their revenues by 22.1 percent a year and TRS by 16.5 percent a year.

The second group exemplifying great firing performance are companies that "super-fired" on a single cylinder (that is, performed in the top *decile* of the sample).[2] The companies in this group, which represents more than a fifth of the sample, delivered CAGR of 19.8 percent in revenue and 14.7 percent in TRS over the period, substantially outperforming the top-quartile single-cylinder companies (with results of 12.6 and 10.3 percent, respectively).[3]

As this suggests, super-firing a *single* cylinder at the top-*decile* level is essentially comparable to firing *two* cylinders at the top-*quartile* level—which is why we include it in our definition of great cylinder-firing performance.

Good performance

As we would expect given the way we've defined our terms, "firing" a cylinder produces higher revenue growth, and the more cylinders you fire, the better your revenue performance. But firing on multiple cylinders is far from being the norm. Let's dig deeper into this.

The threshold for differential performance appears to be *firing on one growth cylinder* while *not misfiring on more than one*. More than a third of our sample met this level of performance, which we characterized as *good*. Companies in this category delivered average revenue growth of 12.6 percent a year and TRS of 10.3 percent. Clearly, firing on one cylinder is a good thing, as long as you're not misfiring on the other two!

Poor performance

The remaining companies—almost half of our sample—either didn't fire on a single cylinder (that is, they were in the second or third quartiles for all cylinders), or they misfired on more than one cylinder (were in the fourth quartile for two or three cylinders). These companies delivered revenue growth of 3.4 percent a year and TRS of 3.6 percent. We classify this level of performance as *poor*.

Firing on more cylinders over time

Do these firing patterns really matter? You may be wondering at this point whether we've stacked the deck. Given the way we've defined "firing" and "misfiring," isn't it only to be expected that companies firing on multiple cylinders should exhibit superior revenue performance?

Let's set aside the handful of three-cylinder companies for the moment. If we look at the rest of the sample, the differences in growth rates and TRS performance across the zero-, one,- and two-cylinder companies are statistically significant at above the 95 percent level. So we can be confident that firing a cylinder is at the very least correlated strongly with differential growth and TRS performance.

But what do these results suggest for an individual company's growth strategy? Which cylinder or cylinders should it choose to fire on? When we isolate the relative power of individual cylinders, our analysis suggests that each contributes on average about 11 to 16 percentage points of TRS over six years, with momentum being the most significant of the three.

Now for a caveat. Our analysis of cylinder firing shouldn't be interpreted as advocating top-line growth at any cost. We aren't suggesting that companies should seek to fire on all cylinders by discounting deeply to win share, making acquisitions at high premiums, and investing wherever they see market growth. In fact, we believe, as we describe more fully in Appendix 2, that there are two ways to grow: rapid growth with stable margins or moderate growth with improving margins. Clearly, to pursue growth with declining profitability is to court disaster.

A six-cylinder engine?

As we noted earlier, a three-cylinder engine has its limitations, but this simple analogy provides us with a good way to compare growth performance. In reality there are *six* growth cylinders that we can identify through our growth decompositions: not just portfolio momentum, M&A, and share gain, but also divestments, changes in portfolio momentum due to M&A, and currency effects.

For some companies the six-cylinder view is crucial, as a net M&A measure doesn't tell the full story. An example might be an active trader that acquires and divests frequently. In such cases it's helpful to separate divestments from acquisitions, and also to isolate the resulting changes in portfolio momentum that would otherwise be attributed to the momentum cylinder. Similarly, as we noted in the previous chapter, the growth performance of companies that operate in many different markets can be profoundly affected by currency fluctuations, so separating out currency effects will be critical to the analysis.

For most companies, though, analyzing growth performance in terms of three cylinders offers sufficient insight without undue complexity.

■ ■ ■

In this chapter, we've depicted the three components of growth as cylinders. Firing on at least one cylinder is associated with boosting growth and driving value, provided you don't misfire on both the others at the same time. Firing on more than one cylinder is even better. And achieving top-decile performance in a single cylinder is about as good as firing on two cylinders.

It's worth taking a step back to judge how well you are firing on multiple cylinders yourself. Your performance is exceptional if you are firing on three cylinders. Your performance is great if you are firing on two cylinders (or top-decile firing on one). Your performance is good if you are firing on one cylinder and not misfiring on more than one. Otherwise, your performance is poor.

As you reflect on your performance, you'll probably form an ambition to fire on more cylinders over time. You may want to ask a few other questions. Which cylinders do your peers fire, and in which parts of your business? As you square your growth aspirations with what's in your current portfolio, in which of the three cylinders would you like to see improved performance?

In the next chapter, we apply this cylinder-firing approach to benchmarking growth performance in a more granular way across an organization.

NOTES

[1] Because companies are required to restate results only for the previous five years when they make important changes to their reporting segments, it's impossible to make consistent segment-level comparisons beyond this period. In future, we hope to be able to add years for the companies already in our database so that we can gradually build up a more detailed longitudinal view.

[2] The companies that "super-fired" are also present in the other four groups. We decided to highlight them to show how much top-decile firing can boost revenue and TRS growth.

[3] These findings were statistically significant at the 90 percent confidence level.

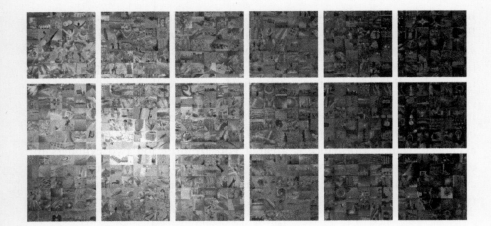

4

A granular company

"I'm astounded by people who want to know the universe when it's hard enough to find your way around Chinatown."
Woody Allen

- You can use cylinder firing to benchmark your growth both at the corporate level and at the granular level

- A growth MRI can help you disaggregate your company's performance so that you understand how your cylinders fire at the segment and sub-segment level

- The challenge for large companies is to ensure cylinder firing across a sufficient number of segments and sub-segments

- Different parts of an organization can fire on different cylinder combinations

S O FAR, WE HAVE INTRODUCED the ideas of granularity and cylinder firing as two independent concepts. We now need to combine the two. In order to get a real sense of your growth performance, you need to judge how well you are firing on cylinders at the granular *segment* level, not just the overall corporate level.

To make this kind of analysis possible, we have developed a tool for conducting growth scans for our clients. We call it a growth MRI.[1] It produces multiple granular views of the business and incorporates several heuristic tests to assist in the analysis. A comprehensive account of the MRI tool is outside the scope of this book, but we have included examples of the kinds of insight it affords in the following two case studies.

Combining cylinders with segments

In order to illustrate how you can apply the cylinder-firing analysis at a granular level, let's look at the case study of a $22.5 billion consumer goods company that we'll call GoodsCo.

GoodsCo is a challenged company as defined in the Introduction: it has a TRS of 5 percent per annum, way below the median, and a revenue growth rate below GDP. The company has been working on a turnaround and has managed to halt the downward slide that it was experiencing until 2000. Between 2001 and 2004, it achieved a CAGR of 3.2 percent (Figure 4.1). But

4.1 GoodsCo's growth development

$ billion

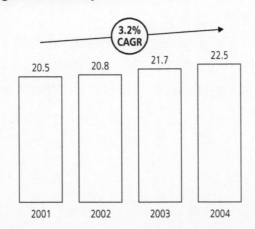

Source: Datastream; company reports; McKinsey analysis

where did it get this growth, and which parts of the business are still struggling?

To find out, we carried out a decomp on GoodsCo, analyzing its revenue components over a five-year period by geographic market and by product category. We combined market research data with the company's filed revenues, so sector revenues are approximations.

At first sight, GoodsCo appears to have produced stable albeit slow growth over the period 2001 to 2004. But let's look at where that growth came from by examining cylinder performance for the five geographical regions in which GoodsCo operates (Figure 4.2).

In the United States, there was strong growth from portfolio momentum, but that was partly offset by a substantial loss in market share. Europe was

4.2 GoodsCo's granular growth decomposition by region

Change in revenue, 2001–04, $ million

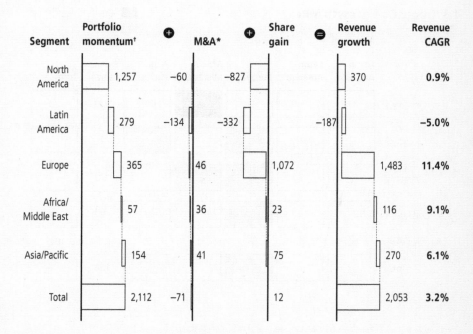

Segment	Portfolio momentum[†]	⊕	M&A*	⊕	Share gain	⊜	Revenue growth	Revenue CAGR
North America	1,257	−60	−827				370	0.9%
Latin America	279	−134	−332			−187		−5.0%
Europe	365		46		1,072		1,483	11.4%
Africa/ Middle East	57		36		23		116	9.1%
Asia/Pacific	154		41		75		270	6.1%
Total	2,112	−71			12		2,053	3.2%

Numbers do not always add up to totals because of rounding
* Including arithmetic CAGR resulting from changes in revenue base due to inorganic activity and share gains/losses
[†] Excluding currency effect
Source: Dealogic; Hoovers; company reports; McKinsey analysis

GoodsCo's growth engine, with a strong organic performance on both share-gain and portfolio-momentum cylinders. Despite positive market momentum, Latin America's performance was hurt by losses on both share gain and M&A. Although Africa/Middle East and Asia/Pacific grew nicely at 9.1 percent and 6.1 percent CAGR, respectively, their absolute contribution to growth was still small.

The picture gets sharper if we dig a little deeper. By disaggregating GoodsCo's reported results further, we can look at its growth MRI in four separate categories across the five geographic regions (Figure 4.3). When we evaluate cylinder firing at this 20-segment level, we get a much more detailed view of what has been happening at GoodsCo.

No fewer than 13 of the 20 segments are registering as poor in terms of cylinder performance; in other words, they are either not firing on any cylinders or misfiring on two or three. Unfortunately, they collectively represent almost 80 percent of the business.

4.3 GoodsCo's growth MRI

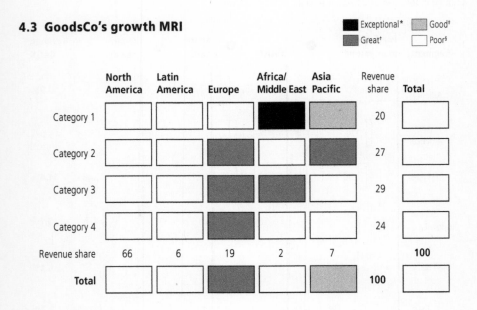

* Firing on all 3 cylinders
† Firing on 2 cylinders, or firing on 1 cylinder at top-decile level without misfiring on more than 1
‡ Firing on 1 cylinder without misfiring on more than 1
§ Misfiring on 2 or more cylinders, or not firing on any

On the positive side, one segment is firing at an exceptional level, although it represents just 0.2 percent of total revenues. Similarly, five segments register as great, representing about 20 percent of revenues between them, while one segment, representing 1.5 percent of revenues, is performing at a good level.

While most categories performed well in Europe, the business is misfiring in its core segments in the Americas.

To put it simply, GoodsCo appears to have a portfolio problem. With the benefit of the growth MRI analysis, we can see that it probably needs to take bold decisions to move into higher-momentum markets. In addition, GoodsCo should consider M&A and divestment opportunities if it aspires to end up with a portfolio of businesses that are firing on multiple cylinders.

Understanding firing performance

Wal-Mart provides a contrasting example, showing how a company can grow at the granular level by firing on multiple cylinders. Its growth story is a remarkable one. When founder Sam Walton died in 1992, the retail giant had achieved just over $40 billion in sales. By the year ending January 2006, revenues had reached $316 billion. Wal-Mart grew by expanding in two mutually reinforcing directions: adding more stores and selling more categories of products and services in existing stores.

From 1995 to 2006, the number of stores rose from 2,558 to 3,856 (Figure 4.4). Despite this growing base, Wal-Mart managed to accelerate the rate of new store openings from over 3 percent a year in the first half of that period to over 4 percent in the second. At the same time as expanding its stores, Wal-Mart also introduced many new service and product categories such as one-hour photo developing, private-label cosmetics, DVD rental, health foods, and office supplies. The reinforcing nature of these two growth paths enabled Wal-Mart to achieve a CAGR in revenue of about 16 percent over the past decade while holding margin steady.

This enviable record doesn't imply, however, that contributions to growth have been uniformly consistent or that the same cylinders are driving growth in different parts of the business. To get a more granular perspective on Wal-Mart's growth, we can divide the business into its standard reporting

4.4 Wal-Mart's expansion
Number of stores*

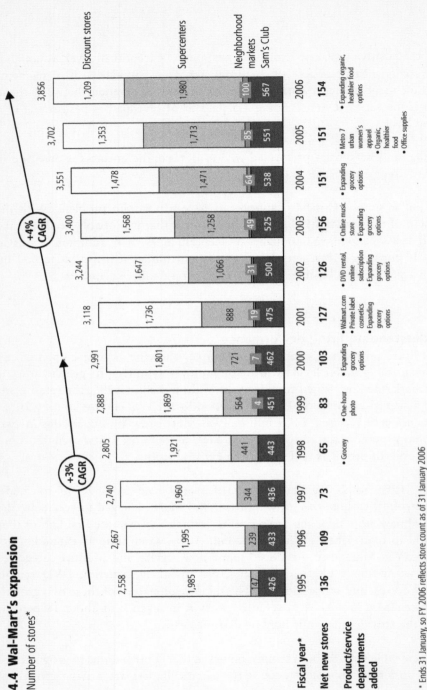

Fiscal year*	1995	1996	1997	1998	1999	2000	2001	2002	2003	2004	2005	2006
Total	2,558	2,667	2,740	2,805	2,888	2,991	3,118	3,244	3,400	3,551	3,702	3,856
Discount stores	1,985	1,995	1,960	1,921	1,869	1,801	1,736	1,647	1,568	1,478	1,353	1,209
Supercenters		239	344	441	564	721	888	1,066	1,258	1,471	1,713	1,980
Neighborhood markets	47				4	7	19	31	49	64	85	100
Sam's Club	426	433	436	443	451	462	475	500	525	538	551	567
Net new stores	136	109	73	65	83	103	127	126	156	151	151	154

+3% CAGR   +4% CAGR

Product/service departments added
- 1998: Grocery
- 1999: One-hour photo
- 2000: Expanding grocery options
- 2001: Walmart.com • Private label cosmetics • Expanding grocery options
- 2002: DVD rental, online subscription • Expanding grocery options
- 2003: Online music store • Expanding grocery options
- 2004: Expanding grocery options
- 2005: Metro 7 urban women's apparel • Organic, healthier food • Office supplies
- 2006: Expanding organic, healthier food options

* Ends 31 January, so FY 2006 reflects store count as of 31 January 2006
Source: Company filings; Hoovers; press reports; McKinsey analysis

segments. For the sake of simplicity we'll keep to a dozen or so segments. In practice, though, a company of this size using its own internal data could probably break down its business into a hundred or more segments.

Working with January 2005 data, we can zoom in on the $285 billion of revenues. First, we can establish the growth cylinder performance of each store format using our decomposition database cutoffs. When we look at the business this way, it's easy to see the importance of the US and the Supercenter (hypermarket) format (Figure 4.5). This combination accounts for $130 billion in revenues and has delivered great cylinder performance. By contrast, the old discount-store format in the US posts bottom-quartile growth and poor cylinder performance.

If we take a step back, it's clear that Wal-Mart as a whole posted a great cylinder performance. To a large extent, this is because the four segments with *great* cylinder performance represent a large part (almost half) of the business, in contrast to GoodsCo's situation. Add in Wal-Mart's *good* performers and you've covered about two-thirds of the company. In short, Wal-Mart fired on cylinders where it mattered the most.

4.5 Wal-Mart's growth MRI

Great* Good† Poor‡

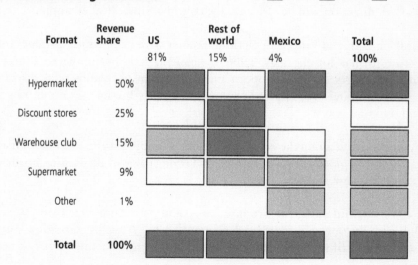

Format	Revenue share	US 81%	Rest of world 15%	Mexico 4%	Total 100%
Hypermarket	50%				
Discount stores	25%				
Warehouse club	15%				
Supermarket	9%				
Other	1%				
Total	100%				

* Firing on 2 cylinders, or firing on 1 cylinder at top-decile level without misfiring on more than 1
† Firing on 1 cylinder without misfiring on more than 1
‡ Misfiring on 2 or more cylinders, or not firing on any

If we then look at the data through a geographic lens, we see that the US, Mexico, and the rest of the world all posted great cylinder performance. However, different regions fired on different cylinders. Whereas portfolio momentum and organic share gain drove growth in the US as a whole, the story in the rest of the world was growth through M&A and share gain, but *not* portfolio momentum.

The MRI confirms that Wal-Mart, unlike GoodsCo, had good or great patterns where it really counted. Moreover, it drew on different cylinders in different countries and acted to improve its portfolio over time—a remarkable performance indeed. Even so, the MRI uncovered opportunities to fire on even more cylinders within various different businesses.

The granularity of choice

If we take a step back, both these examples raise the question of where to compete. On first seeing its growth MRI, a company may feel that it ought to improve its cylinder-firing performance in every cell. But that would be missing the point. Instead, it should view the cells with an eye to addressing "where to compete" choices—which cells to keep, which to emphasize, which to sell—*before* it tackles performance within individual cells.

The finer the granularity of the analysis, the better the insights for informing the growth direction will be. To see why, consider a practical example.

Let's take a high-end European clothing retailer with a successful product line and store format for the mass-affluent segment. It is beginning to saturate the relevant parts of the European market (upmarket commercial districts in major cities) and needs to find new ways to grow. It could set about this in several different ways:

- It could expand along the **geographic** dimension by starting to think of itself as a high-end *global* clothing retailer and trying to grow its existing business by **entering new markets**.

- It could expand along the **product** dimension by defining itself simply as a high-end European retailer and attempting to grow by **targeting other buying needs of the mass-affluent customer** through existing stores or new formats.

- It could expand along the **customer segment** dimension by defining itself as a European clothing retailer and **seeking to attract other customer**

segments beyond its mass-affluent core market. Alternatively, it could stick with its high-end customers but segment this market more finely to find new opportunities for growth.

If it had the management resources and the luxury of time, it could experiment on a small scale with all three options, trying out different combinations and scaling up the ideas that work best.[2] But if it can only focus on one big push at a time, the company will need to evaluate each growth path at a granular level to make an informed choice.

Geographic expansion: From continents to street corners

Let's say the retailer is convinced that there is significant growth potential in the mass-affluent segment outside Europe. In addition, it feels much more comfortable betting on the power of its intellectual property (clothes design, brand, store design and layout) and on the consistency of the tastes of high-end customers around the world than on its ability to create new formats or sell items other than clothes. So it adopts an expansionary global mindset, and its next step is to decide which markets to enter first.

The texture of the market for a high-end clothing retailer starts at the macro level (in which countries or continents is the mass-affluent market growing the fastest?), but goes down to a very granular level, that of neighborhoods or commercial districts within a particular city. This is because urban districts vary so much in terms of their socio-economic mix that choosing the wrong part of town to build your store can prove fatal to your sales growth. Location can easily trump execution; at this level, geography is destiny. A quick tour of the globe serves to illustrate.

Continents. Nominal global GDP[3] grows at 6.2 percent per year. If you strip out inflation, the differences in growth rates between continents are actually quite small. Asia's growth is only 0.3 percentage point faster than that of the world as a whole; Africa's growth is only slightly slower in real terms; and Europe and Latin America trail by just 1 percentage point. Clearly, the real differences are to be found below the continent level.

Countries. Individual countries display greater variation in growth rates than continents do. Asia, for instance, is often labeled as a growth continent, but it doesn't experience rapid growth across the board. China and India may be growing at 8 and 9 percent a year, respectively, but Japan and Indonesia notch up just 1 and 3 percent annual growth. Our retailer may decide to target the US market because the mass-affluent segment represents a relatively large share of the population, but it should also be aware that this segment is growing faster in emerging markets.

States and cities. Let's assume that our retailer decides to enter the US market anyway. It still has a lot of work to do. Some states and metropolitan areas are growing considerably; others are not. If we focus on cities with populations in excess of a million people, population growth rates over the last two decennial censuses (1990 and 2000) range from 0 percent to 3 percent. If we look at affluence, the proportion of people in a city who earn over $75,000 a year can be as high as 41 percent (Washington, DC) or as small as 17 percent (Oklahoma City).

Neighborhoods, commercial districts, streets, and individual sites. At this level of granularity, a company's strategy typically starts to blur with its execution. There is no question that the texture of the market (that is, the level of granularity at which supply, demand, and competition play out) varies from one neighborhood or commercial district to another, and often from one street to the next. In the city of New York, for instance, average per capita income varies enormously by district: in 1999, it ranged from around $8,000 in the Bronx to well above $120,000 in parts of Manhattan. There can be huge differences even within a few blocks. Retailers know that site selection is critical and that a store's sales can depend on whether it is on this street corner or that one and whether it is right on the street or set back. Data at this level is not easily available, but Walgreens and other top retailers have developed sophisticated processes and proprietary data to help them select the best sites.

Product expansion: From categories to SKUs[4]
Now let's say that our retailer is less sure of its products' global appeal but confident that it truly understands its customer base, the mass-affluent segment of the European market. Perhaps it has invested in sophisticated research about what its customers expect from the products they buy or from their shopping experience, and has stumbled onto insights that it can apply to other areas of mass-affluent retailing. Bearing in mind its existing capabilities, it may want to confine itself to non-durable or small durable consumer goods of the type traditionally sold through department stores, such as luxury packaged food, bedding, beauty products, and jewelry. This definition is broad enough to provide significant headroom for growth while still ruling out some areas of luxury retailing, such as sports cars.

As with geography, there is virtually no limit to how granular product selection at the SKU level can go. Imagine that our retailer decides to venture into producing and selling its own brand of beauty products. If it is successful, it may then want to consider entering a series of other new categories, such as fragrances, spa products, nutraceuticals, and beauty services such as facials. Within those categories, it may then decide to vary its offering by store location: for instance, stores in a busy business district could offer express manicures for women on their lunch break, while those in shopping malls could offer one-hour facials for customers with more time.

Customer expansion: New demographics or finer segmentation

On the other hand, perhaps our European clothing retailer feels that its real expertise lies in selling clothing, so it decides to carry on doing just that but to venture into customer segments outside its mass-affluent core. It might choose this strategy if it believes that most of the growth in European retail is going to be outside the affluent segment, and if it is confident enough to take on the discount retailers that already appeal to this market. To reach new segments in this way, some retailers use innovative new formats that link into their brand but avoid diluting it, much as Gap did in 1994 by introducing Old Navy to target middle-class teenagers. Ten years later, Old Navy was generating $7 billion a year in revenue, 42 percent of Gap's total. Banana Republic and Piperlime are other examples of Gap's strategy of targeting differentiated customer segments.

Another option might be for our retailer to stay with the mass-affluent segment it knows so well but to operate at a more granular level within it. Instead of redefining itself, it could look at a finer segmentation of its core market. Is it really reaching everyone it could reach: men as well as women, older people as well as teenagers, children as well as adults? Looking at the multitude of sub-segments within its broad target segment should reveal many opportunities for growth. Gap offers another good example with its introduction of Baby Gap and Gap Kids to reach the children or younger siblings of its core customers.

So what is the right choice for our retailer? Only it can tell—but exploring each of these three growth paths at a granular level will give it a much better chance to pinpoint the most fertile ground for growth, avoid the temptation to opt for the "usual suspects," and find the option that fits its capabilities and organization best.

■ ■ ■

Our analysis of the granular growth decomposition database showed that companies that fired on one or more cylinders achieved higher revenue growth and TRS performance than those that didn't. In this chapter, we've seen how the growth MRI can help you understand this performance at the segment and sub-segment level. But what if you aren't firing on one or more cylinders in some or most of your businesses? What can you do about it? How do you help your businesses to fire on more cylinders over time?

In part II, we'll look at how you can fire on each of the three growth cylinders. We'll then put the elements together to show a compelling way to set your overall growth direction.

NOTES

1 So called because its output resembles that from medical scanners.

2 Here, it is useful to think about the "seven degrees of freedom" concept introduced in M. A. Baghai, S. C. Coley, and D. White, *The Alchemy of Growth* (Orion, London, 1999), pp. 51–60. It provides a framework for thinking about possible growth opportunities within a business at seven levels: selling existing products to existing customers; targeting new customers; introducing new products and services; trying new delivery approaches; reaching new geographies; changing the industry structure; and entering new competitive arenas.

3 We cite real GDP here so as to make a meaningful comparison of growth rates between countries. Throughout most of the rest of the book, we cite nominal output growth at the country level to facilitate comparisons with industry revenue growth rates within that country.

4 Stock-keeping units.

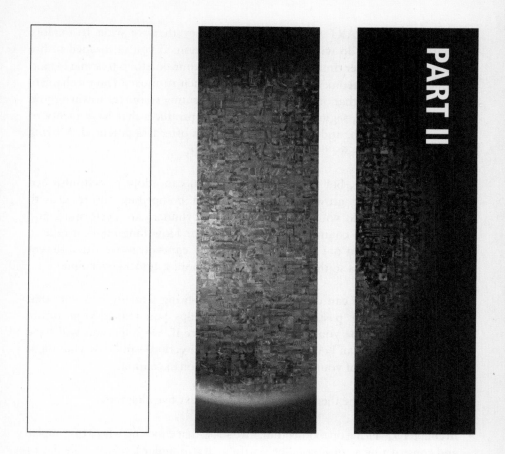

Your growth direction

THE SECOND PART OF the growth journey that we want to explore with you has to do with your growth direction. If you've decided to fire on more cylinders over time, you'll have to shift your portfolio to some extent. The question then becomes where, how, and when to move. The mechanism you need to adopt is that of granular choice: allocating resources toward those businesses, countries, segments, customers, and products that have plenty of headroom for growth, and away from those that offer less potential. Moving may take time, but as we'll show, it often pays off.

The task is daunting, but not impossible. If you can adopt a well-informed perspective on your growth, you can plan a compelling future growth direction. But how do you find out how your cylinders are performing and decide which ones to count on for future growth? How long might it take to move a cylinder from not firing to firing? How can you move the different parts of your business so that they each fire on more cylinders over time?

We'll show how you can develop your cylinder-firing strategy in a way that both builds on your past performance and helps you realize your future potential. By the time you reach the end of part II, we hope you will have concluded that you can "choose" your growth direction—and that you might need to spend more of your time on choice than on execution.

Let's take a look at the themes we cover in the next five chapters.

- In chapter 5, "Firing on momentum," we show that choosing where to compete and constructing a corresponding portfolio at a granular level can take five or more years. We explore the difference between catching a tailwind and creating fresh momentum in the marketplace. We also explain how the hazards of new market entry can be reduced through advance analysis.

- In chapter 6, "Firing on M&A," we show that M&A is the best way to affect short-term growth and examine the way that companies can use advantage to pursue it. As an extreme example, we describe what it is about the operating methods of top private-equity firms that makes them such formidable acquirers.

- In chapter 7, "Firing on share gain," we show that though this is a difficult area to execute well, companies that make bold choices can succeed—and it's just as important to avoid *misfiring* on this cylinder. Although tactical actions can move the needle in the short term, reinventing the business model to gain market share will take some time to yield results.

- In chapter 8, "Mapping your growth direction," we bring the insights about the three different cylinders together and show you how to test the robustness of your strategy over multiple time horizons.

- In chapter 9, "To move or not to move?" we look at the portfolio in the context of the growth cylinders. This reveals that companies in low-momentum businesses have been rewarded for portfolio moves both within and outside their core business, but that high-momentum companies should be cautious about venturing beyond the core.

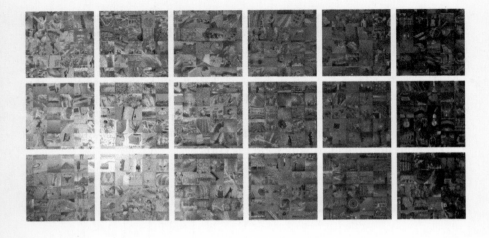

Firing on momentum

"The answer, my friend, is blowin' in the wind"
Bob Dylan

- There are three ways to increase your portfolio momentum: reallocate resources to pockets of high growth, shift your portfolio, or grow your markets

- The biggest driver of momentum is the composition of your initial portfolio

- Shifting your momentum is a marathon, not a sprint, and takes years, not months

- Even so, the top momentum improvers manage to boost their annual momentum growth rates by mid-single-digit percentage point increases over five years

W E'VE ARGUED THAT making the right decision about where to compete is critical. As we saw in chapter 2, portfolio momentum accounts for almost half (46 percent) of an average large company's growth performance, and differences in momentum are large even within industries, often because of the heritage of different business segments. Catching a growth "tailwind" by participating in a fast-growing market segment is obviously an enormous help in achieving high growth.

For a good example, consider Nokia. If we break down the sources of Nokia's growth, we see that almost all of it is driven by portfolio momentum, although the company is also gaining some market share (Figure 5.1). It's clear that it is benefiting from a substantial tailwind: the growth of the mobile phone and mobile equipment markets.

Here we should make an important point: *maintaining* market momentum may sound effortless, but it is not an easy thing to do. In the past few years, Nokia has had its ups and downs in holding on to market share. It took real energy and nous to build a business in an emerging market ahead of other players, and to introduce a huge range of successful phones.

5.1 Nokia's granular growth decomposition

Revenue CAGR breakdown, based on local currency, 1999–2004, percent

Portfolio momentum	7.8
M&A	0
Share gain	0.4
Total revenue growth	8.2

Source: SDC; Hoovers; company reports; analyst reports; McKinsey analysis

If you aren't blessed with strong tailwinds, though, what can you do? Finding ways to increase portfolio momentum is a central issue for many management teams—not to mention a tough challenge, especially in the short term.

To understand how companies improve their momentum over time, we analyzed the performance of the companies in our granular growth decomposition sample between 1999–2000 and 2004–05.[1] Even within this short period, many of the companies changed their momentum. If we classify them according to their ability to fire on momentum, the top quartile of companies—which included BHP Billiton, Daiwa Securities Group, CVRD, Rio Tinto, UPS, P&G, and Samsung—saw their momentum increase by at least 4 percentage points, whereas the bottom-quartile companies experienced a decline of 4 percentage points or more.

All these companies experienced either an acceleration or a slow-down in the markets they started with at the beginning of the five-year period. But only a few of them managed to improve their momentum substantially by moving outside their original portfolio to catch a new tailwind.

We'll now take a look at one of them, the top "improver" among those that made a portfolio shift. In 1993, the Reliance Group was focused primarily on downstream petrochemicals. This area of operations had long sustained the company's high growth rate. However, even by this date Reliance had already committed itself to constructing an oil refinery. This allowed it to move upstream into oil refining, while continuing to grow its core petrochemicals business. Not content with this first diversification, the group quickly moved into three completely new and unrelated sectors: telecom, upstream oil and gas, and biotechnology. These areas were hot spots and, moving when it did, Reliance was able to ride their growth waves. Over the period 1996 to 2006, the majority of Reliance's growth came from businesses outside its core business of petrochemicals. For example, oil and gas contributed to less than 1 percent of revenue in 1996 but contributed to around 57 percent of revenue in 2006.

The next-best case in our sample is that of Tesco, which improved its momentum by 4 percentage points, primarily by shifting an additional 26 percent of its revenues into hypermarkets.

Moving the needle on momentum thus calls for extreme shifts. So it should come as no surprise that almost 95 percent of the changes in momentum among our sample was determined not by portfolio shifts, but by changes in the market growth of the initial portfolio. These changes were caused in turn either by the cyclical nature of the market and its maturing or accelerating growth, or by actions taken by industry players that increase momentum growth in key segments (such as transformational product innovation) or decrease it (such as price wars) (Figure 5.2). This implies that companies that move into high-momentum businesses do so gradually, or early (before market growth rates start to peak), or both. In other words, shifting beyond the portfolio takes time, and is hard to accomplish within a five-year period if you are a large company. But that doesn't mean you should give up.

5.2 Momentum improvement from market growth

Momentum improvement*

$R^2 = 0.95$

Change in market growth†

* Difference between average market momentum in last two years and first two years of period
† Within the segments the company is operating in
Sample: Granular growth decomposition database

How to fire on momentum

In principle, a company can influence the momentum of its portfolio over time in three ways: by reallocating resources internally to pockets of high growth (either within or beyond existing business boundaries); by selecting acquisitions and divestments that affect its exposure to underlying market growth; and by stimulating market growth, for instance, by introducing a new product category.

- **Reallocating resources.** Companies can reallocate resources to pockets of higher growth within their portfolios. This will shift the portfolio mix in the right direction and, hence, increase overall momentum. To be successful, resource reallocation must be based on insights about where growth pockets *will be*—not where they are now. At GE, for instance, CEO Jeff Immelt has announced a $1.5 billion annual investment in energy renewables by 2010. We believe it is helpful to allocate resources from scratch (for instance, by zero-base budgeting) rather than with reference to spending in previous years so as to help direct investment toward the best current and future opportunities irrespective of past allocations. We return to this theme in part III.

- **Acquiring momentum.** M&A can be used to improve the portfolio mix and oost momentum. But acquiring in low-growth segments with the intention of consolidating them isn't necessarily the right approach; companies should always bear higher momentum in mind as one of their objectives. M&A investments always need to be based on a clear understanding of where the growth will come from on the one hand, and whether the assets are correctly valued on the other. We explore M&A in more depth in chapter 6, where we show that shedding low-momentum assets through divestment can have an immediate effect on portfolio momentum.

- **Creating momentum.** To do this, a company can create new markets or expand existing high-growth ones, as we see in the rest of this chapter. Either way, it will need to be skilled at identifying pockets of unmet demand and extending its portfolio of products to reach new customer segments.

Climbing a growth staircase

So how do companies build new businesses in growth markets? In *The Alchemy of Growth*, we introduced the notion of growth "staircases" as a way of describing strategies to build new businesses. When we studied the way successful companies had achieved their growth, what we usually discovered was not a chaotic zigzag of actions but a distinctive staircase pattern with a series of ascending steps that contribute to growth over time. This pattern can be clearly seen in Figure 5.3, which illustrates the building of Johnson & Johnson's Acuvue contact-lens business.

5.3 J&J'S Acuvue staircase

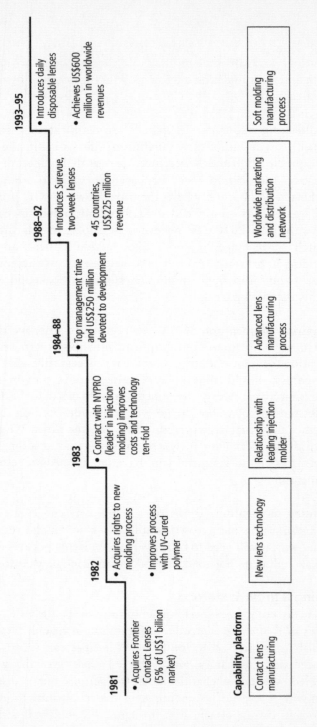

1981
- Acquires Frontier Contact Lenses (5% of US$1 billion market)

1982
- Acquires rights to new molding process
- Improves process with UV-cured polymer

1983
- Contract with NYPRO (leader in injection molding) improves costs and technology ten-fold

1984–88
- Top management time and US$250 million devoted to development

1988–92
- Introduces Surevue, two-week lenses
- 45 countries, US$225 million revenue

1993–95
- Introduces daily disposable lenses
- Achieves US$600 million in worldwide revenues

Capability platform

| Contact lens manufacturing | New lens technology | Relationship with leading injection molder | Advanced lens manufacturing process | Worldwide marketing and distribution network | Soft molding manufacturing process |

While some successful growers couldn't have claimed to know at the outset where their early steps were leading, most had a strong sense of direction about the businesses they were building. They adopted a "one step at a time" approach that usually began with small exploratory steps and evolved towards bigger and bolder ones as they grew more confident of their business strategy. Some staircases reflected huge choices made by CEOs.[2]

Other management specialists have described growth using similar imagery. Michael Treacy draws on sports analogies to make the case for small steps.[3] Gary Hamel describes how "A great idea becomes a commercial success through a recursive process of experimentation and learning."[4]

The growth staircase mirrors the way that entrepreneurs succeed in the real world, often in the face of fierce competition. It recognizes that growth strategy can't be a deterministic exercise but needs to help companies build strong capabilities over time while retaining as much strategic flexibility as possible. Essentially, the staircase approach allows for structured experimentation within a broad but deliberate intent to build a growth business. But how do you decide which growth staircases to invest in?

Beating the odds in market entry[5]

Some writers have argued that growth opportunities that hold out real promise for mature companies are rare. Advising leaders to stop kissing frogs, they claim that success comes from careful selection and a willingness to reject project after project until a good one emerges.[6] A few take the argument to extremes and advise leaders to stick to the core, take less risk, and launch fewer ventures.

Real growth leaders shun this advice. Reflecting on his mistakes in driving growth, Kevin Sharer, CEO of biotechnology company Amgen, described two big pharmaceutical product failures. The first, Kineret, was designed to treat rheumatoid arthritis; the second, Leptin, was intended as a cure for obesity. In both cases, the company significantly overestimated potential revenues. Sharer describes how he went into "submarine mode" and failed to listen to objective voices from the markets. Chastened but undaunted, he maintains "You can't let past mistakes, and the fear of making more, paralyze you."[7]

So the question is not so much "Should we enter new markets?" as "Do we have distinctive insights and capabilities that we can bring to bear on our chosen markets?" A critical issue is whether you can be sure that your choice of market is objective. All too often, executives confronted with a difficult decision rely solely on an inside view and focus only on the issue at hand. In these circumstances, cognitive biases—systematic errors in the way that executives process information—can wreak havoc with market-entry decisions.[8] They persuade executives that their company's skills are more relevant to a new market than they really are, that the potential market is bigger than it actually is, or that rivals won't respond to their entry move.

Consider the following examples.

EMI's CAT scanners

One common error is to underestimate the difficulty of developing new skills. A good example is music producer EMI's venture into CAT (computerized axial tomography) scanners in the 1970s. A researcher in the company's laboratories, Godfrey Hounsfield, had developed the underlying technology.[9] EMI decided to enter this new business despite its lack of experience in the manufacture, sales, and distribution of medical equipment. Rather than partner with other companies to obtain these capabilities, senior management decided to go it alone and build them from scratch.

More than five years passed before EMI launched its first product. Soon after, General Electric, taking advantage of its world-class manufacturing and sales and distribution networks (not to mention 75 years' experience with X-ray equipment), entered the US market. Similarly, Siemens entered first the European and then the US market. Not surprisingly, GE and Siemens became dominant, and EMI exited after sustaining substantial losses.

How many Segways?

A second common error is to overestimate the size of a potential market. When companies are trying to establish how large a market might be, they typically group customers into a number of segments and then make assumptions about pricing and elasticity to estimate what percentage of buyers in each segment they might be able to capture.

An example of how this process can go wrong can be seen in the fate of the Segway, a new two-wheeled vehicle unveiled in December 2001. Although we don't know for sure how the inventor, Dean Kamen, estimated the size of the market, we do know how many Segways he thought he could sell after one year: 10,000 a week. He actually sold just 6,000 Segways in the first 21 months. (We'll consider possible reasons for this later.)

Using reference classes to test entry decisions

As these stories demonstrate, the costs of miscalculation can be heavy. Fortunately, there are practical steps you can take to control cognitive biases in market-entry decisions. What executives need to do is adopt an external perspective, draw on experience of previous market entries, and evaluate opportunities by using common predictors of success. In our experience, combining a robust outside view with an improved inside perspective—one with better assessments of value propositions, capabilities, market size, competitors, market share, revenue, and costs—dramatically raises the odds of making good entry decisions.

You should start by selecting the right reference class to identify the key factors determining successful market entry. This allows you to learn systematically from the successes and failures of other companies; it also counteracts the "confirmation trap" that many decision makers fall into when they look only for information that supports their hypothesis. A broad reference class forces executives to consider more possibilities and more data. Which product attributes and business models have succeeded in the past? Were the winners superior marketers? Did they have outstanding distribution systems?

If your company needs new capabilities to succeed, you should exercise caution and consider using contractual approaches such as joint ventures and licensing to help you secure the missing elements. It's often valuable to ask people who aren't directly involved in making the entry decision—executives from another division, perhaps—to help determine what's needed for a successful entry. Their analysis will be less biased by ingrained knowledge of your current value proposition and skills.

Companies that operate in the pharmaceutical, oil and gas, and film industries understand how important it is to analyze the probability of success and are able to draw on a rich body of past cases to create a reference class. Companies that place product bets less frequently, and with less apparent risk, have fewer internal reference cases to use in comparisons. They may not consider looking at the experience of other companies and industries. Even if they do, they may decide that the benefit doesn't justify the expense. But they are being penny wise, pound foolish: the tens (if not hundreds) of millions of dollars at stake in a typical big-company market entry far outweigh the costs of forming a reference class.

When building a reference class, you should try to include cases that involve as many of the key factors as possible (Figure 5.4). It's even more important

5.4 Developing a reference class

■ Ideal reference class   ◻ Second-best reference class

Ideal reference class	Examples of possible reference classes
Similar business situations where relevant *industries* intersect with relevant *predictive factors of success*	**For EMI** • Companies diversifying into unrelated fields • Medical-diagnostic-imaging companies • Companies in early stage of business life cycle • Technological leaders lacking complementary assets for target market competing against diversifiers with complementary assets for related markets

Possible reference class for the Segway

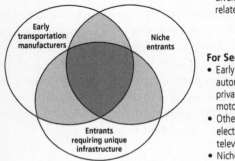

For Segway
- Early transportation manufacturers: automobiles; fuel-cell and hydrogen cars; private planes; bicycles and scooters; motorcycles
- Other entrants requiring unique infrastructure: electric power; telecommunications; high-definition television
- Niche entrants

to uncover failed entries than successful ones, so as to ensure that the reference class approximates the distribution of actual outcomes. The more closely it mirrors the experience of the industry in question, the more valuable it will be to you. That said, it is also useful, particularly if the industry is a new or emerging one, to extend your reference set across different industries.

We can see how valuable a strong reference class can be if we return to one of the case studies. What the Segway management team missed was that the usefulness of the new vehicle would depend on changes to infrastructure. How many cities would allow people to drive their Segway on sidewalks? If potential purchasers had to use roads instead, how many of them would still be willing to buy it? Since the answer to both questions was "not many," very few Segways were sold.

A broad reference class that included conventional automobiles, fuel-cell cars, hydrogen cars, and other infrastructure-dependent technologies such as high-definition TVs and telephones might have revealed that securing purchasers' right to ride the Segway in cities was of paramount importance. After all, it took decades to create the roads, power grids, networks, and standards necessary for cars, electric lighting, telephone services, and cell phones to become ubiquitous.

■ ■ ■

We've seen in this chapter that it *is* possible to increase momentum. Some of the iconic names in business manage it year after year. They find momentum and ride it just as an aircraft catches a tailwind. But there the analogy ends. The skill for a large corporation lies in constructing a "staircase" of business-building steps so that it can climb from one to the next without ever slowing pace. This calls for insight, big choices, and the objectivity that comes from using the right reference classes.

For some companies, shifting momentum may take too long or be too much to ask. We now turn our attention to the second growth cylinder, M&A.

NOTES

[1] Two-year averages.

[2] An example is the move by Intel's Andy Grove into microprocessors, which we describe in the Conclusion.

[3] See Michael Treacy's opinion piece in the *Harvard Business Review*, July–August 2004, pp. 29–30: "Home runs can certainly win baseball games. But constantly swinging for the fences doesn't make good sense—not when bunts and singles can generate robust growth."

[4] G. Hamel and G. Getz, "Funding growth in an age of austerity," *Harvard Business Review*, July–August 2004, p. 82.

[5] This section draws heavily on an article of the same name by J. T. Horn, D. P. Lovallo, and S. P. Viguerie in *The McKinsey Quarterly*, 2005, number 4, pp. 34–45.

[6] For an interesting discussion on this topic, see A. Campbell and R. Park, "Stop kissing frogs," *Harvard Business Review*, July–August 2004, pp. 27–8.

[7] See the interview by Paul Hemp in *Harvard Business Review*, July–August 2004, p. 73.

[8] Behavioral economists have written extensively about the impact of cognitive biases on financial markets and on a wide range of decisions. See C. Roxburgh, "Hidden flaws in strategy," *The McKinsey Quarterly*, 2003, number 2, pp. 26–39, for an overview of the relationship between cognitive biases and strategic mistakes, as wel as a partial summary of the literature on this topic.

[9] This is not to suggest that EMI had not made a major innovation: Hounsfield won a Nobel Prize for his work in 1979.

6

Firing on M&A

"Certainly there are lots of things in life that money won't buy,
but it's very funny—Have you ever tried to buy them without money?"
Ogden Nash, "The Terrible People"

- The average large company gets 31 percent of its revenue growth from M&A

- More than 50 percent of acquirers are rewarded in the long term even after paying a premium to the seller

- M&A needs to be matched by judicious and timely divestments, especially of businesses showing early signs of demise

- Companies can learn a lot from private-equity firms, which now account for almost 30 percent of buy-outs

- The real question isn't whether M&A is good or bad, but whether you are good at M&A

IN PART I, we showed that M&A plays a crucial role in the growth of large companies. Judging by the volume of M&A activity out there, we might conclude that M&A is high on most executives' agendas. There are obviously a lot of CEOs who believe that M&A can create value.

Yet conventional wisdom would have it otherwise. Academics and management consultants have long been skeptical about M&A. Studies suggest that most mergers and acquisitions destroy value; some cite failure rates as high as 70 or 80 percent. Of course, we all know cases that have ended in disaster. Yet despite the studies and the anecdotal evidence, many CEOs continue to pursue M&A. So what do they know that academics and consultants don't?

Studying the studies

To understand why many CEOs take a different point of view, it helps to look at the studies themselves. Most studies don't really tell us whether M&A creates value. Admittedly, it's a difficult question to answer. The studies that stand up to the closest academic scrutiny measure "announcement effects": statistically significant stock-price moves in a narrow trading window around the time of a deal announcement (say, the five days immediately before the announcement and the five days after it). The idea is that the deal is probably the most important fact on investors' minds during this period, so that any stock-price fluctuations are likely to be influenced by their reactions to it.

There's a problem with this approach, however. The only information that investors have to go on when a deal is announced concerns price and the identity and nature of the participants. Important though these factors are, they are far from the whole story. The most important factor, the outcome of the transaction, can't be known in the announcement window; it will depend on the integration and performance of the businesses involved, something that may be impossible to judge until years later.

But let's accept the method for the moment and study what happens in the announcement window, as the market isn't completely wrong. Let's look at how a typical analysis is carried out. The basic idea is to examine a population of announced deals and to calculate stock-price reactions to each deal during the announcement window. Any moves that are small (within one standard deviation) are deemed insignificant and excluded from the results as "noise" within daily trading. The remaining group, the deals where statistically significant price moves have occurred within the window, are then compared to establish the nature of the announcement effects.

Be warned: you need to take these calculations with a pinch of salt. To see why, let's take a look at the market reaction to the M&A deals in Figure 6.1.[1] Look at the data one way, as we've described in the previous paragraph, and you end up with a 58 percent failure rate. In other words, if we exclude the 46 percent of "neutral" reactions that weren't statistically significant and take the 53 percent that were, 31 percent of these (equivalent to 58 percent of the whole sample) had negative reactions, and only 22 percent (42 percent of the whole sample) had positive ones.

However, if you look at the deals a different way and factor the "neutral" reactions back in, the 58 percent failure rate dwindles to just 31 percent for the sample as a whole. In other words, almost 70 percent of the deals analyzed were viewed either neutrally or positively by the market, and *not* negatively. This example illustrates how opposite conclusions can be drawn from the same data.

6.1 Same data, different interpretations

Percent of M&A deals by abnormal return range*

Neutral to positive market reaction

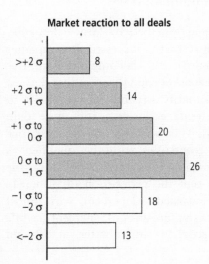

Market reaction to all deals

>+2 σ	8
+2 σ to +1 σ	14
+1 σ to 0 σ	20
0 σ to −1 σ	26
−1 σ to −2 σ	18
<−2 σ	13

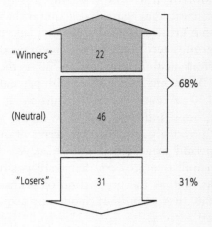

Reported results

"Winners"	22	68%
(Neutral)	46	
"Losers"	31	31%

Numbers do not always add up to 100% because of rounding
* Abnormal returns in excess of beta-adjusted S&P returns; significance is abnormal return as a multiple of time-adjusted sigma, which is the standard deviation on log normal daily returns (60 trading days prior to announcement)
Sample: Top 102 US companies by revenue and market capitalization as of 1994

If you then extend the window by a year and look at the stock prices of the same population of companies (a step that doesn't pass muster with academics, since it introduces noise from other sources into the stock price), an interesting result emerges. Among those classified as "winners" according to stock-price movements five days either side of the announcement, 39 percent had *lower* stock prices a year later, whereas 52 percent of the "losers" had *higher* stock prices.

Put all this together and what it means is that once you take into account neutral reactions, the chance of a statistically significant negative reaction is only about 30 percent. Moreover, if you fast-forward, the chance of a positive outcome is almost as high as that of a negative outcome in the long term.

While there is no shortage of M&A failures, it seems likely that the risks of M&A have been overestimated somewhere, somehow.

Leaders do more M&A than you realize

Our growth decomposition database shows that the average large company gets nearly a third of its growth—3.1 percentage points a year—from M&A.[2] For a $35 billion company, that's more than $1 billion in acquired revenue each year. Note that this contribution to growth is *net* M&A, so it also takes into account divestments carried out within the time period.

Moreover, a review of the growth strategies pursued by large companies suggests that aggressive acquirers have been at least as successful as companies that grow organically. We divided our sample of 100 US companies into four groups according to the percentage of their market capitalization that derived from acquisitions: up to 30 percent (primarily organic growers), 30 to 70 percent and 70 to 150 percent (moderate acquirers), and more than 150 percent (primarily acquisitive growers). Then we took each of these four groups and analyzed how many of the companies within it qualified as "positively rewarded" in terms of outperforming their peers in TRS over the period measured (Figure 6.2). We found that the proportion of primarily acquisitive growers that were positively rewarded (42 percent) was almost as high as the proportion of primarily organic growers (49 percent), while the two groups of moderate acquirers scored a little better, at 50 and 60 percent.

One key difference between acquirers that were positively rewarded and those that were not was the ability to change operating performance. In a sample of ten companies, operating margins rose for *all* the positively rewarded

6.2 Are aggressive acquirers rewarded?

Percent of positively rewarded companies* among aggressive acquirers, moderate acquirers, and primarily organic growers†

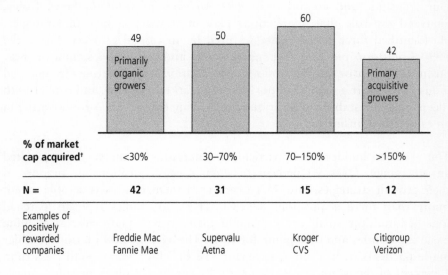

% of market cap acquired†	<30%	30–70%	70–150%	>150%
N =	42	31	15	12
Examples of positively rewarded companies	Freddie Mac Fannie Mae	Supervalu Aetna	Kroger CVS	Citigroup Verizon

* Those that outperformed peers in TRS 1994–2004
† Measured at time of acquisition, allowing for cumulative percentages to exceed 100%
Sample: Top 102 US companies by revenue and market capitalization as of 1994
Source: Compustat; McKinsey analysis

acquirers during the period, and fell for four out of five of the negatively rewarded group.

It's clear, then, that M&A can succeed: on average, just over half of companies are rewarded in the longer term. Not only that, but they succeed after paying a significant premium to the seller. This suggests that over time the stock markets learn which companies make good acquisitions and reward them accordingly.

So the question becomes one of confidence and capability. How well do you think you do M&A? Let's see what we can learn from successful growers.

How growth companies use M&A

Saying that M&A can be successful and that acquisitive companies are frequently rewarded doesn't tell us *how* companies use it to grow. We are often asked whether companies should favor large deals or small ones. We believe that both have their role: large deals mainly in industry consolidations and divestitures and small in platform building. As we see in chapter 8, the right M&A strategy for your company will depend on your growth direction.

Our colleague and co-author of *The Alchemy of Growth*, Steve Coley, analyzed the role that acquisitions play in supporting growth strategies. He identified three broad strategies used by successful growers during the 1990s: *platform building* (expanding scope and creating a significant new business segment or activity), *roll-up/consolidation* (consolidating a fragmented industry to create a significant position in a market segment), and *core growth* (deepening an established position in a growing market and/or innovating in an established business).

The platform builders were particularly interesting in the way they created an advantage. Over 90 percent of them used acquisitions in support of their growth strategies, and 75 percent used them to a considerable extent (more than three acquisitions a year). These companies typically patched together multiple small deals to build their growth platforms, assembling basic capabilities and then going for scale. The average new platform builder made 65 deals over a ten-year period, 58 of which were small (less than 1 percent of the acquirer's market cap). By contrast, Coley's broader sample of high-growth but low-TRS companies made just 44 deals on average, 34 of them small.

In creating an advantage, successful platform builders typically begin with small acquisitions and increase the size of their commitment to the platform over time, thereby managing the risk. Some 60 percent of all initial acquisitions in these new growth staircases accounted for less than 20 percent of a company's total investment in the new platforms. That is to say, they were entry acquisitions that were followed by other moves.

Also noteworthy was the role that large acquisitions played. The average size of the largest acquisition made by a platform builder was 17 percent of its market cap; for the high-growth low-TRS companies, it was much larger, at 40 percent.

Let's now take a look at one company that has turned the making of acquisitions into a fine art.

The building blocks of growth

CRH's growth is a truly remarkable story of how a company can manage granular acquisitions. Since its formation in 1970 following the merger of two Irish building materials companies, it has grown to almost €15 billion in revenue and €1.3 billion in net profit, with a market capitalization of €17 billion. It operates in some 2,600 locations across 26 countries with over 65,000 employees. Thanks to its impressive compound annual growth rate of almost 19 percent since 1970, if you had invested $100 in 1970, your stake would be worth over $50,000 today.

CRH has stuck to the same formula for a quarter of a century. It has grown primarily by acquiring small- to medium-sized businesses at a good price to build leading positions in local markets. A typical deal improves the local industry structure and leaves room for CRH to add value by injecting global know-how and capital for further investment. The company has made hundreds of acquisitions in the past 25 years, spending around €1 billion a year on them in the past five years alone.

The business is operated through largely autonomous local business units that match the granularity of the market. These units are clustered in broad product groups in key markets. This represents the right level of granularity for CRH for two reasons. First, the construction industry is one where transport costs are high and customers and tradespeople are local, so it makes sense for business units to be local too.

Second, most of the acquisition opportunities targeted by CRH are also local businesses run by owner-entrepreneurs. In most cases, CRH managers pursue a patient courtship with these owners, knowing that at some point they will be keen to cash out or pass the business to the next generation. CRH offers them a unique proposition: join the CRH federation, pocket the cash, and continue to run the business. Since price is only one part of the value proposition, the company leaves room for the acquirer to capture value from the deal. It also taps into a unique talent pipeline of proven entrepreneurs, many of whom stay with CRH and move into more senior roles.

CRH's decentralized structure is fundamental to its M&A process. The deal pipelines are long—up to ten years—and depend on local relationships in a way that few M&A departments could match. Moreover, a typical acquisition is so small that it wouldn't even register on the radar screen of most centralized M&A teams. By combining local managers with a team of seasoned deal makers in each region, CRH has devised a winning formula. Its deal pipeline is extensive, stretching not only into the small local markets where the company already operates but also into adjacent markets where it might choose to operate in the future.

Not every deal that CRH does is small, though. The regional managers in each product group also keep a look-out for larger deals. They have 15 regional development teams reporting to them, all staffed with experienced deal makers who execute the transactions. This combination gives CRH a unique portfolio advantage in attracting and executing deals in the building materials industry.

In 2003, it carried out 41 deals for a total of €1.6 billion. One was the largest in its history: the purchase of Cementbouw, a leading Dutch manufacturer and distributor, for €700 million. The average size of deals, however, was less than €20 million.

Once it acquires a business, CRH expects it to follow standardized reporting procedures and to adhere to performance measures that it tailors to the market and the capital intensity of the business. It also expects dual citizenship: though local businesses are run largely autonomously, connections are made across the organization in order to share best practices and exploit the scale of a global business. It says of this arrangement:

> "Experienced operational management are given a high degree of individual responsibility. This local autonomy, within Group guidelines and controls, helps accommodate national and cultural needs and capitalizes on local market knowledge. The Group's size and structure is leveraged to drive margin improvement and earnings growth. Product-based best practice teams promote performance improvement through the sharing of experience, technologies and ideas."[3]

CRH's ability to grow its business deal by deal at a local level while exploiting both traditional scale benefits and unique portfolio advantages has created one of the most remarkable and consistent growth stories of recent times.

Don't forget divestment

M&A isn't just about acquisitions, of course. In *Good to Great,* Jim Collins argues that successful leaders need to have a "stop doing" list as well as a "to do" list.[4] Divestment is the "stop doing" aspect of growth improvement. And just as executives tend to focus more on their "to do" lists than on their "stop doing" lists, divestment is often overlooked as a way to create value.

Let's look at an example. In 1994, ITT Industries was a diversified conglomerate with holdings ranging from hotels to defense electronics. It decided to concentrate on just two segments that had growth potential and were aligned with its capabilities: defense electronics and fluid technologies (pumps, mixers, and valves). It spun off the rest of its portfolio, creating substantial value for shareholders. ITT now had a strong operational focus in segments with favorable growth conditions. In essence, it had shrunk to grow (Figure 6.3).

ITT didn't qualify as a growth giant by our criteria: by 2003, its revenues had reached only 70 percent of their 1994 level. However, the company did increase its annual TRS by 18 percent during the portfolio transition, and the remaining businesses are growing rapidly, by an average of 18 percent over the past three years. To sum up ITT's performance over the course of ten years, we could say that it made a strategic decision to exit businesses with relatively low growth potential in order to position its portfolio for higher growth during the next cycle.

6.3 ITT's revenue breakdown
Revenue by segment, 1994–2006, percent

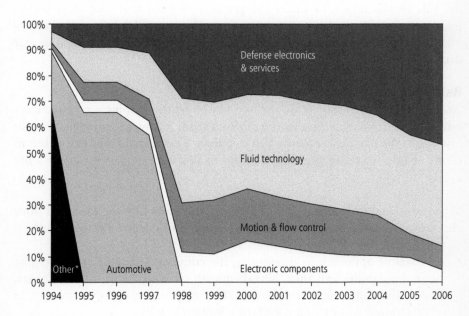

* Insurance (70%), hospitality & entertainment (25%), and communications & information services (5%)
Source: Annual reports; McKinsey analysis

Not many companies use divestment as part of their growth strategy; indeed, executives should probably do much more of it than they do. During the 1990s, nearly 60 percent of the largest US companies completed no more than two divestments exceeding $100 million[5]—numbers that contrast sharply with those for M&A.

So why are divestments so rare? For one thing, they are difficult: those involved in the decision often face the loss of their own jobs; layoffs and worker buy-outs incur real costs; the separation of a division often leaves behind an overhead burden. Another reason lies in the psychological biases that affect decision making: they cause companies to ignore warning signals, to avoid adjusting goals to reflect changing circumstances, and to continue to invest beyond the opportunity for return.[6]

Not only do companies do relatively little divestment, but when they do, they tend to wait too long. When we analyzed the challenged companies from the Introduction that decided to sell, we found that early sellers fared better than late sellers. Another analysis suggests that exit decisions are most often taken at the troughs of business cycles—not the ideal time to sell, as prices are likely to be at their lowest.[7] All too often, divestment decisions are made during a fire sale or shutdown, or under the pressure of persistent long-term under-performance and consequent scrutiny from investors.[8] Understanding this—and putting in mechanisms to compensate for it—is critical to making exit decisions well.[9]

Balancing acquisitions and divestments

Acquisition and divestment are the two key levers for shaping a corporation's business portfolio over the short to medium term. As always, timing is critical; not just in the narrow sense of when to pursue a particular transaction, but in terms of how to tailor portfolio activity to the stage of a corporation's life cycle.

When we analyzed moderately diversified companies,[10] we identified four characteristics associated with managing a corporation's portfolio successfully:

- A proactive approach to monitoring the company's current and emerging internal capabilities and matching them with external changes in technology, regulation, and consumer behavior that might open up opportunities in related industries or make use of the company's skills.

- The rapid divestment of businesses that show early signs of possible failure.

- The prompt "liberation" of successful new businesses after the opportunities for internal synergies have been realized.

- The active and continuous trading of business portfolios.

Companies with focused, mature business portfolios are logical candidates for acquisition-based diversification. A critical first step is to make a realistic and candid assessment of your capabilities. More diversified companies with low expectations of value creation would benefit from focusing their portfolios. Diversified companies, even those capable of generating high growth and commanding high investor expectations, should be aware of the maturation trajectories of their business units and think about when it makes sense to divest them, rather than waiting until their value begins to decline and they become harder to sell.

The active and balanced trading of assets is important. One study showed that companies that manage their corporate portfolios actively (those in the top third of total M&A activity) create 30 percent more value over the long term than the more passive portfolio managers do. And for mature companies, strategies that involve both acquisitions and divestments outperform those that focus on one or the other.[11]

Although divestment detracts from growth in the short term, it's interesting to look at why some moderately diversified companies liberate businesses early. In 2001, BellSouth and SBC placed their wireless assets in a joint venture that became Cingular Wireless. With their complementary service footprints, the two companies established a national wireless brand and went on to acquire AT&T Wireless in 2004, thereby creating the largest wireless operator in the US. BellSouth's chairman and CEO, Duane Ackerman, explained the logic of this acquisition by pointing to the impact it had on his company's revenue growth rate: "We have the highest exposure to the highest growth segment in the industry." By liberating its captive wireless properties, BellSouth placed them in what became a much stronger strategic position.

Lessons from private-equity firms

The extreme case in balancing acquisitions and divestment is exemplified in the practices of private-equity firms. In recent years, private equity has become much more important: almost 30 percent of buy-outs (the A of M&A) now go to private-equity companies. Whether they will continue on this roll is not the issue. What concerns us here is their distinctive approach to M&A: they sell almost as quickly as they buy, which gives them a unique set of advantages. We believe there is much that corporations can learn from this approach.

Long-term (not incremental) focus

Managers often complain about the market's relentless pressure on improving earnings quarter by quarter without fail. They have a point: if you take historical data for margins, revenue cash flows, or any other measure of performance you care to examine, there is hardly any performance pattern that is consistent quarter after quarter. In fact, there is barely any difference between volatile patterns and more stable ones in terms of TRS, as Figure 6.4 shows.

One reason why managers are so nervous about quarter-by-quarter performance is that companies that issue quarterly earnings guidance find markets swift to punish them if they miss their pre-announced quarterly targets. They issue the guidance despite this risk because they believe that the increased transparency will reduce the volatility of their stock price and/or increase their earnings multiple. However, a recent study calls this view into question. It looked at 4,000 publicly traded companies from 1994 to 2004

6.4 Volatility in earnings growth barely affects TRS

Percent

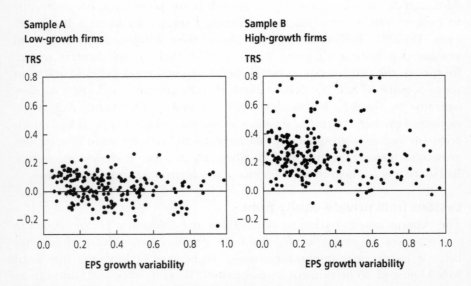

Sample A
Low-growth firms

Sample B
High-growth firms

Sample: 739 US companies with EPS estimate, TRS, and beta available for 1991–2000, excluding financial services firms
Source: Compustat; SDC; Bloomberg; McKinsey analysis

and found no difference in valuation multiples or volatility between companies in the same industry that did and didn't issue quarterly guidance. [12]

Unlike the wider market, private-equity firms tend to act on a time frame that is measured in years rather than quarters. Henry Kravis of private-equity firm KKR observed that:

> "The trouble with corporate America today is that everything is thought of in quarters. Analysts push [companies]: 'What are you going to earn this quarter?' [Whereas] we say to the management of companies, 'You are here today. Where do you want to be five years from now, and how are you going to get there?' It may very well mean taking a step backwards. But believe me, in five years, we are going to have a company that is much more productive, efficient, and competitive."[13]

Granular investment insight

The advantages enjoyed by private-equity firms start from the way they gather the information they need for M&A. Conventional wisdom has it that markets are perfect and that all available information is traded upon, yet in reality the texture of the market is far more granular than the information available in the wider market. Though the market is quick to act on information released in a company's quarterly and annual updates, these updates can never do justice to the detail and complexity of the company's performance at sub-industry and category levels. Moreover, updates never look ahead for more than a couple of years, whereas the company itself will often plan and invest on a much longer time horizon.

A private-equity firm is not restricted to the information provided to the market. Because it has access to data rooms and management interviews when conducting due diligence, it is able to obtain information that is far more granular than that available to public-company investors.

As we explain in chapter 13, there are ways for large companies to build "insight engines" similar to those used by private-equity firms to drive their information advantage.

Attention to the assets

Because investment insight is so important, the amount of attention you give to an asset matters a lot, particularly when you are trying to understand how it performs at a granular level. Private capital, including family capital, often has an advantage over other owners in the time and attention it gives to its assets.

A typical private-equity partner devotes most of his or her time to purchased assets, and the rest to buying additional ones. Compare this with the practices of a typical board director and it looks like an awful lot of time, especially since the average private-equity partner has no more assets to look after than the average director, who may attend only six to ten board meetings a year. In addition, private capital usually draws on extensive analytical and other kinds of support.

High incentives

The scale of the incentives provided by private-equity firms often gives them another advantage over the corporate world. Consider VNU (now Nielsen), a mid-sized market-research company originating from Europe but operating mainly in the US. Partly because of the differences between US and European business cultures, incentives had always been an issue. But when a private-equity consortium bought VNU and appointed David Calhoun, a former top executive at GE, as CEO, it awarded him an incentive package worth hundreds of millions of dollars. This introduced a completely different culture into the company in terms of both executive selection and incentives.

We've found that private-equity firms are now regularly outpacing corporations in the incentive structures they offer, giving them a clear edge in attracting and motivating talent.

■ ■ ■

Both M&A and divestment are important tools for shaping the portfolio to facilitate more sustainable growth. There is evidence that active and balanced M&A strategies create value. Yet surprisingly few companies make full use of divestment.

Private-equity firms throw down a gauntlet for corporations: they have a highly aggressive, highly diversified model of both acquisition and divestment, and yet they still produce a decent return after paying substantial premiums. The success of their ventures suggests that corporations could create a lot more value through M&A than they might imagine.

We will return to the M&A theme in chapter 13, and describe in greater detail how some companies build M&A engines to pursue a large number of transactions.

NOTES

[1] The data derives from an analysis we made of the top 75 US companies by market cap and the top 75 by revenue as of 1994. After overlaps were eliminated, 102 companies remained.

[2] See Figure 2.4.

[3] CRH annual report 2003, p. 1.

[4] J. Collins, *Good to Great: Why some companies make the leap . . . and others don't* (HarperCollins, New York, 2001).

[5] This point is based on an analysis of the 200 largest US companies (by market capitalization) in 1990 that still existed in 2000.

[6] J. Horn, D. Lovallo, and P. Viguerie, "Learning to let go," *The McKinsey Quarterly,* 2006, number 2, pp. 65–6.

[7] R. E. Caves, "Industrial organizations and new findings on the turnover and mobility of firms," *Journal of Economic Literature,* 1998, volume 36, number 4, pp. 1947–82.

[8] N. W. C. Harper and S. P. Viguerie, "Are you too focused?" *The McKinsey Quarterly,* August 2002, special edition, *Risk and Resilience,* pp. 29–37.

[9] J. Horn, D. Lovallo, and P. Viguerie, "Learning to let go," *The McKinsey Quarterly,* 2006, number 2, pp. 65–6.

[10] N. W. C. Harper and S. P. Viguerie, "Are you too focused?" *The McKinsey Quarterly,* August 2002, special edition, *Risk and Resilience,* pp. 29–37.

[11] J. P. Brandimarte, W. C. Fallon, and R. S. McNish, "Trading the corporate portfolio," *McKinsey on Finance,* number 2, autumn 2001, pp. 1–5.

[12] P. Hsieh, T. Koller, and S. R. Rajan, "The misguided practice of earnings guidance," *McKinsey on Finance,* 2006, pp. 1–5. The article also examined what happens to companies that decide to begin issuing guidance. It compared the volatility and multiples in the year that guidance starts to those in the previous year, and then compared any observed changes to those observed in the rest of the industry. Again, it found no benefit to the companies that issued quarterly guidance.

[13] Interview with American Academy of Achievement, 12 February 1991.

7

Firing on share gain

"The strongest principle of growth lies in human choice."
George Eliot, Daniel Deronda

- Market-share gain is not the main driver of growth and differential growth performance, but it is still important

- In the short term, gaining market share can boost revenue growth

- Gaining substantial share is difficult to achieve and even harder to sustain

- To do it, you need either an advantage that stands out a mile or the ability to change the rules of the game

S WE'VE SEEN, market-share gain is *not* the main driver of either growth or differences in growth performance. Our analysis shows that over a five-year period, it explains only about 21 percent of the difference in growth performance within our sample of large companies.

But that's not to say that share gain is unimportant. In the short term, actions that boost market share can also boost revenue growth. Indeed, if we shrink the timeframe we considered in chapter 2 to a single year, share gain becomes much more important. Similarly, across one-year periods, share gains and losses account for 26 percent of differences in growth performance in aggregate, spiking to as high as 33 percent in a single year.

In addition, market-share performance is always important from a company's point of view because loss of share tends to be judged harshly. Your share loss is your competitor's share gain. In a world that often judges a company's performance against that of its peers, CEOs are seldom forgiven for a deteriorating share trajectory.

Finally, a loss of market share may lead to a reduction in margin. As we describe in Appendix 2, the "grow" path requires margins to be maintained or increased. In this sense, losing market share could mean that growth doesn't create shareholder value.

A tough task

So gaining market share is important. It's also extremely challenging. Among the companies in our granular growth decomposition sample, only about one in ten achieved substantial share gain. By this, we mean that they derived more than 4 percentage points of their overall annual revenue growth from share gain (note that this *doesn't* mean they gained 4 points of market share a year!).

That so few companies attained this level of performance shows how difficult it is to obtain strong growth by firing on this one cylinder alone. The task becomes even more of a challenge if you are in a sector that isn't benefiting from a tailwind because all the players are likely to be focused on share battles.

When we look at the market-share performance of the companies in our growth decomposition database, we find that the share gainers and losers tend to fire or misfire on share across the board. In other words, winners do well in most (79 percent) of their segments, while losers perform poorly in most (77 percent) of theirs (Figure 7.1).

It's important to note, though, that 80 percent of companies gain or lose only a small amount of market share in aggregate. To get a real sense of what's happening, you have to look deeper to find the segments that are firing and the ones that aren't. In this sense, share firing is very granular for most companies: if your market-share performance varies from one segment to another, you're unlikely to be firing on the share cylinder at the company level.

Since achieving growth through share gain is so difficult, a company that has chosen this route must have a clear understanding of how to succeed at it.

7.1 Market-share performance by segments

Percent of segments gained or lost by group

Group	Segments lost	Segments gained	Share of sample companies
Strong share gainers (more than 4.3% of annual revenue CAGR from market share)	−21	79	10%
Slight share gainers (up to 4.3%)	−36	64	38%
Slight share losers (up to −4.3%)	−61	39	42%
Strong share losers (more than −4.3%)	−77	23	10%

Sample: Granular growth decomposition database

Learning from the winners

The top fifteen share gainers in our sample from 1999 to 2005 did succeed in gaining substantial share. The contribution to annual revenue growth made by share gain ranged from 6 to 20 percentage points (Figure 7.2). Given such substantial shifts, it's fair to say that these companies transformed the markets they were competing in. But how did they do it?

7.2 The top share gainers

Contribution to annual revenue growth rate, 1999–2005, percentage points

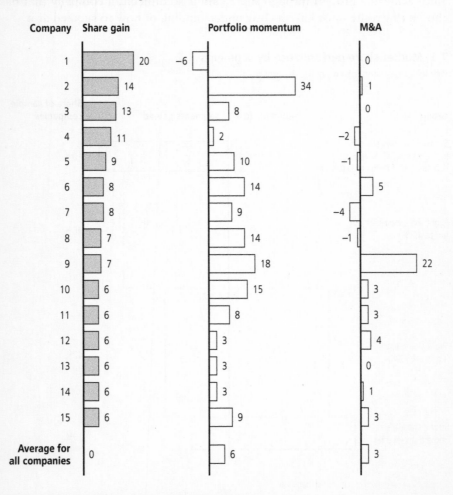

Source: SDC; Hoovers; company reports; analyst reports; McKinsey analysis

Before a company can gain share, it obviously needs some kind of edge over those companies from which it takes share. When we analyzed the top fifteen share gainers, one thing stood out: they've all made big choices—strong commitments to create distinctive (and possibly disruptive) business models—on the basis of insights or distinctive advantages. Not all big choices are rewarded by share gain, of course. However, it does seem that fortune favors the brave, or at least those with expansive mindsets.

To illustrate this, let's take a quick glance at five of the fifteen star performers.

Dell: Fresh thinking about the supply chain

Dell's share gain is the result of its distinctive insight into the evolution of the computer hardware industry, coupled with its advantage in supply-chain management, which has been well documented.[1] By selling direct to customers, it was able to grow organically at 13 percent in a market that was itself contracting (by 6 percent between 1999 and 2005).

Dell used its insight to make a big choice about the nature of its business model and its approach to the supply chain before putting in the operational work needed to make it happen. If all that hard work had been directed toward a "me too" approach, Dell's growth history would have looked very different.

Valero: High-complexity refining

As we saw in chapter 3, Valero is one of the rare companies that fires on all growth cylinders. In the period between 1981 and 2005, Valero made a huge bet by investing in heavy-crude refining. The capabilities and insight it built over two decades paid off when commodity prices skyrocketed.

The company bought its first refinery in Corpus Christi, Texas, in 1981. The refinery was designed to process heavy, sour grades of crude, which are much more complex to refine than the more popular lighter, sweeter grades. Valero committed $1 billion to upgrading the refinery and began to build capabilities for producing clean fuel (reformulated gasoline) using sour crude and heavily discounted residual fuel.

Its decision to acquire refineries that others found unattractive stemmed from top management's insight that environmental regulations would increase the demand for clean fuel. This commitment paid off in revenue terms: from 1999 to 2005, Valero's markets grew by 18 percent CAGR and organic share gain by 7 percent CAGR.

Valero's capability is not confined to capturing market share and tapping into a booming market. It also uses M&A extensively and has developed skills at turning around acquisitions—even troubled ones such as Orion Refining, which it acquired at a bargain price. By making the right granular choices and building the right capabilities, it has been able to create a clear advantage over competitors in the industry and gain significant market share.

Toyota: Quality at affordable prices

Toyota's performance is exceptional: it has gained share in all of the 19 markets in which it operates, apart from two small segments in Asia (outside Japan). When it comes to share gain, North America is by far its most important market, and represents almost half the total increase.

The company claims its advantage lies in its ability to offer high quality and reliability at affordable prices. It achieves this through its commitment to the Toyota Production System, which pioneered lean manufacturing methods that have since been adopted in many other industries around the world. This radically different approach to operations is undoubtedly a key factor in explaining Toyota's share gain.

Centrica: Changing the retail energy game

Not every company that achieves substantial share gain is as well known or possesses such global reach as Toyota. Consider Centrica, which has achieved a remarkable turnaround largely through its advantage in its UK operations.

In the 1990s, Centrica (then the retail arm of British Gas) suffered heavy market-share losses following the deregulation of its industrial and residential gas businesses in the UK. But the tide turned in 1998. Although its share of the residential gas market was still dwindling, the company took advantage of the opening up of the residential electricity market to attack regional incumbents. Its expansion was successful: five years later, Centrica had become the market leader, with a share that had soared from zero in 1998 to 24 percent in 2003.

Centrica's advantage was twofold. First, it had privileged assets: its customer base in the gas business and its brand recognition. Even though it had lost substantial market share, Centrica was still serving about 80 percent of UK households at the time it launched its electricity offering. This put it in a privileged position to offer its customers both gas and electricity.

Which brings us to the second source of advantage: Centrica's insight that a dual-fuel offer would be a key success factor and that it was well placed to provide such an offer. History proved it right: market research published in 2001 revealed that consumers choosing a utility provider rated a dual-fuel offer as the second most important factor after price.

Samsung: Betting on new technology

In recent years, Samsung Electronics has had a stupendous track record in share gain, especially in the telecommunications and semiconductor segments. Our granular growth decomposition analysis reveals that these two segments account for an overwhelming part of its share gain between 1999 and 2005. Although we agree with commentators that great branding is one source of Samsung's stellar performance, especially in consumer electronics, we don't think it is the only one. We would also point to the big choices made by Samsung's chairman Kun-Hee Lee—choices based on his insight into the market on the one hand and a set of truly exceptional growth capabilities on the other.

Let's hone in on telecommunications, which contributed more than half of Samsung's total share gain. In this segment, the two major choices it made were to commit to CDMA[2] technology and to adopt a "fast-integrator model"[3] that allowed it to test and develop new products quickly, so helping it to gain share through rapid innovations in a high-momentum competitive arena. It's hard to beat the combination of a powerful business model and a favorable tailwind.

Samsung's ability to exploit the fast-integrator model stems not from a one-off effort to improve manufacturing efficiency, but from a distinctive operational competency. So ingrained is its execution focus, that if you were to remove it, you would no longer recognize the company.

Shaping your own destiny

All these examples illustrate that if a company is to achieve substantial share gain, it must make big choices that create advantage. This calls for an expansive mindset. Dell took its direct model into new markets and new products. Valero capitalized on its carefully constructed advantage in complex refineries. Toyota pushed its lean manufacturing system into new segments and countries. Centrica used its knowledge as a gas supplier to expand into electricity. Samsung exploited its ability to take new products to market at unprecedented speed.

If we look at the top fifteen share *losers*, we naturally see a very different picture. All suffered losses in annual revenue growth: between 5 and 15 percentage points a year. Some of these companies were deliberately exiting certain sub-segments because of poor performance, as Corning did in telecommunications and Fujitsu in components. But most had failed to respond to attacks from others. For instance, First Pacific Company Ltd, a diversified Hong Kong–based company with businesses including consumer food products and telecommunications, didn't respond to new entrants selling below cost and was overtaken by new business models.

Rather than shaping their destiny through big choices, the share losers were driven by the market. Here lies an important difference between winners and losers. While big gains require big choices (nearly 80 percent of share-gain winners had a distinctive business-model advantage), you don't have to make a big choice to qualify as a loser, nor do you need a historically distinctive *dis*advantage. Adopting a passive posture may well be enough. In our sample, half of the share-gain losers had a distinctive disadvantage, while the other half stumbled on execution.

Segment size matters (but not just in the way you think)

As we've explained, our granular growth decomposition is derived at a segment level. This means that a company's share gain or loss is calculated as a weighted average of the difference between its own organic growth rates and the growth rates of the underlying segments. When we look at the leading winners and losers, we find that more often than not, as we saw in Figure 7.1, they tend to exhibit strong or weak market-share performance across most of their segments.

In this case, segment size matters as well: we find that the larger segments dominate the aggregate revenue impact. Needless to say, strong or weak share-gain performance in a large business has a big impact on revenue; it's a numbers game. But the upshot is important as well as obvious: small market-share shifts in large segments have a disproportionate effect on the total picture for your company.

When we cut market-share performance by segment size, we see the greatest share extremes in smaller segments, with contributions to annual revenue growth as high as 23 percent and revenue loss as high as 33 percent. However, the biggest impact on revenue growth rates comes from segments representing more than 30 percent of a company's total revenues (Figure 7.3).

Short-term wins

We mentioned that market share matters more over shorter time frames. In the space of a single year, market-share performance can be responsible

7.3 How changes in segment share hit revenue
Percent

Strong share gainers				Strong share losers			
Segment size*	Share gain		Revenue creation	Segment size*		Share loss	Revenue destruction
<10		23	1	<10	−33		−2
10–20		22	3	10–20	−11		−2
20–30	14		4	20–30	−6		−1
30–40	7		2	30–40	−7		−3
40–50	5		2	40–50	−7		−3
50–60	9		5	50–60	−5		−3
60–70	6		4	60–70	−5		−3
70–80	6		5	70–80	−4		−3
80–90	9		7	80–90	−8	−7	
>90	10		10	>90	−5		−5

* As a percentage of total revenue
Sample: Granular growth decomposition database

for as much as 33 percent of differences in company growth. What does this mean?

Many companies pull performance levers that boost revenues quickly: think of transaction pricing, sales stimulation, and even the launch of a new product range. When successful, such actions drive revenue growth and show up in our growth decomp as share gain. The problem is that these short-term revenue-boosting measures rarely make much difference to a company's fundamental growth trajectory; instead, they eventually get competed away. That's why market share is less important in our five-year analysis than in our one-year analysis where most companies are concerned.

The message is clear: use tactical actions to boost revenues whenever you can, but don't expect your overall growth trajectory to be driven by market-share growth unless you have a genuine advantage across a sufficiently large cross-section of your company.

In debates about market-share performance, most companies (and researchers) face a challenge of definition. The relative roles of market-share gain and market momentum depend on the level of granularity at which you view a particular market. If you use an aggregated market definition, you will tend to see more market-share gains and losses. At a more granular level, on the other hand, some of these gains and losses will reveal themselves to be momentum differences across growth pockets. Our view—and a major theme of this book— is that a fine-grained view, say at the G4 level, can help companies understand growth opportunities better and, hence, make more appropriate choices.[4]

■ ■ ■

If you're hoping to drive growth through substantial and sustained share gain, you'd better back that expansive thinking with some source of advantage that sets your company apart from the pack, whether it derives from truly superior insight or truly distinctive capabilities. If you don't, you'll find your competitors' execution soon matches yours; your market-share performance takes a dive; and your shareholders lower their expectations, stalling your growth program.

NOTES

[1] See, for instance, J. P. Womack, D. T. Jones, and D. Roos, *The Machine that Changed the World: The story of lean production* (Rawson Associates, New York, 1990) and M. Dell and C. Fredman, *Direct from Dell: Strategies that revolutionized an industry* (HarperCollins, New York, 1999).

[2] Code division multiple access, an alternative to GSM.

[3] This model is characterized by the rapid integration of standard components, software, and platforms from third parties and a high degree of flexibility in meeting operator and market demands. In 2003, for instance, Samsung marketed 138 different mobile phones on the basis of 78 different platforms. This was not achieved at the expense of development time, since the interval from concept to shipping was reduced from fourteen months in 1997 to just five in 2002.

[4] We'd be the first to admit that identifying the drivers of market-share gain (or performance gain in general) is treacherous research terrain, and we wouldn't claim to have overcome the problems fully in this analysis. It's true that companies with distinctive advantages have gained share by making big choices, but that doesn't mean that making big choices—even with the benefit of insight and advantage—will necessarily lead to distinctive market-share performance.

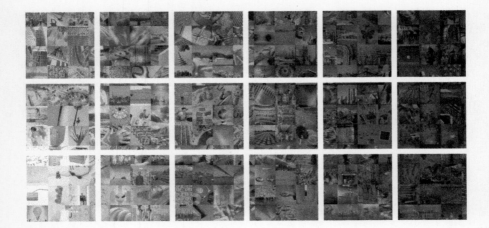

8

Mapping your growth direction

"And she's buying a stairway to heaven"
Led Zeppelin

- A compelling growth strategy is one that is clear about which cylinders will drive growth in each time horizon

- Plotting the cylinders horizon by horizon yields nine "how to" strategies that can be used to define alternative growth paths

- The growth map provides a structure for setting and communicating a growth direction and charting the actions for pursuing it

IN *THE ALCHEMY OF GROWTH* we introduced the "three horizons" framework to help business leaders look ten or more years ahead when they are formulating and articulating their growth direction. We argued that companies seeking sustained and profitable growth need a pipeline of business creation that comprises actions across all three horizons at once (Figure 8.1), and we described how the horizons could be cascaded down to leaders at all levels in an organization.

The point of the three horizons was to encourage and assist executives to evolve their portfolios over time. Since we introduced the framework, companies have adopted it to make a thorough analysis of their strategic opportunities so as to arrive at the right growth themes. Unfortunately, though, we have seen many organizations (and their advisers) use our framework loosely and thus arrive at growth strategies that aren't sufficiently robust.

8.1 The three horizons

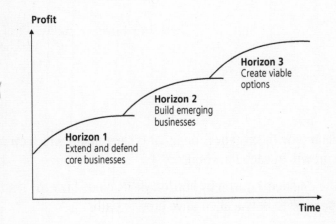

To avoid this problem, companies need to assess how their sources of advantage in each of the three cylinders match the granular opportunities in the marketplace. Fair enough, you may think, but how do you figure it all out? We have developed a new tool, the growth map, to help with this task. It provides a much more disciplined way of approaching the three horizons framework.

The growth map

As we've seen in the last three chapters, each of the three cylinders can be used to drive growth in a company. If we combine the three cylinders with the three horizons framework, we arrive at the growth map: a tool for ensuring that we apply the necessary rigor when we set our growth direction and for charting the actions we must take to pursue it.

Let's take a look at the growth map illustrated in Figure 8.2. The columns in the grid correspond to the three horizons of growth. It's important to note that the "clock" for the horizons will differ from company to company. If you're in a hyper-growth market such as consumer electronics, horizon 3 may be only a couple of years away; if you're in a slow-moving resource industry, on the other hand, you may not see horizon 3 initiatives become mature businesses for a decade or more. This means that you'll need to form a view on the right timing of horizons for your organization and markets *before* you start to set your growth direction.[1]

The rows in the grid correspond to the three growth cylinders we explored in previous chapters. The benefit of mapping cylinders against horizons is that it forces you to think clearly about how to deliver growth over time. How will you use portfolio momentum, M&A, and share gain to extend and defend your core businesses in the near term? How will firing on the three

8.2 The growth map

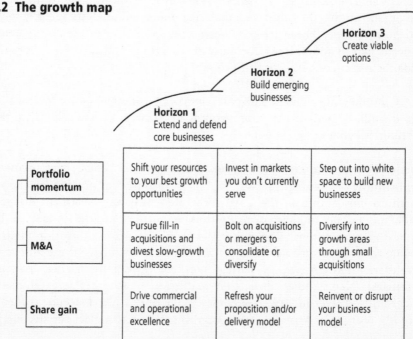

	Horizon 1 Extend and defend core businesses	Horizon 2 Build emerging businesses	Horizon 3 Create viable options
Portfolio momentum	Shift your resources to your best growth opportunities	Invest in markets you don't currently serve	Step out into white space to build new businesses
M&A	Pursue fill-in acquisitions and divest slow-growth businesses	Bolt on acquisitions or mergers to consolidate or diversify	Diversify into growth areas through small acquisitions
Share gain	Drive commercial and operational excellence	Refresh your proposition and/or delivery model	Reinvent or disrupt your business model

cylinders build your emerging businesses in the medium term? And how will you create viable options for the long term? Will your growth direction lead you to fire on more cylinders in years to come?

To answer these questions, you'll need to form objective, dispassionate judgments about your sources of advantage horizon by horizon. This is becoming more and more difficult for large companies to do well. You should include a broad set of competitors in your reference class: for instance, include private-equity firms in the reference class you use to evaluate your M&A cylinder. What you may regard as a clear source of advantage may, when put to the test, turn out to be no such thing.

The growth map helps you to compare different options for improving your cylinder firing on the basis of your source of advantage, and to assess how effectively these options will drive revenue growth in each horizon. We've already taken a cylinder view of your growth direction in previous chapters; let's now work systematically through the growth map to see how it can help you set your growth direction horizon by horizon.

Horizon 1: Extend and defend core businesses

As we saw in *The Alchemy of Growth,* horizon 1 is concerned with the heart of the organization—the businesses that customers and analysts identify with the corporate name. These are core businesses for a reason: they drive near-term performance and account for most of the profits and cash flow that will provide the resources necessary for growth.

But how should you extend and defend your core businesses? More specifically, which cylinder(s) will drive your growth in horizon 1? Let's look at the opportunities cylinder by cylinder.

- **Portfolio momentum: Shift your resources to your best growth opportunities.** Companies can use their resource allocation to boost portfolio momentum in the short term. Redeploying investment dollars, leadership talent, and even decision-making authority to the units with the highest growth potential helps put the weight of the organization behind raising the average growth rate. With additional resources, these units can accelerate their growth in critical markets (especially in fast-growing countries). New studies show that reallocating resources is a relatively under-utilized lever in large companies.[2] One of our pharmaceutical clients recently reorganized one of its country operations to reflect the decline in the influence of physicians and the increase in the influence of pharmacies. Despite much resistance, the physician sales force was cut by 30 percent and resources were redirected to a new dedicated pharmacy team.

- **M&A: Pursue fill-in acquisitions and divest slow-growth businesses.** The M&A action plan in horizon 1 typically consists of supplementary acquisitions that deepen the positional advantage of a company's existing businesses. These acquisitions may round out a product offering, supply missing capabilities, or otherwise protect the business from competitors. One of our telecom clients recognized it had a gap in its distribution capabilities as it moved from selling mostly mobile products via retail outlets and call centers to selling broadband. It needed a door-to-door salesforce that could reach critical mass quickly; acquisition was the logical way to fill the gap.

- **Share gain: Drive commercial and operational excellence.** Though keeping up with the competition is critical to profitable growth, market-share outperformance is often difficult to achieve in horizon 1. As we argued in chapter 7, it typically involves improving basic execution or leveraging a business-model advantage to compete hard for share across all segments.[3] In the short term, a company can pull a number of tactical levers to affect market share, such as transactional pricing, sales stimulation, and better market segmentation and customer targeting. These are critical levers for improving short-term earnings, but our analysis reveals that they seldom have much impact on a company's overall growth trajectory.

To illustrate the importance of short-term portfolio-momentum and market-share improvement, let's look at Delta Airlines. Since late 2005, the company has been switching to smaller aircraft and reducing mainline capacity in its domestic operations, and shifting toward more international flights. It cut domestic capacity in the first half of 2006 by 15 percent and increased international capacity by 20 percent, adding 50 new routes to more than 20 cities. The turnaround has yielded promising early results. For the first half of 2006, revenue from international flights was up by 24 percent on a year earlier, and domestic revenue rose by 5 percent despite the cut in capacity. Delta emerged from bankruptcy in April 2007.

Short-term improvements like those mentioned above can readily be implemented in horizon 1, and often drive both momentum and share gain.

Horizon 2: Build emerging businesses

While horizon 1 addresses the businesses that are at the heart of today's organization, horizon 2 looks at the emerging businesses that may one day transform it. Even though substantial profits may be years away, these businesses should be at the top of any forward-thinking executive's mind. They may prove to be as profitable as horizon 1 businesses in time.

However, emerging businesses will need considerable investment in both time and capabilities, so the primary focus for horizon 2 should be on building new streams of revenue. Yet this is becoming increasingly difficult for a large company to achieve systematically and repeatedly, as Geoffrey Moore deftly described in a recent *Harvard Business Review* article.[4] In the M&A arena, for instance, the rise of private-equity firms and special-purpose acquisition companies has made competition even more intense. Many companies that have squared up to top private-equity firms in an acquisition race and lost are left wondering what they could have done differently.

Let's now look at the second column in the growth map. Which of the three cylinders will be most powerful in driving your company's growth in horizon 2?

- **Portfolio momentum: Invest in markets you don't currently serve.** Capabilities that have been built up in existing businesses represent a source of advantage that can be exploited to move into new markets. Supermarkets have followed this growth strategy over the years by driving costs out of the supply chain, passing on a share of the savings to consumers through price reductions, and expanding from traditional dry grocery into adjacent categories such as fresh food, alcohol, pharmacy, general merchandise, and even financial services.

- **M&A: Bolt on acquisitions or mergers to consolidate or diversify.** The M&A initiatives in horizon 2 tend to involve bigger moves designed to secure advantageous positions in key markets. Acquisitions of compatible businesses or outright mergers can be used to purchase revenue in promising areas, including those in adjacent markets.

Such deals account for many of the big headline-grabbing transactions such as mergers in the oil and pharmaceutical industries and consolidation in the European energy and utilities sector. Take National Grid Transco, a UK-based utility. In 1999, 80 percent of its revenues came from electricity transmission in its home market. The company then dramatically expanded its US presence by making three large acquisitions in two years. It also broadened its domestic portfolio by merging with Lattice Group, a UK gas transmission and distribution company, in 2002. By the end of 2005 its top-line revenues had risen to nearly six times their 1999 total, a CAGR of 34 percent, while TRS had grown at 6 percent. This part of the growth map also includes less conspicuous deals such as acquisitions by big technology companies of small ones with complementary products that can benefit from their sales and marketing clout.

- **Share gain: Refresh your proposition and/or delivery model.** In order to deliver a sustainable step change in market share in horizon 2, companies need a value proposition that is far superior to that of competitors, as we saw with Dell and Toyota in chapter 7. This involves more than product innovation; it embraces such things as retailers investing in format renewal, technology companies rewiring their salesforces to deliver integrated solutions rather than independent products, and integrated telecom incumbents bundling fixed telephony, mobile, and broadband at a substantial discount.

Horizon 3: Create viable options

Horizon 3 looks beyond emerging businesses to the embryonic options on future growth. These initiatives may be small, but they serve to test possible business activities and investments that may yield profits in the long term. As we discussed in *The Alchemy of Growth,* horizon 3 initiatives are the research projects, market tests, pilots, alliances, minority stakes, and memoranda of understanding that have the potential to yield businesses with horizon 1 levels of profitability if they prove successful.

Horizon 3 initiatives are not for dreamers, though. Clearly there are any number of possible future endeavors that a company pursuing growth could investigate. The challenge it faces is to nurture those that show promise while dropping those with diminishing potential in a disciplined manner. This may sound reminiscent of what venture capitalists do, but there is an important difference. A company creating viable options in horizon 3 isn't simply venturing with the intent of seeing a few of its portfolio investments strike gold. Rather, it is making a commitment to build horizon 2 businesses within its chosen arenas over the next few years by learning and taking a series of steps up a staircase.

So which cylinders will drive your growth in horizon 3?

- **Portfolio momentum: Step out into white space to build new businesses.** Sometimes portfolio moves are triggered by insights about the emergence of an entirely new business segment or the disruption of an existing one. In such cases M&A isn't an option since the business (or business model) doesn't yet exist. A company wishing to enter has no choice but to build a new business. One example is an energy company moving into the production of renewable-energy equipment such as fuel cells. Another is Apple's decision to sell music via its iTunes online store to both Mac and Windows users. This marked an innovative and disruptive business-building move that leveraged a whole set of advantages Apple had acquired through the success of its iPod and computer ranges. The company made a similar move more recently when it entered the mobile telephony market with its iPhone.

As we saw in chapter 5, improving your portfolio momentum often takes time. Companies should bear this in mind when they make their horizon 2 and, particularly, horizon 3 investments.

- **M&A: Diversify into growth areas through small acquisitions.** In horizon 3, M&A moves are typically smaller and more measured. They involve forays into uncertain terrain where attackers are deploying new business models that disrupt the economics and positional advantage of traditional incumbent businesses. These forays can be viewed as important first steps along the path to future growth strategies. Some companies have accepted that the market is better than any individual company at innovating, and that buying early-stage businesses can be a better investment than backing internal R&D or business-building efforts. In accordance with this belief, they operate large business-development teams that build deep relationships with venture capitalists, academic institutions, and research communities to identify new opportunities early and establish a position as the preferred partner for commercialization.

- **Share gain: Reinvent or disrupt your business model.** A reshaped business model is likely to take some time to produce share gains.[5] And few large companies are good at disrupting their own markets at the likely cost of product cannibalization, earnings dilution, and channel conflict. It's no surprise that Amazon was created by a new entrant and not an existing bricks-and-mortar bookstore. When the major airlines introduced their own low-cost carriers in an attempt to emulate the success of discount point-to-point players such as Southwest and Ryanair, they were following this strategy. Most have struggled to pull it off. Yet successful reinventions do happen. A mortgages attacker that had reached the limits of penetration with its own products successfully reinvented itself as a mortgage broker to disintermediate the established banks.

Mapping your growth

In *The Alchemy of Growth*, we reported the results of our research into thirty great growers. In fact, we derived our three horizons model by analyzing the growth directions and strategies that these companies adopted. By plotting this pattern onto our growth map, we arrive at the classic *Alchemy* model shown on the left of Figure 8.3. Although it didn't use these specific terms, it emphasized the importance of firing on the market-share gain cylinder in horizon 1, M&A in horizon 2, and momentum in horizon 3.

By adding the three growth cylinders to the three horizons framework, we can go beyond this model to identify various other patterns for companies to consider when choosing their growth direction:

- **Private equity.** Private-equity firms pursue M&A as an engine of growth in horizons 1 and 2. Because of their preference for scale and leverage of cash flow, they don't tend to seed M&A options in horizon 3.

- **Venture capital.** Venture-capital firms pursue horizon 3 investments almost exclusively, but they also actively push the share-gain lever to drive growth in existing investments.

- **Organic.** Some companies shy away from inorganic growth. In the high-tech sector, for example, many firms drive growth through share gain in horizons 1 and 2, while spending on R&D to create a pipeline in high-momentum areas.

- **Turnaround.** Companies undergoing a turnaround need to concentrate on shifting their portfolio momentum. They do this in all horizons organically, but also rely on game-changing M&A (including divestments) in horizons 1 and 2.

- **Acquisition-based growth.** Over the past decade, companies in some growth sectors have become interested in collaborative horizon 3 models. Instead of growing their own options, they acquire their new businesses by working with specialists such as venture-capital firms. This growth pattern resembles the old *Alchemy* model but with inorganic growth replacing portfolio momentum in horizon 3.

- **Strong tailwind.** Some companies are carried along by a strong tailwind that helps them make a big growth spurt. Their growth pattern is an additive one: share gain in horizon 1 plus M&A in horizon 2 plus portfolio momentum in horizon 3.

8.3 Growth map patterns

☐ Primary contributor to growth

Original pattern

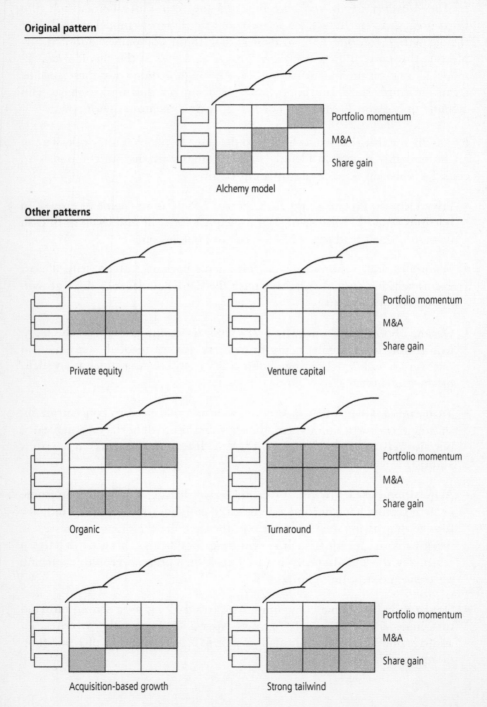

Alchemy model

Other patterns

Private equity

Venture capital

Portfolio momentum

M&A

Share gain

Organic

Turnaround

Portfolio momentum

M&A

Share gain

Acquisition-based growth

Strong tailwind

Portfolio momentum

M&A

Share gain

Each of these patterns has a compelling logic in terms of how and why the different cylinders contribute to growth in the different horizons. That, in the end, is the critical test for any growth map. However, this is not an exhaustive list; many other growth directions are possible. In fact, it can be well worth experimenting with alternative growth maps so as to trigger an informed debate about which direction to choose.

■ ■ ■

We end by quoting Theodore Levitt. He described the first requisite of leadership as knowing precisely where one wants to go and making sure the whole organization knows it too:

> "Unless a leader knows where he is going, any road will take him there. If any road is okay, the chief executive might as well pack his attaché case and go fishing. If an organization does not know or care where it is going, it does not need to advertise that fact with a ceremonial figurehead. Everybody will notice it soon enough."[6]

His words are as true now as when he wrote them more than 40 years ago, and sound an apt note for today's leaders as they set a direction for growth.

NOTES

[1] For a detailed discussion of how the timing of horizons can vary by context, see *The Alchemy of Growth*, chapter 2.

[2] In a 2006 UCLA working paper, "The hand of management: Differences in capital investment behavior between multi-business and single-business firms," D. Bardolet, D. Lovallo, and R. Rumelt found that a significant proportion of company assets yield insufficient profit to cover their cost of capital or sustain growth. The problem is more acute in multi-business firms (39 percent of assets) than in single-business firms (20 percent). These assets could be "seeds" (early growth businesses that show promise) or "weeds" (businesses with limited prospects). Either way, firms should think carefully about resource allocation. In an unpublished study, the same authors found a correlation between capital allocation in the current period and the last of between 0.77 and 0.92, suggesting that firms reallocate resources only to a limited extent, at least in the short term.

[3] P&G's share gain described in chapter 10 is a prime example of this.

[4] G. A. Moore, "To succeed in the long term, focus on the middle term," *Harvard Business Review*, July–August 2007, pp. 84–90.

[5] For more on this, see, for example, C. M. Christensen, *The Innovator's Dilemma: When new technologies cause great firms to fail* (Harvard Business School Press, Boston, Mass., 1997).Christensen described the specific case for disruption (a paradigm-shifting innovation that redefines the market away from incumbents).

[6] T. Levitt, "Marketing myopia," *Harvard Business Review*, July–August 1960, pp. 45–60.

9

To move or not to move?

"You gotta move"
"Mississippi" Fred McDowell

- All growth strategies involve choices about moving—or where, when, and how to evolve the portfolio mix over time

- Whether you should move depends on whether you have low- or high-momentum growth

- Economic downturns create great opportunities for portfolio moves, yet few companies seize them

- Adjacencies alone don't determine whether a move will succeed or fail; leveraging a distinctive advantage is what really matters

IN 1971, Mick Jagger sang the Rolling Stones' cover version of "You gotta move" on their *Sticky Fingers* album. Some 35 years later, at the 2006 Super Bowl half-time show, he was still moving. Not a bad model for corporate performance. But the Stones have moved while staying true to a particular style of music.

Another rock star, Madonna, has also sustained her performance across decades. But she has adopted a different approach. As well as keeping moving on stage, she has constantly reinvented herself by moving into new areas such as acting, writing children's books, and designing clothes—never afraid, it seems, to try something new.

So when does it make sense for corporations to shift their mix of businesses? Should you aspire to be like the Rolling Stones or Madonna; growing within your core businesses or venturing into new ones? If you find yourself with a low-momentum mix, should you consider shifting to a more promising portfolio? What if your portfolio already has high momentum? The question of whether, when, and how to move is the subject of this chapter.

Who moves?

Portfolio shifting happens more than you might imagine. Among our two-cycle growth giants from the Introduction, roughly 70 percent pursued growth by exploiting opportunities in their core businesses, including consolidation and rollups. The remaining 30 percent diversified their scope, building at least one major new business or making a major geographic expansion (defined as growing from less than 5 percent to more than 15 percent of sales) during the period.

We found similar results in a study of a broader group of companies that we conducted a few years ago. Among 201 growth "stars," 37 percent built new growth platforms while 63 percent pursued either core growth or roll-up strategies.[1] Both studies found extensive use of acquisitions among diversifiers and platform builders alike. So moving—both inside and beyond the core—is common and figures prominently in successful growth.

Consider the case of Virgin (Figure 9.1). Richard Branson started his first business venture, *Student Magazine,* in 1968 at the tender age of 16. Two years later, he moved into music and entertainment by selling records through mail order, and founded the Virgin brand. He opened the company's first record shop in 1971. By the late 1970s, Virgin had diversified in the world of entertainment by setting up a publishing company and opening nightclubs in

9.1 Evolution of Virgin's portfolio
1968–2006

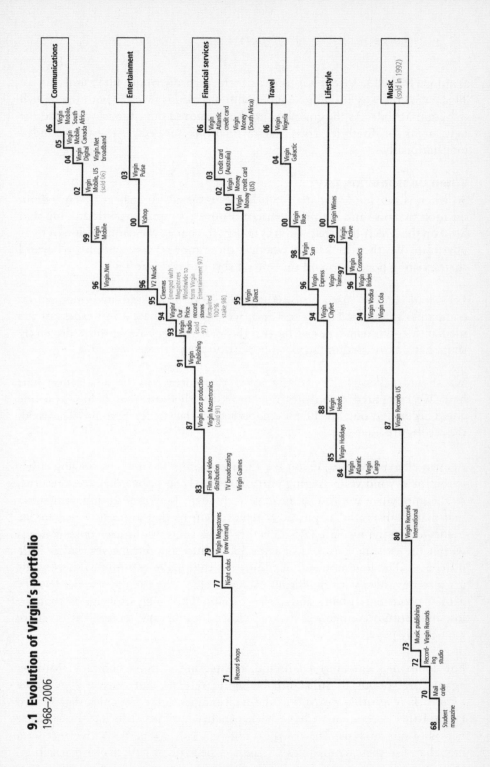

Communications

06 Virgin Mobile, South Africa
05 Virgin Mobile, Canada
04 Virgin Mobile, US (sold 06)
  Virgin.Net broadband
02 Virgin Mobile
99 Virgin.Net
96 Virgin Publishing

Entertainment

03 Virgin Pulse
00 Vshop
96 V2 Music
  Cinemas (merged with Megastores Worldwide to form Virgin Entertainment 97)
95 Virgin/ Our Price record stores (acquired 100% stake 98)
94 Virgin Radio (sold 97)
93 Virgin Publishing
91 Virgin post production
  Virgin Mastertronics (sold 91)
87 Film and video distribution
  TV broadcasting
  Virgin Games
83 Virgin Megastores (new format)
79 Night clubs
77 Record shops
71

Financial services

06 Virgin Atlantic credit card
  Virgin Money (South Africa)
03 Credit card (Australia)
02 Virgin Money credit card (US)
01 Virgin Money
95 Virgin Direct

Travel

06 Virgin Nigeria
04 Virgin Galactic
00 Virgin Blue
98 Virgin Sun
96 Virgin Express
  Virgin Trains 97
94 Virgin Citylet
88 Virgin Hotels
85 Virgin Holidays
84 Virgin Atlantic
  Virgin Cargo

Lifestyle

00 Virgin Wines
99 Virgin Active
96 Virgin Cosmetics
  Virgin Brides
94 Virgin Vodka
  Virgin Cola

Music (sold in 1992)

87 Virgin Records US
80 Virgin Records International
73 Music publishing
72 Record-ing studio Virgin Records
70 Mail order
68 Student magazine

London. In 1983, Virgin Vision was formed to distribute films and videos. This paved the way for a move into communications in 1999 with the launch of Virgin Mobile. As the company gradually moved out of music and into the new areas of lifestyle, travel, and financial services, it also expanded internationally.

When does moving pay?

So when is moving associated with higher returns? To answer this question, we took the low- and high-momentum companies in our growth decomp that fired on the M&A and share-gain cylinders to change the composition of their portfolio. We then looked at whether these moves were within or beyond their existing portfolios and the impact this had on their TRS.

Let's look at the matrix of returns for both low- and high-momentum companies (Figure 9.2). In each case, we measured the TRS in excess of the median for different types of moves: those driven by M&A, those driven by share gain, those within the existing portfolio, and those beyond it.

We should acknowledge straight away that there may be a selection bias here. We compared companies that moved with those that didn't, and one could argue that only the better companies get the chance to move. That said, the results are interesting.

Against all expectations, if you are a low-momentum company, moving either within or beyond your existing portfolio is likely to bring you excess returns, so the imperative for you to move is fairly high. Low-momentum companies that make substantial acquisitions achieve returns that are 3 to 4 percentage points above the median TRS. Whether these acquisitions are consolidations within the existing business or expansions into new businesses makes little difference. The low-momentum companies that make substantial share gains are also rewarded with significant excess returns at the slightly higher level of 5 to 6 percentage points above the median. This analysis suggests that for low-momentum companies, moving either by inorganic expansion or share gain clearly pays.

For companies catching a tailwind, the picture is more complex. Moving again corresponds to substantially higher returns, but *only if they move within their existing portfolio*. The high-momentum companies that moved beyond this core seem to have been penalized, at least during the six-year period of our analysis. The reason is not yet clear, but perhaps investors set a high bar for these companies to meet expectations and avoid distraction.

9.2 Moving pays
Excess median TRS,* CAGR 1999–2005, percent

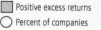

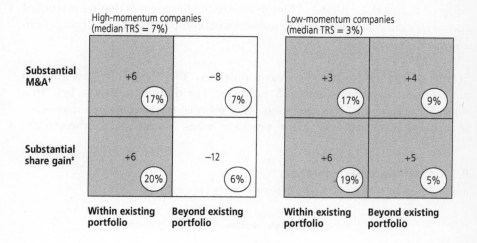

High-momentum companies
(median TRS = 7%)

Low-momentum companies
(median TRS = 3%)

Substantial M&A†

	Within existing portfolio	Beyond existing portfolio
	+6 (17%)	−8 (7%)

Substantial share gain‡

	Within existing portfolio	Beyond existing portfolio
	+6 (20%)	−12 (6%)

	Within existing portfolio	Beyond existing portfolio
	+3 (17%)	+4 (9%)
	+6 (19%)	+5 (5%)

* The difference between the median TRS of the companies in a quadrant and the median TRS of the entire high-momentum or low-momentum sample
† M&A contributes more than 4 percentage points to revenue CAGR (top quartile)
‡ Share gain contributes more than 2 percentage points to revenue CAGR (top quartile)
Sample: Granular growth decomposition database

Indeed, strong momentum automatically sets the bar high for any move; if you think about it, moving off a tailwind would actually *slow* your growth unless you moved onto an even stronger tailwind.

We should also note the significance of the core business in the returns of any large company. If a diversifying move is seen as an indication that the core is running out of steam, investors may lower their expectations.

Don't stop in a downturn
Another key aspect of when to move relates to the economic cycle. Most CEOs consider moving during upturns. When the economy is growing strongly, leaders have the capacity to focus on growth. In a downturn, on the other hand, moving may be the last thing on their minds. As revenues slow and margins are squeezed, management switches its focus to cutting costs to maintain earnings. M&A is often out of the question. Growth and low-priority investments are deferred; the company protects its balance sheet.

The impact of this behavior is shown in a detailed analysis of our growth decomposition database. We identified segments that had experienced significant upturns or downturns, and looked at the strategies companies adopted during these periods.[2] Our most striking finding was that 60 percent of companies did not move at all in a downturn, compared to only 40 percent in an upturn (Figure 9.3).

When companies adopt defensive postures, they virtually give up on acquisitions. Even fewer make divestments. The thinking seems to be: "In a downturn, stay put." We also found that most of the acquisitions that occur in upturn segments take place precisely when prices are at their peak.

9.3 Downturns induce paralysis

Reaction to upturn or downturn in a major segment, percent of companies*

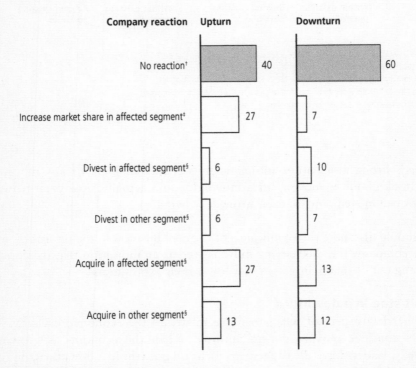

Company reaction	Upturn	Downturn
No reaction[†]	40	60
Increase market share in affected segment[‡]	27	7
Divest in affected segment[§]	6	10
Divest in other segment[§]	6	7
Acquire in affected segment[§]	27	13
Acquire in other segment[§]	13	12

* Companies can have more than one reaction, so totals exceed 100%

† Took none of the actions below

‡ Share gain in top quartile (i.e., 3.3% for both 2002 and 2003)

§ Sum of acquisitions (divestitures) for segments in period 2002–04 represents more than 11% (14%) of 2001 sales (corresponds to 2.5 years of acquisitions at top inorganic quartile rate and 3 years of divestments)

Although every executive knows the maxim "Invest in a downturn," hardly any seem to act on it.

So it seems that faced with economic downturns, most companies go into reactive mode, seeking to smooth out the cycle's impact on their earnings by cutting costs and selling assets. But the best growth companies don't do that. They view a downturn as a time to increase their lead and make acquisitions. They pounce on the opportunities it creates with an alacrity that is the stuff of legends: think of General Electric's speedy dispatch of an army of deal-makers to Asia after the financial markets took a downturn in 1998.

Our analysis of the growth decomposition database shows that failing to respond to changing market conditions destroys shareholder value in both upturns and downturns. It also shows that in an upturn, the way to create the most value is to increase your market share in the segments affected. Not surprisingly, as prices rise, divestments create slightly more value than acquisitions.

In a downturn, divestments destroy shareholder value while acquisitions at favorable prices create value. In fact, our analysis shows that *firing the M&A cylinder is the most value-creating step you can take during a downturn*. And yet, as we've seen, only a small minority of companies manage to seize this opportunity.

There may be a good reason for their inertia. We have some evidence that in short time frames the market rewards this cyclical behavior and thereby reinforces it. But over longer periods, the market favors growth. This doesn't mean you should go on a spending spree in a downturn and tighten your belt in an upturn. Rather, you should time your entries and exits judiciously, using insights about the cycle itself.

It is worth pointing out that if you look at the different profitability patterns that we describe in Appendix 2, only the companies with rapid growth and stable margins or moderate growth and high margins will be in a position to take advantage of this opportunity. Those choosing the high payout path are unlikely to have the means to invest in a downturn unless they can change shareholders' expectations.

In short, counter-cyclical investment works well. Arguments that growth is risky in a downturn fly in the face of the evidence.

Advantage, not adjacency

When we think about moving, it's hard to avoid the topic of diversification. Ever since the conglomerates of the 1960s were dismantled, the argument over diversification versus focus has simmered on, with one side arguing for growth and expansion, the other for atomization and concentration. Much has been written on this topic, and we're not planning to add too much to it here.[3] Suffice to say that our earlier research has shown that a moderately diversified business model—that is, a corporate portfolio with several businesses at various stages of maturity—can perform just as well as (or better than) a focused company while affording better prospects for long-term growth and performance. The model for moderate diversification is a corporation that is skilled at developing, growing, culling, and liberating businesses over time, rather than one that slavishly adheres to a focused portfolio (Figure 9.4).

Adopting an expansive mindset is essential when you are trying to broaden your growth opportunities. In 1960, Theodore Levitt published an article in the *Harvard Business Review* that is now regarded as a classic. "Marketing

9.4 Model for moderately diversified company

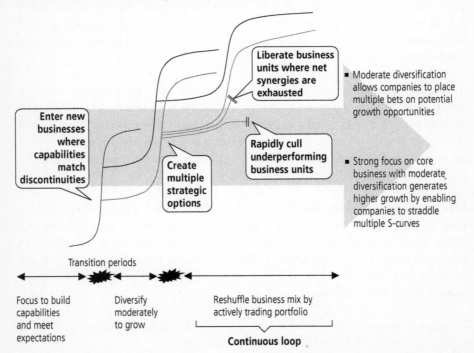

Liberate business units where net synergies are exhausted

Enter new businesses where capabilities match discontinuities

Create multiple strategic options

Rapidly cull underperforming business units

- Moderate diversification allows companies to place multiple bets on potential growth opportunities

- Strong focus on core business with moderate diversification generates higher growth by enabling companies to straddle multiple S-curves

Transition periods

Focus to build capabilities and meet expectations

Diversify moderately to grow

Reshuffle business mix by actively trading portfolio

Continuous loop

myopia" posed the question: "What business are you really in?" Levitt imagined what would have happened if buggy-whip manufacturers had defined themselves as being in the transportation industry.[4] While the buggy whip itself may have had little chance of survival, its manufacturers consigned themselves to a doomed path by failing to define their business more broadly to allow for innovation and encourage a culture of change.

One company that illustrates the power of an expansive mindset is Gillette. It made the leap from a narrow definition of its market—men's razors and blades, in which it commanded a 60 percent market share—to a much broader one. By redefining its business as personal use and personal care products, in which it had a 5 percent market share, it opened the door to tremendous growth opportunities that were consistent with its capability platform.[5] Its expansive mindset enabled it to move from the segments in which it was comfortable to whole new areas of business.

But how do you develop an expansive mindset? Whatever industry you are in, the challenge is the same. As the story of the European retailer in chapter 4 illustrates, to expand your field of view you need to go broad, then focus. The issue, of course, is *how* broad, and *how* focused. Where do you set the outer limits for your field of view? And how granular do you need to be within it when it comes to segmenting the broader market, setting priorities, and making entry decisions?

As a general rule, we suggest that when mapping out a growth direction, you define your market sufficiently broadly that your market share is no more than 5 percent. You can then evaluate the 95 percent of the market that is new to you at a G4 level of granularity. You should focus your attention on the pockets of growth with the highest prospective momentum growth rates where your capabilities already give you an advantage over your competitors. We call this the "5/95" rule.

You may object that all this is flying in the face of corporate orthodoxy, which dictates that you should focus on your core portfolio and venture into new businesses only if they are close to it. One variation on this theme has it that you should measure the distance from your core portfolio by counting up the number of new business dimensions, or "adjacencies." For example, moves toward new customers, new markets, and new products would add three new dimensions or adjacencies to your business and therefore create a distance of three.[6] The greater the distance, the more complicated and challenging the growth opportunity is assumed to be.

Although there is some truth in the idea of distance—no business can succeed in an activity to which it is fundamentally unsuited—the adjacency concept is flawed, and can be misleading. In fact, adjacency is often used as a proxy for familiarity. Consider private-equity companies, which often ignore adjacencies altogether. Some build extremely diversified portfolios, using their advantages to make successful moves into unrelated businesses and creating value through the disciplines of operational improvement, deal structuring, and financing.

So distance need not doom a move to failure. Companies that are trying to decide where to compete and how to acquire substantial market share should base their decisions on the distinctive advantages they possess. When it comes to expanding into new businesses, *advantage trumps adjacency*.[7]

■ ■ ■

In terms of where you grow, moving either within or beyond your core portfolio tends to pay if you happen to be a low-momentum company. On the other hand, if you're lucky enough to have a portfolio with high momentum, set a high bar for moving outside your core. When you are evaluating potential moves, don't let yourself be seduced by high-growth segments in which you have no particular advantages. Ensure that your search process is sophisticated enough to consider the *real* power of your advantage, and not just the distance from the core. And don't let a downturn deter you; it may offer a great opportunity to put a clear distance between your company and the rest of the pack.

NOTES

[1] Based on an unpublished study, "The importance of new platforms in shaping growth," Steve Coley et al., McKinsey & Company, December 2003.

[2] From our granular growth decomposition database, we identified the companies that had made significant moves during the period under measurement and made detailed segmented decompositions. Of the segments we identified, we focused on those that accounted for at least 10 percent of company sales. We then identified "upturn" segments that had market growth in 2002 and 2003 of at least 40 percent and 3 percentage points above the average for 2000 and 2001. We also identified "downturn" segments using a mirrored set of criteria.

[3] See, for instance, N. W. C. Harper and S. P. Viguerie, "Are you too focused?" *The McKinsey Quarterly*, August 2002, special edition, *Risk and Resilience*, pp. 29–37.

[4] T. Levitt, "Marketing myopia," *Harvard Business Review*, July–August 1960, pp. 45–60.

[5] See chapter 4 in *The Alchemy of Growth*.

[6] For a description of the adjacency methodology, see C. Zook, *Beyond the Core: Expand your market without abandoning your roots* (Harvard Business School Press, Boston, Mass., 2004).

[7] In his new book, *Unstoppable: Finding hidden assets to renew the core and fuel profitable growth* (Harvard Business School Press, Boston, Mass., 2007), Chris Zook has shifted his argument away from his more rigid prescription for adjacency-based growth toward finding and exploiting the hidden assets or advantages that already exist within a company and leveraging them for growth.

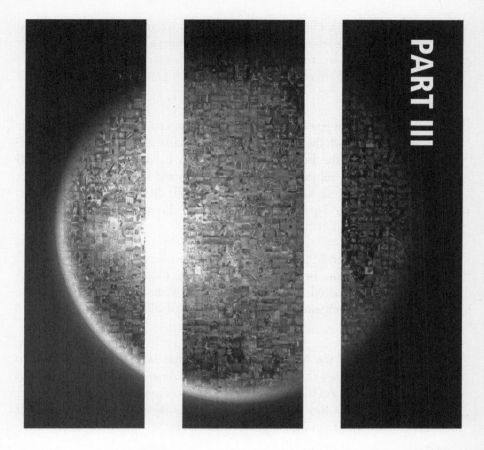

PART III

Your growth architecture

S O FAR THIS BOOK HAS focused on strategy: we've presented the facts on growth and what they imply for large companies aspiring to grow. In this third and final part, we turn to how companies can act on these strategic insights by making changes in their design and operations—or what we call their "architecture."

This is the third big choice on the growth journey, and the point at which our focus starts to shift from the science to the art of management. Our perspectives in parts I and II of the book are derived from hard analysis, but part III necessarily draws on subjective experience and case studies. We don't offer recipes or prescriptions since the answers will differ from company to company. We do offer a powerful way to think about architecture and how you design your company for growth.

It's *your* experience and judgment that count in translating these ideas into practical changes in your organization. Our goal is to help you by highlighting the key principles involved, introducing frameworks based on these principles, and offering some compelling examples by way of illustration. And then it's up to you.

The main message of the next few chapters is that large companies need to organize to manage growth at a granular level while also realizing the benefits of scale. This may sound like a scary prospect. You may well object: "It's fine in theory, but I've got lots to do. How can I possibly manage a hundred or more growth units? The complexity will drown me!"

We don't think it will. We believe it *is* possible to manage growth at a granular level without increasing complexity for the CEO. Our systematic approach to bringing the different elements of the architecture of growth together— what we call "cluster-based growth"—may even make your life simpler. The increased transparency can help you avoid the cat-and-mouse games that divisions so often play with the corporate center, freeing you to concentrate on getting your business units to fire on more cylinders over time.

There are five chapters in this section.

- In chapter 10, "The architecture of growth," we examine the key dimensions of granularity and scale and show how they can be applied to strategy development and organization design. We also present a simple framework that you can use to assess how well your own company is designed for growth.

- In chapter 11, "Looking in the mirror," we help you test how well your overall architecture reflects your growth direction. This calls for a frank appraisal of the current state of your company and an objective review of your starting point for the growth journey.

- In chapter 12, "A blueprint for granularity," we show that granularity opens up opportunities in management and that a successful blueprint needs to leverage the scale of the organization to increase granularity. We also explain how to find the "sweet spot" of granularity for your markets and what that implies for your organization design.

- In chapter 13, "Building scale platforms," we look at how you can improve your cylinder firing by building two growth platforms: an M&A machine to drive a larger volume of deals and an insight engine for generating superior insight and foresight about growth opportunities.

- In chapter 14, "Cluster-based growth," we describe our systematic approach for managing granular growth at a large organization. We describe how the approach was adopted at Deloitte Australia and extend the methodology to a range of other industries from retail banking to energy and higher education.

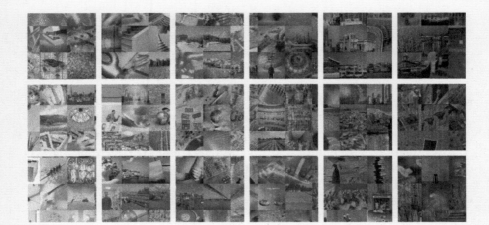

10

The architecture of growth

"Architecture is one part science,
one part craft and two parts art."
David Rutten

- Scale and granularity are not opposed: scale enables granularity, and granularity doesn't necessarily inhibit scale

- To deliver both granularity and scale, a company must design its strategy and organization model to create an architecture for growth

- *Strategy* involves both the company's overall growth direction and the specific actions it takes to capture granular opportunities

- *Organization design* entails creating scale platforms and a granular blueprint that matches the texture of the market

IN 1989, CERN, the biggest particle physics laboratory in the world, was grappling with a problem. It was constantly losing collective knowledge about complex experiments as researchers left the organization. Newcomers would take months to get up to speed. A member of staff, Tim Berners-Lee, noted that "if a CERN experiment were a static once-only development, all the information could be written in a big book."[1] But constant staff turnover, coupled with the dispersal of expertise across thousands of people, made such an undertaking impractical.

So Berners-Lee went on to develop a system that would enable individual documents to be shared and connected according to their topic and mutual relevance. Every user would have the ability to create new content, publish it, link it to existing content, and access a multitude of databases.

His creation, the World Wide Web and its associated standards and protocols, is a perfect example of a system architecture that enables both maximum granularity and maximum scalability. By providing any user anywhere in the world with the means to write and publish new content and combine it with existing content, it allowed for the granular production of information. By establishing a common format for writing and accessing documents that anyone could use, it promoted scale. Moreover, the flexibility of this new medium allowed users to convey not just text but also images and sound, enabling the release of massive amounts of existing as well as new information to the world at large.

Precisely because the World Wide Web combined granularity (any individual can use and contribute to it) with scale (any document is accessible to anyone and can be linked to any other published content), it opened up possibilities for new business models and new channels of discussion and collaboration. It has had and is still having an immense impact on research, communication, the media, businesses of all types, and governments the world over.

Scaling up

Big companies are getting bigger. Between 1984 and 2006, the average market value of the most valuable 150 companies in the world increased almost fourteenfold, from $6 billion to $83 billion.[2] Over the same period, average net income per employee grew from $9,000 to $49,000, and average revenue increased almost fivefold to $53 billion. So why are we arguing for granularity? How does that square with the insatiable quest for scale?

First, let's establish what scale is. We've found that many organizations hold rather a simplistic view: they assume that greater size automatically confers scale benefits. It's true that increased size *often* brings lower unit costs, but not always. Sometimes small is better: Nucor changed the rules of steel manufacture when it discovered that building mini-mills a fraction of the size of competitors' integrated mills could give it a 20 percent cost advantage. And we should remember that the cost/benefit curve is just that: a curve, not a straight line.

We often hear clients claiming a scale advantage over competitors merely because they are bigger. One bank claimed that having 20 percent more branches than competitors gave it a scale advantage in distribution—until it did the sums and realized that the economics of the extra 20 percent hardly differed from those of the first 80 percent. Similarly, packaged-goods companies in concentrated retail sectors like those in the UK and Germany have discovered that mergers undertaken to build scale don't necessarily give them more leverage over retailers. That's because scale alone doesn't affect the structural advantage that retailers enjoy. Only the ability to build stronger brands and offer innovative products can give the packaged-goods companies an edge.

However, we don't dispute that sheer size confers some advantages, particularly in terms of the balance sheet. Only the major oil companies have the liquidity to take on the task of developing new regions, which demands huge upfront investments, involves great technical complexity, and often exposes players to substantial political risk. Only the big global brewers have the earnings streams to wear the years of losses that have so far characterized the Chinese beer industry. Only the leading global banks have balance sheets that allow them to bet billions on minority stakes in banks in developing nations. And as private-equity firms raise larger and larger sums of money, genuine scale benefits will belong only to the true global giants.

Scale *and* granularity
So how does scale fit with granularity? If scale is to provide a platform for growth, it needs to be an enabler of greater granularity. This is exactly what we see happening in many industries as companies harness the power of information technology.

Consider the telecom industry. A few years ago, a typical mobile operator would have offered consumers a choice of five or six different plans and then focused on promoting them. Today, some of our clients create a profile of each customer down to his or her individual P&L. They use this profile in combination with a campaign-tracking tool to run hundreds of campaigns each week in order to stimulate usage. Their focus has shifted to the lifetime value of each individual customer.

Rather than following a static campaign plan, these companies learn from results, adapt, and evolve. If a customer phones to cancel her account, she is directed to someone in the "save" team who understands her pattern of usage, knows exactly what she is worth to the company, and uses this information to make her an offer designed to keep her as a customer. This whole process exploits a level of granularity in market information that would have been unthinkable just a few years ago. Technology has enabled companies to build scale in their customer-service capability that flattens out the cost of acting at a granular level.

This takes us to an important point: in today's world, *scale and granularity are no longer in opposition*. Things have moved on since Henry Ford offered the Model T in any color so long as it was black. He was fierce in his defense of standardization because it was the source of assembly-line efficiency; any variation would negate scale. For him, granularity was the enemy of scale. Mass production demanded absolute conformity in assembly.

The IT revolution has changed all that. Scale enables granularity, and granularity doesn't necessarily inhibit scale.

Strategy + organization = architecture

A robust strategic direction is the starting point for growth. There's unlikely to be much disagreement about that. But as most CEOs know all too well, there's a big difference between working out a strategy and being confident you can deliver it.

This is where the idea of architecture comes in. We are by no means the first to apply it to companies. Much of the existing work focuses on the various elements in an organization and the need to ensure that they are in alignment, which is a very important idea.[3]

Here, though, we want to focus on architecture as the integration between design objectives (strategy) and design execution (organization). We use the term "growth architecture" to describe a simple framework for ensuring that your strategy and your organization model are both designed to deliver granularity and scale. Most CEOs we know see themselves as the "architects" of their organization, working to develop the right strategies for their businesses and to design the organization they believe will best deliver them.

We can represent architecture in terms of a simple two-by-two matrix, with strategy and direction on one side and scale and granularity on the other. To these four elements we add a fifth, management processes, which we represent as a circle to reflect the need for alignment and linkage between the other elements. Let's look at each of these in turn (Figure 10.1).

- The **growth direction** reflects the company's aspiration to fire on multiple cylinders across all three time horizons.

- The **granular strategy** describes "staircases" of moves designed to capture granular growth opportunities and build real advantage.

- **Scale platforms** enable a large company to exploit the advantages of its size and distinctive capabilities.

- The **granular blueprint** aims to create an organization that matches the texture of the market.

- **Management processes** such as strategic planning, resource allocation, and performance management are used to link the other elements together.

10.1 The architecture framework

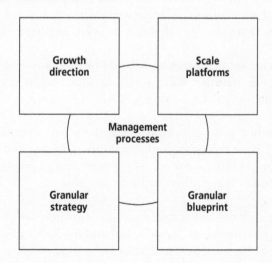

The art in architecture

As we showed in part II, conventional wisdom about growth leads many companies to overlook the importance of making granular choices about where to compete. Though their CEOs are working incredibly hard to rally their organizations for growth, they lack a complete understanding of the sources of future growth and the challenges of the market. As a result, these companies have an architecture that appears to be geared chiefly to execution, not growth.

Admittedly, getting it right is very difficult. As with real architecture, the best designs blend science with art. Where growth is concerned, we have laid out the science and shown that much of it challenges the incremental way that many organizations think about growth. But that takes us only so far. Senior management still needs to take a leap of faith and use its judgment to blend this science with the art that will be needed for an enduring result.

There is no single architecture that leads to successful growth. What we hope to do here is provide a practical framework that will help you apply your judgment and experience to design the right growth architecture for your business.

Test your direction

So far, this book has focused on strategy, principally corporate strategy. We have introduced the growth map as an aid to help you set your growth direction. It enables you to consider alternative sources of growth and balance them across the three horizons. The growth map is just a tool, though. You need to make sure that your growth direction is compelling by *testing* it.

First, challenge whether the direction is based on any real insight or foresight about the way your industry will evolve. Is your insight superior to your competitors', or no more than the standard industry view?

Second, test whether your direction is based on an accurate view of the distinctiveness of your resources and capabilities. Be harsh on yourself: all too often an inflated sense of our edge over competitors prompts us to make risky strategic choices that fail to live up to our hopes.

Third, make sure that the implications of your direction are clear in terms of the trajectory of your financial performance and the levels of investment you expect. Dissonance between you and your key stakeholders on the shape of the financials is one of the fastest ways to stall a growth program.

The best way to communicate a growth direction to your wider organization is to describe in detail what it will mean in practice. People want to know what they will be asked to contribute. So your work on setting a strategic direction is not complete until each theme or major element in the overall growth direction has been broken down into detailed strategies that are readily actionable. That is to say, the growth direction needs to be cascaded down the organization and translated into specific strategies for each level to act upon.

If we think back to the levels of granularity described in chapter 1, a granular strategy needs to translate growth themes into winning plays at a G4 or G5 level for each step in the growth staircase.[4] For organic growth, this usually involves thinking through the right sequence of market moves and resource investments. For inorganic growth, it means designing a detailed acquisition strategy with specific targets identified for at least the first year.

Work on your organization model

If overestimating the benefit of sheer size is the first mistake many companies make, overestimating the synergy between different businesses is the second. Executives seem to have a bias toward synergy that can lead them to force business units to cooperate even when the benefits are far from clear. Opening up this debate inevitably raises questions about the role of the corporate center in multi-business companies. Much academic work has been done on this topic, some arguing for activist corporate centers and some casting doubt on whether they perform any better than the capital markets.[5] We won't attempt to summarize the arguments here. Theory aside, though, we would argue that if you are sitting in the corporate center of a multi-business company, you need to work out what portfolio advantages your company has.

The major private-equity players are pretty clear about this. They believe that they bring deal-structuring and governance advantages that allow the businesses they own to focus much more effectively on pulling the levers that create value. These advantages include lifting quarterly earnings pressures and allowing companies to plan for performance over a horizon of three to five years; removing many of the compliance burdens of being publicly listed; and structuring incentives so that managers can enjoy a more substantial share of the value created.

Whether or not private equity remains in the foreground of business activity, it's hard for public companies to ignore the impact of its governance model. If you are a senior manager in a public company, you need to be able to say how your governance model allows the potential benefits of the corporate center to be realized. One simple way to test for value is to ask whether scale will enable more units to fire on more cylinders over time. In chapter 13, we describe how some large organizations have developed scale engines for insight and M&A to serve precisely this purpose.

P&G: A GREAT GROWTH STORY

The late 1990s were tough times for consumer-goods companies. Retailers were getting bigger. In the five years to 2003, the market share of the top 10 US retailers grew from 30 to 55 percent.[*] In Europe, similarly, the top five retailers had market shares of 65 percent in Germany, almost 70 percent in the UK, and about 80 percent in France. With size came greater buying power and a stronger influence on pricing.

At the same time, consumers were defecting. Long-established brands were losing ground to private labels, especially in Europe's food and household-goods markets. To make matters worse, media consumption was fragmenting, making traditional advertising channels such as TV less effective at communicating brand messages.

Even US giant Procter & Gamble was not immune to these pressures. In 1998, its then CEO, Durk Jager, announced a six-year global reorganization plan, Organization 2005, which was designed to help the company bring innovative ideas to market more quickly.[†] But in March 2000, a combination of rising raw materials costs and continued price pressures forced the company to issue an earnings revision.[‡]

The financial markets reacted savagely. In a single day, P&G's market value fell by a third: the largest drop in the company's history,[§] and one that contributed some 142 points to a 374-point fall in that day's Dow index.[¶] By 10 March, the stock price had fallen below $53, a 55 percent drop from its January high of over $118.[**]

Three months later, P&G appointed A. G. Lafley as its new CEO. He announced a comprehensive plan to turn around the company's fortunes by building big brands, investing in innovation, deepening customer partnerships, reducing costs, and improving cash management. Together, these measures paved the way to recovery. Between 1999 and 2005, P&G grew its top-line revenue from $38 billion to $57 billion,[††] at a compound annual growth rate of 6.9 percent.

How did it achieve this transformation? To find out, we need to break down the growth into inorganic, portfolio momentum, and organic share gain. P&G gained 1.5 percent a year from M&A, 3.5 percent from portfolio momentum, and 1.9 percent from market share. Currency effects seem to have had a relatively small impact, reducing portfolio momentum by approximately 0.5 percent a year (from 4.0 percent). Over the period, P&G's portfolio momentum increased significantly: from 1 percent in 1999–2000 to around 5 percent by 2005–06.

The strategy for growth

To understand P&G's success, we need to drill down a level deeper to look at product categories. Our granular growth decomp shows that of the absolute revenue growth for the period ($18.6 billion), the biggest contributions came from beauty care and healthcare, which both grew at around 18 percent (Figure A). In beauty, P&G fired strongly on the M&A cylinder with its acquisitions of Clairol and Wella, as well as on portfolio momentum, while in health it fired on share gain and portfolio momentum.

Figure A P&G's growth decomposition by product category

Change in revenue, 1999–05, US$ billion

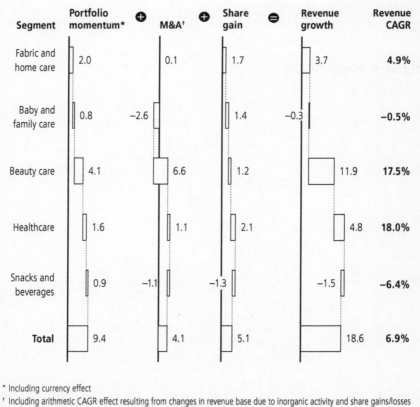

Segment	Portfolio momentum*	⊕	M&A†	⊕	Share gain	⊜	Revenue growth	Revenue CAGR
Fabric and home care	2.0		0.1		1.7		3.7	**4.9%**
Baby and family care	0.8	−2.6			1.4	−0.3		**−0.5%**
Beauty care	4.1		6.6		1.2		11.9	**17.5%**
Healthcare	1.6		1.1		2.1		4.8	**18.0%**
Snacks and beverages	0.9	−1.1		−1.3		−1.5		**−6.4%**
Total	9.4		4.1		5.1		18.6	**6.9%**

* Including currency effect
† Including arithmetic CAGR effect resulting from changes in revenue base due to inorganic activity and share gains/losses
Source: Dealogic; Hoovers; company reports; McKinsey analysis

Clearly, growth was driven by P&G's "where to compete" choices. In 1999, branded players in categories such as snacks were finding it hard to protect their margins against encroaching retailers. In the company's 2004 annual report, Lafley described P&G's strategy as shifting to "faster-growing, higher-margin . . . businesses that are growing ahead of both industry averages and P&G target growth rates." Health and beauty were prime examples. Moreover, they were categories in which brand and innovation played a strong role, and in which P&G had a relatively low share.

During the same time period, P&G also divested low-growth businesses: JIF peanut butter and Crisco cooking oil from its snack and beverages portfolio, and in Australia, Milton infant hygiene from baby and family care. The extent of P&G's portfolio shift between 1999 and 2005 can be seen in Figure B. Healthcare's revenue contribution doubled from 7 to 14 percent, while beauty care's rose from 19 to 34 percent. Since P&G was a company with $38 billion in revenues in 1999, this represented quite a dramatic reshaping of the portfolio.

Figure B Portfolio shift
Revenue mix, 1999–2005, percent

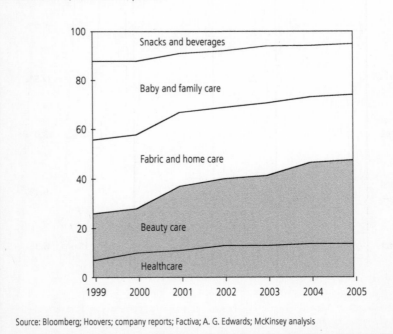

Source: Bloomberg; Hoovers; company reports; Factiva; A. G. Edwards; McKinsey analysis

Since then, P&G has made another big move, spending $57 billion to acquire Gillette in 2005. The purchase added men's and women's grooming products to P&G's presence in health and beauty. It also added the Duracell business, which could prove a tougher arena in which to maintain an edge through branding and innovation.

And the search continues, as Lafley promised in the 2005 annual report:

"We will continue to invest in new businesses, with emphasis on entering or creating categories adjacent to existing P&G categories. We have identified more than $20 billion of opportunity in categories that are growing an average 6 percent per year with P&G-average margins."

Between 1999 and 2005, P&G's cost of goods fell from 49 to 46 percent of sales. Over the same period, the company became markedly more capital efficient: while sales increased by 50 percent from $38 to $57 billion, invested capital stayed virtually unchanged at about $14.5 billion.

These cost reductions yielded increased cash flows that were directed toward M&A, geographic expansion, capability-building efforts, and advertising expenditure (which rose from $3.6 billion in 1999 to $5.9 billion in 2005). At the same time, P&G earned a reputation for excellence in customer management. By 2005, according to its annual report, US retailers were ranking it top in six out of eight key categories: clearest strategy; most innovative; most helpful consumer and shopper information; best supply-chain management; best category management; and best marketing.

Not just strategy, but organization

Though P&G made crucial strategic decisions over this period, they weren't the whole story. Equally important was the way it built the organizational capability it needed to integrate deals and drive market-share growth in health and beauty. The pure growth rates of the different segments are one side of the coin; the assessment of the margin attractiveness of each segment and the ability to capture the growth potential are the other.

The first and perhaps most important organizational change carried out by P&G was the new structure it announced in 1998. The company was reorganized as one seamless global organization comprising global business units (GBUs), market development organizations (MDOs), a global business services organization (GBS), and corporate functions. Though the implementation of this structure caused disruptions that probably contributed to the missed earnings in 2000, the model itself proved a winner, helping P&G bring its scale to bear in local markets: "We're now able to capture the benefits of focused, smaller companies through dedicated GBUs while capturing the go-to-market strengths and capabilities of a $50 billion company."[‡‡]

The relationship between the global business units and the market development organizations is central. Each MDO team focuses P&G's portfolio of brands at the granular level on local markets, consumers, retailers, supply chains, and governments. It is this local knowledge and expertise that is critical to execution. The MDOs concentrate solely on winning in these local markets but are aligned with the GBUs through objectives covering top-line growth, market share, cash, costs, and value creation.

The GBUs are charged with developing a growth direction through clear long-term growth strategies for individual brands. Their role is to bring scale by identifying consumer needs common to multiple markets across the world, and to extend brands and product innovations quickly to them. They focus exclusively on gaining leadership in their individual industries and are measured in terms of TRS.

The third element in the structure is global business services, which aim to provide services and technology innovation to the businesses at best-in-class costs, quality, and scale.

The advantage of this structure is that it eliminates inefficient overlaps. The MDOs are free to focus all their resources on local customers without duplicating product innovation, sourcing, advertising, and other activities led by the GBUs. This benefit is multiplied across categories, markets, and trade channels. Lafley claims that "We can reap the benefits of global scale while acting like a local company everywhere we compete." This is not just rhetoric; the numbers back him up.

As P&G reshaped its organization, it revised its expectations of managers. Extensive changes took place in the top ranks, producing a relatively young but experienced team. Lafley recounts:

> "We very quietly changed over half of the leadership team . . . . Almost all of us have now managed a business in at least two major regions of the world. Most of us have handled a developing region and a developed region, so we are far more knowledgeable about how to operate in different markets."[§§]

Managing granularity at scale
P&G was smart to focus on health and beauty—categories where private-label penetration is lower and retailers' supply-chain muscle less developed, and where

branding and innovation mark out the winners. As Lafley explained, "Branding is more important than ever—and big leading brands are more valuable than ever. In a sea of choices where confusion reigns, consumers value the reliable promise of their favorite brands. This plays to our strength: branding is in P&G's DNA."

P&G set out to use its global scale to build better customer management, innovation, and marketing capabilities. Other consumer companies also saw these areas as key to success and rationalized their brand portfolios to focus their capabilities on fewer products, believing that they would reap the benefits of greater scale. But P&G saw that more of the same was not enough, and set out to transform its global capabilities to win in local markets.

- **The innovation platform.** Lafley comments, "In an environment of rising consumer expectations, relentless competition, and rapid technological change, innovation becomes more important than ever. . . . In a global world, innovation can come from anywhere at any time. We have totally, dramatically, changed the way we set about innovation. We are trying to become more comfortable with the fact that it doesn't have to be the technology in the product that acts as the starter for innovation." Previously, each division innovated independently; now all innovation was brought together at scale into a single process and tracked at every stage. "At the end of every month I have a pretty good idea of what we have in the pipeline through all the different stages, across all the businesses."

  P&G now looks to acquire between a third and a half of its product innovations from outside; not necessarily through acquisition, but through partnerships or even technology exchanges with competitors. This approach, which it calls "Connect and Develop," has led to the successful launch of a number of new products including Olay Regenerist, Swiffer Dusters, and Crest Spinbrush. Between 2004 and 2006, P&G introduced more than a hundred new products that had been developed at least partly outside the company.[¶¶] As Larry Huston, vice-president for innovation and knowledge, explained, the company is now "scouring the world for proven technologies, packages, and products that P&G can improve, scale up, and market either on its own or in partnership with other companies."[***]

  Lafley claims that this approach to innovation confers a distinct market advantage: "We can compete on multiple fronts simultaneously without spreading ourselves too thin; we can deliver a higher frequency of new products across multiple markets; we can plan long term globally while focusing locally on superior execution every day."

- **The brand platform.** P&G took equally radical steps in shaping its brand organization. It brought greater standardization and discipline to its brand strategy and extended its timeframe for marketing initiatives, abandoning its old quarter-by-quarter approach to put more emphasis on longer-term results. Brand managers were rewarded for delivering growth and extending the brand over time. Accordingly, brand plans switched from a one-year horizon to two-year forecasts with projections for the following three to five years. In addition, the time frame for promotions became two to three years instead of one to two. This new longer-term perspective also enabled P&G to improve its performance evaluation since the impact of managers' actions and decisions could be judged more accurately over an extended period.

NOTES

* A. G. Lafley, "Chairman's letter to shareholders," P&G annual report 2003. All other quotations in this box come from the 2004 annual report.

† See www.pg.com.

‡ As reported by cnnmoney.com.

§ At the close of trading on 6 March 2000, P&G's stock was quoted on the NYSE at $87.44. The next morning, its price opened at $58. The overnight fall, when adjusted for dividends and splits (from $37.92 to $26.46 for the same period), was 30 percent (Yahoo finance).

¶ As reported by cnnmoney.com.

** On 12 January 2000 P&G's shares peaked at $118.37 before closing at $117 (adjusted for a 50.6 split) (Yahoo finance).

†† P&G's acquisition of Gillette in 2005 fell outside the period we studied.

‡‡ This and subsequent quotations from A. G. Lafley come from the 2004 annual report unless otherwise indicated.

§§ Egon Zehnder, interview with A. G. Lafley (www.egonzehnderknowledge.com).

¶¶ Larry Huston and Nabil Sakkab, "Connect and develop: Inside Procter & Gamble's new model for innovation," *Harvard Business Review,* March 2006, pp. 58–66.

*** Ibid.

Applying the architecture framework

To illustrate the value of placing our discussion of architecture into a formal framework, consider the story of Procter & Gamble in the text panel. We believe P&G's growth architecture was extremely well designed for both granularity and scale:

- The company's **growth direction** was clear: it made a portfolio shift toward higher-margin health and beauty categories to capitalize on its strengths in branding and innovation.

- This direction translated into **granular strategies** for product categories, customers, and markets.

- P&G's **scale platforms** included innovation and marketing capabilities, as well as world-class support services.

- The **organization blueprint** created global product categories to exploit P&G's scale, and local market development organizations to cater to the particularities of each market.

- Finally, P&G's CEO made subtle but important changes to **management processes,** including extending the tenure of brand managers and revamping talent development and incentives.

■ ■ ■

A key element in any company's growth journey is the design of its architecture, as P&G's story illustrates. Like the growth strategy, the organization model must deliver both granularity and scale. In the next chapter, we help you look in the mirror to see whether you have an architecture that is designed for growth.

NOTES

[1] Tim Berners-Lee, "Information management: A proposal," CERN, March 1989, May 1990.

[2] Measured in 2003 US dollars.

[3] See, for example, R. S. Kaplan and D. P. Norton, *Alignment: Using the balanced scorecard to create corporate synergies* (Harvard Business School Press, Boston, Mass., 1996).

[4] As we explained in chapter 5, the staircase approach introduced in *The Alchemy of Growth* continues to be the best way to think about growth strategy at the business-unit level since it incorporates a time dimension that is often lost in short-term strategic planning.

[5] See, for example, P. Kontes, "A new look for the corporate center: Reorganizing to maximize value," *Journal of Business Strategy*, volume 25, number 4, 2004, pp. 18–24.

11

Looking in the mirror

"Mirror, mirror, on the wall:
Who is the fairest of them all?"
Snow White

- CEOs intending to drive growth will benefit from a solid, fact-based understanding of their companies' current architecture

- There are several common patterns of architecture that apply to companies at different stages in their growth journey

- By looking in the mirror and making a full and frank appraisal of your architecture pattern, you can assess your own starting point more reliably

IN THE LAST CHAPTER, we looked at a company that had an architecture designed to support growth. But P&G is far from the norm. Most organizations are geared to performance, not growth. And most CEOs inherit an organization that is something of a mishmash: a patchwork of compromises and evolutionary decisions rather than a single considered design that aligns all functions and business units in pursuit of a common goal.

Yet a complete redesign is hugely disruptive to an organization. What most companies need, rather, is a set of decisive interventions that can build on their strengths and help align their organization with their new strategic direction. But how should they go about this task?

Looking in the mirror

We believe that any CEO intending to drive growth would benefit from a solid fact-based understanding of the current state of his or her company's architecture. It's especially important to test how well the growth direction has been reflected in the other architectural elements. By "looking in the mirror," as we call it, you can make a full and frank appraisal of each element, uncover any gaps, and reflect on what you need to do to produce a unified and consistent design that will stimulate growth. Let's remind ourselves of what our framework looks like (Figure 11.1) before we consider each element in turn.

Growth direction. Begin by reviewing your overall growth direction. To what extent is it based on granular market insights? Does it signal an intention to fire on certain cylinders in each of the three horizons? If it *doesn't* include an aspiration for above-GDP growth, are you planning to deliver adequate levels of performance improvement or capital return instead?

Scale platforms. Now turn to the sources of scale that define your company's competitive advantage. Do you have robust plans for building the scale platforms that your growth direction demands, and for systematically generating market insight and driving M&A?

Granular blueprint. Next, examine your organization chart. Does its level of granularity match the texture of the market? Have you appointed the right leaders in pivotal roles? Do they have the necessary decision rights and accountability?

Granular strategies. Consider your granular business strategies. Are they going to generate the growth you expect in terms of share gain, portfolio momentum, and M&A? If you are shifting your portfolio, have you avoided the characteristic pitfalls that frustrate new market entries?

11.1 Using architecture framework

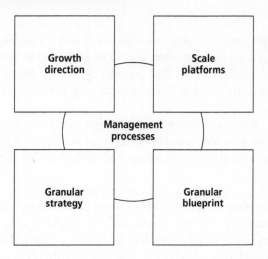

Management systems. Lastly, think about the key management processes and systems in your company, especially those relating to resource allocation and performance management. Are they working to align the other architecture elements in a mutually reinforcing way? Do they help you manage the business at a fairly granular level?

These overarching diagnostic questions give you a sense of what looking in the mirror involves. To do the job properly, you need to reflect on about a dozen questions for each of these five elements. That should give you a good picture of how well your current architecture is designed for growth.

Common patterns in architecture

To help with this task, we have identified some of the most common architecture patterns. (Note that in the diagrams below, we've used shading to identify elements of the architecture that are designed for growth.) As you read about the patterns, consider which one sounds the most familiar to you— it's probably the pattern that represents your company best.

Out of synch

 We call the first basic architecture pattern "out of synch" not because a company exhibiting it suffers from poor performance but because the elements of its architecture are not aligned with its growth direction or with one another. The company may once have had an architecture designed for growth, but not any more. Perhaps its growth direction is no longer compelling or has become obsolete.

This pattern is often seen in companies that face major discontinuities in their core business or have a longstanding engine of growth that finally runs out of steam. A retailer could exhibit this pattern when its roll-out of a proven format to new locations reaches maximum density, for instance.

The top priority for a company with this pattern is to set a new growth direction based on granular market insights. It will probably need to make substantial changes to align the organization with this new direction.

Ivory tower

Another common pattern is the ivory tower. This company has made thoughtful plans for its growth journey. It has used superior insights about the future of its industry to chart a compelling direction, and has probably communicated it internally and externally. However, the direction has not yet been translated into the rest of the architecture, so that granular business strategies and an appropriate organization structure are lacking.

This pattern is frequently encountered when leaders are clear on a particular growth direction but the company is slow to act on it. If a company decides to expand into Asia, say, but has no senior executives with experience in the region and no granular market-entry strategies, its plans are likely to stay on the drawing board. The challenge for an ivory tower company is to identify leaders who can focus attention on translating the growth direction into granular strategies.

Top down

This pattern occurs when leaders have managed to commit the top level of their company to a compelling growth path and have even managed to build a set of central scale advantages, but haven't yet managed to push the growth agenda through to the operating levels. In other words, they are off to a good start but there is a long road ahead.

This pattern is often a transitional state in a growth program: the impetus for change has begun at the top and will be driven down the organization over time. But problems arise if the process gets stuck in top-down mode. It's also advisable for leaders to avoid making announcements that raise people's expectations too far, since fulfilling them may take a long time.

If P&G had looked in the mirror in 2001, it would have seen that it fitted this top-down pattern. It had a clear growth direction and solid scale platforms, but its business-unit strategies and organization still reflected its old model. It took the company a few years to fill in the bottom two elements of architecture. Once it had done so, it had a robust architecture for growth.

Bottom up

This pattern is the hallmark of misaligned top leadership. It shows a company where the business units are driving growth, yet there is no growth direction or scale platform at the top. Such a company is vulnerable to attack by private-equity firms out on a hunt. The pattern is not sustainable since the company is incapable of identifying emerging market opportunities or making a shift in its portfolio mix.

The burden of action typically falls on the board of directors, which will need to question the effectiveness of corporate executive leadership and take remedial measures. The good news is that the business-unit fundamentals are usually strong so a revitalized leadership can often add value very quickly.

Left-brained

A company that is highly strategic and analytical but isn't pulling the organizational levers at its disposal will exhibit this pattern. It has a set of granular business strategies that are consistent with a compelling overall growth direction, but this strength is undermined by inconsistent and ineffectual approaches on the organization side of the framework.

This pattern is quite common, especially in large companies. Sophisticated planning processes and analysts' unquenchable thirst for reporting focus leaders' minds on perfecting strategy, while the organizational initiatives needed to implement it don't get the attention they deserve. Put simply, the company doesn't yet walk the talk.

The challenge for a left-brained company is to restore balance by developing its right-brain capabilities. The first step is to review the organization design and produce a blueprint that matches the growth direction and strategies. The second step is to design central capability-building initiatives to bolster its performance. Finally, the company needs to achieve harmony between the four elements of its architecture by aligning growth-enabling processes (especially operating disciplines and performance management) so that they drive superior execution of its strategies.

Right-brained

 This pattern is the mirror image of the previous one. The right-brained company's strengths lie in organization design and the development of capabilities and resources for growth. Its leaders see strategy as something that emerges from great design, and devote their energies to creating a high-performing organization. In short, they put structure before strategy.

More often than not, right-brained companies enjoy some initial success as various corporate-wide initiatives (six sigma, talent engagement, learning) take hold. In time, however, the lack of a growth direction and business strategies starts to tell. Rudderless, they slow down and stagnate, ending up in a kind of Brownian motion.

We think the right-brained pattern is rarer than the left-brained, although it can be found in industries that are not highly dynamic or prone to disruption, where leaders are less likely to shift strategies or make big moves. A notable example is Thermo Electron under the Hatsopoulos brothers.[1] In both cases, structure drove strategy, not the other way around.

The challenge for right-brained companies is to wake up before it's too late. A sense of urgency or a burning platform is needed to force leaders to re-examine their growth direction and business strategies.

Designed for growth

 This pattern is a big improvement on previous ones. With four out of the five architectural elements in place, the company is in great shape to turn its attention to securing its long-term health. The main challenge that remains is to align the key growth-enabling elements in order to sustain growth.

This pattern is most often found in companies that are on a growth streak. Their challenge is to institutionalize their success beyond the life of the current winning formula (and the current leadership). Their priority is to build an insight machine that can identify emerging trends in a systematic way and to allocate resources to building the scale platforms they need to evolve and succeed in the long term.

Fully resonating

 This final pattern represents the pinnacle of growth: that rare beast, the growth giant. Not only has it aligned its strategy and organization for granular growth, but it has also managed to create a robust set of management systems that will enable it to reconfigure itself in response to external market shifts.

If we look back a decade at the 30 great growers identified in *The Alchemy of Growth,* only five proved capable of sustaining their growth and adjusting to the subsequent economic downturn.[2] That meager success rate highlights the magnitude of the challenge of sustaining profitable growth over decades.

Now we turn to a case study that highlights how important it is to understand a company's readiness for growth and to identify elements in its architecture that need to be strengthened or realigned.

The Unilever story

In February 2000, Unilever announced that it was embarking on a program to drive market-share growth by rationalizing its portfolio to focus on its 400 leading brands. "Path to Growth," as the program was called, was to be supported by other initiatives: the development of new electronic channels, the creation of a more integrated supply chain, the simplification of support functions, and the divestment of underperforming businesses.

Five years later, with revenue still at the 1999 level of €41 billion, Unilever admitted defeat. It acknowledged that "Our Path to Growth strategy delivered strong profitability, improved margins, capital efficiency and cash flows but not sustained growth. And we were losing market share."[3] In fact, Unilever had lost 2.9 percent a year in organic share while gaining 1.4 percent growth a year from its acquisitions net of divestments and 1.7 percent from its portfolio momentum. In terms of our three cylinders, it had misfired on portfolio momentum and organic share, and was neutral on inorganic growth.[4] It was high time to look in the mirror.

All in all, Unilever had lost market share worth almost €8 billion in five years, paradoxically while pursuing a strategy that had share gain as its primary objective. The company made a number of mistakes. Its growth direction—rationalizing the brand portfolio to grow market share—was clear but targeted the hardest of the three growth cylinders. But not much else of the necessary architecture was in place. In fact, Unilever seemed to be exhibiting the ivory tower pattern we described above.

The 400 brands were expected to drive growth but they weren't given new strategies at a sufficiently granular level. Specifically, in the view of many industry observers, Unilever focused too much on brands and not enough on categories and countries. In the end, although many of the 400 brands did grow substantially by entering new categories, too much of that growth was at the expense of other Unilever brands in those categories. Similarly, Unilever wrongly assumed that size would automatically translate into global scale benefits, for example, in purchasing and R&D. But many of its efforts were hampered by a cumbersome organization model with two chairmen, overlapping accountabilities, long chains of command, and a predominantly regional focus.

Recognizing these shortcomings, Unilever announced a change of direction under its new CEO, Patrick Cescau. In the company's 2005 annual report, he described three areas in need of particular attention:

"First, to make our portfolio work harder for us, with sharper priorities and resource allocation. Secondly, better execution, especially in the areas of marketing and customer management. And, finally, create a more agile 'One Unilever' organization, aligned behind a single strategy, with the right people in the right jobs, delivering quality and speed of execution."

Unilever set out to have much clearer priorities about where to grow, emphasizing "precisely which categories, segments and brands in which countries will drive growth."[5] It decided to place much more emphasis on developing and emerging markets such as India, China, and Russia, and on healthy living and personal care product categories. (Note that these were among the portfolio shifts that had worked so well for P&G.)

Finally, recognizing that its organizational design was partly responsible for the failure of the Path to Growth program, Unilever redesigned its organization around three pillars: categories, regions, and functions. Categories were responsible for driving brand development and strategies, and for focusing innovation on fewer bigger ideas. Regions were accountable for deploying brands and innovations at the local level and for managing customers. Functions were integrated under the One Unilever program so that common practices and standards could be instilled across all of them. Finally, Unilever abandoned its unusual dual-chairman structure. At the end of this process, it was much closer to being designed for growth. As we go to press, the results look positive, with growth and margins both picking up.

■ ■ ■

Now it's time for *you* to look into the mirror. Out of the eight patterns we've described in this chapter, which one best represents your company? What does that imply for your priorities in your growth journey?

Looking in the mirror can be disturbing as well as enlightening. Even so, we have seen chief executives glean valuable insights that help them to begin or accelerate their growth journey and produce a robust architecture for growth.

You can use this exercise as a powerful lens to help your management team discuss issues connected with your architecture. We have seen it provoke interesting debates that bring to the surface the different perspectives adopted by different executives. The challenge then becomes one of finding ways to bring together the various architecture elements in a coherent design.

We have already described the strategy side of architecture in earlier chapters. We now turn to the right-hand side of the framework from Figure 11.1. The next chapter examines the granular blueprint before we turn to scale platforms and portfolio advantages in chapter 13.

NOTES

[1] For a detailed description of the Thermo Electron case, see R. Foster and S. Kaplan, *Creative Destruction: Turning built-to-last into built-to-perform* (Pearson, 2001).

[2] Namely Acer, CRH, Hutchinson Whampoa, Nokia, and Wells Fargo.

[3] Annual report, 2005.

[4] Note that the appreciation of the euro against the dollar and Latin American currencies meant that currency effects had a severe impact on Unilever's portfolio. Our estimate is that the portfolio would have grown almost 3 percent faster, at around 4.6 percent, if currency effects had been excluded. They cost the company as much as €8 billion in revenue. So can Unilever claim that it was merely unlucky to be denominated in euros? Yes and no. Clearly currency effects cost it a great deal, but equally its portfolio momentum declined over the period, from a growth rate of 14 percent to 3 percent if we include currency effects, or from 6 to around 2 percent if we exclude them. So regardless of currency effects, Unilever's "where to compete" choices caused its portfolio momentum to decline.

[5] Annual report, 2005.

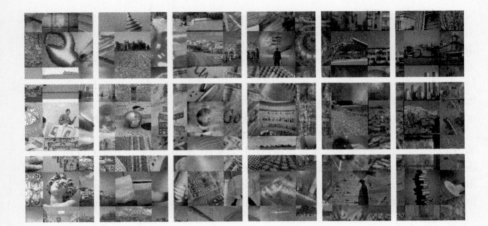

12

A blueprint for granularity

*"A cookbook must have recipes, but it shouldn't be a blueprint.
It should be more inspirational; it should be a guide."*
Thomas Keller, chef and restaurateur

- A successful blueprint needs to increase granularity *and* leverage the scale of the organization
- It allows "where to compete" choices, M&A decisions, and resource allocation to take place at the right level of granularity: one that exploits the texture of the market without sacrificing the benefits of scale
- Granularity need not increase the complexity of running a company; it increases transparency and can help focus actions and interventions

D URING THE IRANIAN hostage crisis in 1979–81, US president Jimmy Carter authorized a rescue bid called Operation Eagle Claw. The plan was to bring forces in by helicopter to free the hostages being held at the US embassy in Tehran. Unfortunately, two of the eight choppers lost their way when an unforeseen low-level sandstorm blew up, while a third suffered a mechanical failure and had to drop out. The failure of the mission not only intensified the standoff but also affected the US election: nine months later, Ronald Reagan marched into the White House.

According to security expert Howard Schmidt,[1] the failure of Operation Eagle Claw was largely due to the Americans' unfamiliarity with the conditions on the ground. It turns out that the sand in Iran has a different texture than the sand back home in the Arizona desert. It was this difference in granularity that stopped the choppers from reaching their destination and ultimately doomed the whole mission. Here we have a tragic but vivid metaphor for the importance of addressing the right level of granularity in strategic planning.

One of the toughest challenges for a large company is working out how to motivate thousands of employees and enable them to contribute to the growth of the organization by pursuing granular opportunities. The difficulty lies in the fact that operating in large groups typically reduces people's sense of collective identity and increases the incidence of "free-riding."[2] A blueprint for granularity is, in part, an antidote to the lack of ownership and sense of personal involvement that often plagues large organizations. As Jack Welch put it when describing the challenge at GE:

> "Our dream, and our plan, well over a decade ago, was simple. We set out to shape a global enterprise that preserved the classic big-company advantages—while eliminating the classic big-company drawbacks. What we wanted to build was a hybrid, an enterprise with the reach and resources of a big company—the body of a big company—but the thirst to learn, the compulsion to share, and the bias for action—the soul—of a small company."[3]

Designing an organization blueprint to accommodate greater granularity is far from simple. Indeed, most organization models are explicitly designed to obstruct granularity—to create spans and layers to aggregate information and decision making to what is seen as the right level for senior managers. Think of a typical large company that has its business units focus on market share while keeping its M&A decisions and "where to compete" choices for the corporate center. With a design like that, it has little chance of operating at a granular level. The multitude of opportunities to make small deals and shift the portfolio won't even make it onto management's radar screen.

To overcome the shortcomings of a structure like this, some thinkers have advocated less hierarchical and more distributed organization models.[4] Others have proposed fairly rigid processes for designing the right architecture.[5] And, indeed, a number of companies have managed to design organization models geared to exploiting granular growth opportunities in a systematic manner. Most successful models don't simply atomize the business into small units and have them all report individually (although some CEOs may opt for this route). Rather, companies make a careful analysis of the level of granularity required for success in their business and then produce an optimized organization model that allows them to engage in "where to compete" choices, M&A decisions, and resource allocation at that level.

Finding the sweet spot

But how do you know what the right level of granularity is? The guiding principle is that it should allow your company to exploit the texture of the market but without sacrificing the benefits of scale. We call this the "sweet spot." When a tennis player hits a ball with the sweet spot in the middle of the racquet, it flies through the air with surprising power and minimum vibration. In much the same way, operating your business at the sweet spot of granularity magnifies the effectiveness of your actions to achieve growth.

Over the past decade, the deregulation of markets and advances in information technology are likely to have increased the level of granularity at which you should be managing your business and driving your growth strategies. To see why, let's look at a traditional retailer, a bookstore. The bookseller's objective is to decide which categories of book to stock and to allocate space to them in a way that optimizes the revenue per unit of shelf space. At a certain point, the marginal revenue from adding another category of books no longer justifies the extra cost of the space (or the confusion for customers as they try to find their way around the store). To enforce discipline, revenue or profit per square foot or meter is rigorously tracked and compared across categories.

Conceptually, the problem looks like Figure 12.1 (which may remind you of your first economics class). As you begin to target your market segments in more granular ways, the sales benefits typically increase quite quickly, but then start to taper off as you add smaller and smaller variations. On the costs side, the most efficient business model would offer no variation at all. When you

12.1 Locating your sweet spot

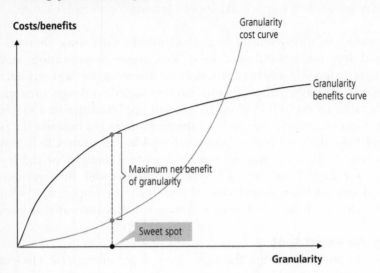

add complexity by catering to a broader range of customer needs, the costs (like the bookseller's inventory) begin to rise quite sharply. The intersection of these two curves is the sweet spot for granularity in your market.

The impact of new technology

It's interesting to see how the internet has moved the sweet spot of granularity in the book business during the past decade or so. Unlike our traditional bookseller, Amazon isn't constrained by a physical storefront; customers using its website can choose from some 3.7 million titles (by way of comparison, a typical Barnes & Noble superstore stocks about 100,000 books). With no bricks-and-mortar presence, a fully developed and scalable IT platform and infrastructure, and many of its books delivered not from its own warehouse but via a virtual supply chain, Amazon is able to act in a much more granular way at very low marginal cost. By analyzing the goods that individual customers buy, it develops a picture of their needs and interests so that it can email them with personalized offers and recommendations.

Indeed, Amazon exemplifies what has been called "the long tail":[6] a market that has been reshaped by the internet into a small number of "big hits" (popular products such as Oprah's latest book-club choice) with a long tail of niche items now readily available for the first time. Not many bookshops are likely to stock a title as obscure as *Tattooed Mountain Women and Spoonboxes*

12.2 Moving your sweet spot

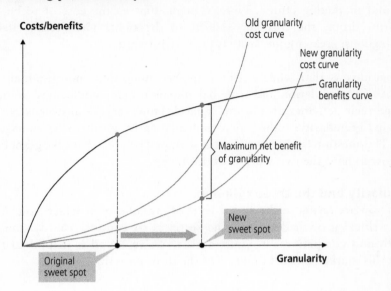

of *Daghestan,* but Amazon can (and indeed does at the time of writing, at least in the UK).

Of course, bookselling isn't the only business that's being reshaped by new technology. In emerging markets, technology is enabling businesses to build scale rapidly while continuing to operate in a very granular way.

Consider a couple of examples from China. Ping An, the country's second-largest insurance company with more than 30 million customers, is able to manage a fragmented sales force of about 200,000 agents by using a mobile-based sales management platform, thus overcoming the lack of fixed-line telecom infrastructure in some regions.

China Merchants Bank, one of the country's most successful financial services firms, wanted to ensure that its distribution footprint followed pockets of GDP growth but was wary of the quality of published data and the time it took to get it. So the bank used night-light aerial photography to identify the brightest areas, reasoning that they were where the economic growth was. It then targeted these key markets in its growth plans.

When technology is harnessed in ways like these, the curves we examined in Figure 12.1 are reshaped to look more like those in Figure 12.2. As demand fragments, more tailoring may be required to achieve the same benefit from sales and marketing efforts. Note, though, that as the cost of technology platforms drops, the cost curve shifts to the right. The overall effect is unambiguous: greater granularity is the way forward.

The paradox is that while markets are becoming ever more granular, the pursuit of consolidation and scale has impaired many companies' ability to manage their activities at a granular level. However, the answer is not just increased granularity; rather, increased granularity needs to be managed *at scale*. The question is where to have the scale and where to have the granularity, and how to have the two work in concert.

Granularity and the three cylinders

When you are trying to define the level of granularity at which you should make critical growth decisions, the secret is to consider the dynamics of growth and competition in your market. We've found it helpful to think about this market context in terms of the three growth cylinders.

If you are reflecting on *portfolio momentum,* for instance, it's important to understand where you need to look to find significant variations in the growth rates of different market segments. Should you make your "where to compete" choices in terms of product categories, consumer segments, geographic markets, or some other dimension? Once you have identified the right dimension, you then need to establish the right level of granularity within it.

When Procter & Gamble looked at its innovation processes, it decided that the right level of granularity for planning new products was not countries or even brands, but global customer segments. It took the view that consumers' affluence and aspirations have more influence on their consumption habits than the country they happen to live in. So P&G centralized all its innovation under global category managers, bringing global scale to bear on new product development while preserving its ability to operate effectively at the level of individual countries. New products now reach local markets in 18 months, rather than the three years typical under the old structure. This is a good example of a scale advantage that enables increased granularity.

If you turn then to the *M&A* cylinder, you need to understand whether your M&A opportunities are likely to be in big businesses or small ones, and whether your organization model is geared to capturing them. As we saw in chapter 6, a decentralized structure helped one large company, CRH, to identify and execute a large number of small acquisitions.

Finally, if you look at the *share gain* cylinder, you need to understand whether critical investments in capital expenditure and operational budgets in your market are typically made in small chunks or big lumps. At what level of granularity do your competitors differentiate their business models?

The answers to these questions are not often found at the highest level of an organization. Yet many CEOs are handed information aggregated at this level, thus losing transparency and forfeiting opportunities to influence key decisions. That's why successful executives spend so much time asking questions and grilling direct reports to get behind the averages and find out what is *really* going on and what is hidden from view.

Think for a moment about the opportunities that would open up before you if only you could see into your organization at a far more granular level than you can today. Imagine the advantages you would gain if your organization blueprint enabled you to act in a more focused, precise, and nuanced way than your competitors.

Designing your organization blueprint

All well and good, you may think, but how can a fully stretched management team take on all this extra complexity? Don't worry: we don't know many CEOs who have time on their hands, so we aren't suggesting that you drown in ever more detail. We aren't talking about drilling deeper in operational reviews. We want to encourage you to tap into *the key decisions that drive growth*: choices about where to compete and what to buy.

Let's be frank: it may be downright impractical to try to manage everything at a G4 or G5 level. Aggregation is often needed to ensure that a unit has the critical mass for managing such things as its talent and its cost structure, as well as for controlling its resources so that it can justifiably be held accountable for its performance. Working through this tradeoff is the key challenge in designing an organization blueprint. Fortunately, you can use several organizational levers to help you.

Structure is the most obvious and often the most effective of these levers. Your organization blueprint will need to show how business units are grouped; how many layers of management are needed; and which functions are to be shared or centralized and which devolved into the business units. The test here is whether the benefits of sharing and centralization genuinely outweigh the benefits of focus and unambiguous accountability.

How you group the business units and what you call them also matter a great deal. Think about the lens you use to get the clearest view of your business when you are gauging its growth potential. Is it product? Customer segment? Geography? It's interesting to note that as you "go narrow" along one of these dimensions to define granular units, you can also "go broad" along others to create headroom for growth. Remember that the way you define the market in which you participate can open up (or close down) growth opportunities, as we saw with Gillette.

However, structure isn't the only organizational lever you have at your disposal. There are various other ways of managing an organization at a granular level that don't involve breaking it up into ever smaller pieces. In some cases executives can be highly effective at making granular decisions within an organization that isn't granular in structure at all. They adopt non-structural mechanisms such as incentives, management processes, and cultural norms to support or complement the organization design and make the model work as a whole.

Another crucial non-structural lever is people. CEOs pursuing growth need to take a fresh look at their talent management. Because growth initiatives take time to deliver real impact, the managers chosen to lead them may need to stay in post for three to five years instead of the usual 18 months or so. Looking further ahead, companies need to create a leadership pipeline that will generate a sufficient number of growth leaders at the right level of granularity.

When you design the blueprint for your organization, your experience, judgment, and insight into the texture of the market and the nature of your company are critical in making the right decisions. We wouldn't presume to be prescriptive about the number of layers or spans of control your company may need other than to say that they shouldn't lead to aggregation and averaging. Although the choices are yours to make, it can be instructive to see how others have tackled the challenges. To this end, we'll now turn to an example of a successful granular blueprint at a retail bank.

Putting a blueprint into practice

Over the past ten years, the ANZ Banking Group has been the strongest performer of the big four Australian banks, which together account for around 80 percent of the market. The industry as a whole has enjoyed a strong tailwind: low inflation and rapid economic growth (in which Australia leads the OECD) have generated annual consumer credit growth of around 9 percent over the past fifteen years.

In the second half of the 1990s, ANZ embarked on what was to become a remarkable transformation. By 2006 it had lifted both staff and customer satisfaction to industry-leading levels, increased revenue in its core banking business to A$10.2 billion (US$7.7 billion), almost tripled profits to over A$3.7 billion (US$2.8 billion), and slashed its cost/income ratio from 65 to 45 percent. Recognizing that consumer lending offered lower risks and high growth, ANZ divested its riskier businesses to focus on growing the consumer business. In 1997 this comprised just over a third (36 percent) of its portfolio; by 2003 it accounted for over half (55 percent).

A critical part of the transformation was ANZ's redesign of its organization to enable it to operate at a much more granular level than its competitors. CEO John MacFarlane saw retail banking as an inherently granular business: "Customers identify with *their* branch or *their* relationship manager. Staff identify with *their* team or *their* business."[7] This meant that the right level of granularity for ANZ was the individual branch. But it saw that operating individual branches as business units wouldn't work, since product specialists and wealth advisers had to be shared between several branches, and a larger arena than a branch was needed if the company was to attract (and pay for) the talent it needed at a local level.

So MacFarlane assembled ANZ's thousand or so branches into a hundred community-based businesses, each comprising between eight and fifteen branches and headed by a local CEO. These businesses, each with around a hundred employees, were small enough to be connected to local communities and to preserve a sense of ownership among staff, but large enough to be capable of attracting and rewarding the right talent for local CEO positions. These CEOs had the freedom to appoint their own product and wealth specialists and make their own decisions on local marketing and opening hours.

ANZ's monolithic product organization was also split into fifteen or so business units. MacFarlane explains:

"The creation of many individual business units within ANZ, and the removal of bureaucracy and layers of management, gives more responsibility to people to recognize customers' needs and develop those businesses. In 1997, we had as many as nine layers of management between the CEO and front-line staff who serve customers; today there are just four."[8]

All of ANZ's local competitors have one or two more layers to their organizations despite having undergone major structural reforms.

What enabled ANZ to manage with a leaner structure was the clarity of decision rights and the improved accountability that it achieved through its successful cultural change program. But its executives emphasize that none of this would have been possible without the reporting to support it. Profitability was reported at the individual branch level and aggregated to the cluster level—something that anyone who has ever worked in a bank will recognize as a remarkable accomplishment.

The question that needs to be asked, however, is whether greater granularity sacrificed the benefits of scale that ANZ enjoyed. The answer is an emphatic no. In fact, the bank was able to reduce its total expenses while cutting its cost/income ratio by 20 percentage points and boosting its revenue by about 40 percent. The flattening of its organization structure was a key element in all this, but just as important were its big investments in systems, account check processing, and risk management. They enabled the bank to operate at a level of granularity that matched the market while still enjoying scale benefits.

■ ■ ■

Devising a blueprint for granularity doesn't involve sacrificing the benefits of scale. On the contrary, a successful blueprint needs to leverage the scale of the organization to increase granularity. ANZ took great care to ensure that its design was well suited to serving the needs of many different local communities.

This leads us to the subject of our next chapter, which shows that granularity need not inhibit the advantages of scale and that scale can, if managed properly, bring advantages to granular organization.

NOTES

[1] In an unpublished interview in 2007.

[2] Many celebrated thinkers have studied such problems. Winner of the Nobel Prize for Economics, Thomas Schelling, showed in his book *Micromotives and Macrobehavior* (W. W. Norton, New York, 1978) that small but deliberate changes in micro-incentives can contribute to vastly different macro-outcomes. Mancur Olson, a pioneer in the integration of politics into economics, examined the effect of pockets of co-operation (or coalitions) on the overall behavior of large populations in his book *The Logic of Collective Action* (Harvard University Press, Cambridge, Mass., 1965). Organizational theorist Albert Hirschman reflected on the need to create opportunities for meaningful expression and contribution (which he called "voice") in order to secure individuals' loyalty and prevent their defection (*Exit, Voice, and Loyalty*, Harvard University Press, Cambridge, Mass., 1970).

[3] Jack Welch in General Electric's annual report, 1995.

[4] See, for example, Ori Brafman and Rod A. Beckstrom's book *The Starfish and the Spider: The unstoppable power of leaderless organizations* (Portfolio, New York, 2006).

[5] See, for example, J. R. Galbraith, *Designing Organizations: An executive guide to strategy, structure, and process* (Jossey-Bass, San Francisco, California, 2002).

[6] See C. Anderson, *The Long Tail: How endless choice is creating unlimited demand* (Random House, London, 2006).

[7] ANZ annual report, 2003, p. 6.

[8] ANZ annual report, 2002, p. 15.

13

Building scale platforms

"If the shoe fits, you're not allowing for growth."
Robert N. Coons

- A scale platform allows a large company to exploit the structural advantage of its size across multiple business units and markets

- Traditional scale platforms such as networks and brands are designed to boost scale advantages and improve operational efficiency and effectiveness

- Two new scale platforms—insight engines and M&A engines—can help large companies gain advantage across all their businesses

IN THE TRADITIONAL view, large companies create a competitive edge through scale advantages, often connected with cost and sometimes with scope. We believe that scale can also produce benefits for granularity. CEOs frequently object that increased granularity would undermine the advantages of scale. But it *is* possible for large companies to retain the benefits of scale while operating in a more granular fashion. They can do so by developing scale platforms that enable granular units to fire on more cylinders over time.

The role of the granular blueprint is to unleash the entrepreneurial energy and accountability of an army of small communities to pursue granular growth opportunities in the marketplace. The role of the scale platform is to ensure that a large company realizes the advantage that derives from its size by building systematic capacity across multiple business units to manage greater granularity.

Rethinking scale

Designing your architecture for granular growth demands that you transcend traditional notions of scale. It's not simply a matter of lowering costs (though a low cost position can, of course, be a critical driver of growth). Sometimes scale platforms are based on distinctive operating capabilities such as an outstanding supply chain. They can also derive from a company's formal and informal processes. A scale platform might, for instance, be built on processes that generate market insight, support decisions linked to that insight, drive performance, and shift the portfolio over time. Examples might include CRM (customer relationship management) or business intelligence systems. In a knowledge economy, scale platforms can be based on better ways to build knowledge or talent across a portfolio.

Many of the companies that leverage scale platforms do so to improve operational efficiency and quality control and to reduce costs: consider Wal-Mart's supply chain, UPS's physical delivery network, and Toyota's lean management system. Others, such as P&G, PepsiCo, Johnson & Johnson, and Pfizer, have created scale platforms that produce direct top-line benefits in areas such as branding, innovation, and alliance building.

Some scale platforms are designed to improve both the top and the bottom line. GE, for example, has focused recently on driving commercial excellence across its portfolio. This will complement the scale platforms traditionally associated with the company, such as talent development, performance management, insight, and M&A. The thrust behind commercial excellence was prompted by GE's realization that there was $5 billion of discretionary pricing in appliances alone. CEO Jeff Immelt says, "It was the most astounding number I'd ever heard—and that's just in appliances. Extrapolating across our business, there may be $50 billion that few people are tracking or accountable for. We would never allow something like that on the cost side."[1]

It's important to remember that the sources of scale advantage can change over time. Having set your growth direction across the three horizons, you should question whether your current scale platforms will continue to be sufficient, and for how long. Given the cylinders you have decided to fire on in horizons 2 and 3, might you even need entirely new scale advantages?

Rather than examine each type of scale platform in detail, we'll now focus on the two that are most helpful in improving your cylinder-firing performance over the medium and long term. The rest of this chapter examines how you can build an *insight engine* (to fire on your portfolio momentum cylinder) and an *M&A engine* (to fire on inorganic growth). Insight engines enable companies to identify and pursue, in a highly systematic way, a much larger number of growth opportunities at the G4 and G5 level. M&A engines enable companies to identify and execute, again in a highly systematic way, a much larger volume of mergers and acquisitions.

Building an insight engine
Insight into potential sources of growth is essential when companies are constructing and managing a portfolio of granular strategies. Without insight into future growth, companies will follow the growth trend rather than ride it from the start.

There are many techniques for garnering insights, and some of the best stories are about accidental or serendipitous discoveries. But the key to building a scale platform is to create an insight engine that can generate insights regularly and systematically from both the people and the processes in the organization. Broadly speaking, either companies can change some of their existing core processes (such as performance reviews) so that they uncover more market insight, or they can create parallel "overlay" processes dedicated to insight generation. Either way, the purpose of an insight engine is to funnel new knowledge, ideas, and perspectives gathered from multiple sources into the strategic management of the company and its portfolio.

Let's examine these two different approaches. Both offer practical ways to gather granular insights from the whole organization.

Redesigning management processes

What happens in a typical performance review? Managers explain their business at an aggregate level and the CEO and executive team try to dig deeper to understand what's really happening. But the dialogue seldom gets to where it needs to go.

An average business unit has a multitude of product lines, markets, R&D projects, and marketing programs. Even if the BU head manages to run through the high-level financial and operating numbers for most of them, there may well be a heap of talent issues for the CEO to tackle next. Amid so many competing claims, the discussion of the outlook and risk never gets beyond "what you should expect from my business unit next quarter, and why we may not meet that expectation." Hardly any time is devoted to talking about the underlying texture of the market, or the drivers of growth and profitability across the different component businesses, or how these drivers are changing. A rich opportunity to involve the CEO in making portfolio choices and allocating resources at the level where growth and profitability actually take place is wasted.

One solution is to structure management dialogues so that they *do* reflect the granular texture of the markets—and, even more important, the decisions that affect the business. At one large semiconductor company, performance dialogues focused on the four business units. However, the CEO realized that these discussions weren't reaching the underlying drivers of the business. The company had more than 50 underlying portfolio segments, each of which ran four or five major R&D programs. In effect, there were some 300 individual performance cells. Not only that, but the cells generated very different rates of return on R&D investments, yet this was not reflected in the allocation of funds.

The focus on the four business units meant that the decisions that drove overall growth, such as the program-by-program allocation of R&D, were lost in the aggregate figures and therefore invisible to the CEO. Similarly, any market insights that were evident at the cell level were buried in the aggregation. Once the CEO understood this, he demanded a far more granular conversation about performance and strategy.

The first step was to get a clearer view of the 300 or so separate cells and to open up direct dialogues with the heads of the 50-plus portfolio segments. The second step was to make sure that these dialogues would inform future choices and not just dwell on past performance. In R&D, for example, the company traditionally focused on whether the ratio of investment to sales was similar to that of previous years, and how it compared to competitors' numbers. While this seemed a reasonable approach, it failed to take account of a crucial fact: that the company's chances of success varied significantly across the 300 performance cells.

Today, dialogues with the CEO go beyond static performance measures and benchmarks and address the most important questions: the probability of winning in the market cell by cell; whether resources need to be reallocated; and whether it is time to exit a market altogether. These discussions require deeper intelligence on the markets and on the nature of competitors' sources of advantage. After restructuring its performance reviews, the company reallocated 30 percent of its R&D resources to markets where it had a strong winning play. Two years later, it is growing significantly faster than the broader market.

Some managers worry about the amount of time that this management approach demands. "How can I possibly look at 300 cells and still add value? If I have to do this job, why do I need a business-unit manager?" In our experience, though, going for greater granularity in reporting actually saves time rather than squandering it.

How can this be? It's because the critical issues affecting growth are brought to light *immediately,* making the dialogue between the executive board and the business unit much more specific and thus much closer to the reality of both the market and the internal organization. The dialogue can then focus on solving the problems facing the business unit without undermining its accountability for executing the agreed solution. In most cases, the *number* of issues discussed doesn't increase, but the *specificity* and *quality* of those issues rises dramatically.

Adding overlay processes

Companies that don't wish to change their processes can instead augment them to achieve greater insights into their markets and performance. Consider the case of Johnson & Johnson.[2] In the mid-1990s, it faced a new Democratic administration seeking to reform healthcare. Major change seemed imminent, and this increase in political risk was matched by an increase in managed care.

In order to be ready for potential reforms, J&J launched its "FrameworkS" process to garner superior insight into what might happen and how it could respond. The process represented a huge commitment for the company: it demanded a significant investment of time from the executive board and other senior managers as well as involving hundreds of other employees. J&J broke down the problem into different dimensions, dedicated separate teams to each one, and interviewed a large number of industry players including insurers, healthcare providers, consumers, equipment providers, and regulators. Extending across several quarters, the process integrated all the information gained from thousands of dialogues to produce an unprecedented level of insight into the US healthcare market.

Johnson & Johnson continues to use a similar process today. It requires each participating employee to produce insights into issues that have been identified or to develop responses to them. Though the complexity of sorting through so many insights is considerable, the benefits are compelling: J&J reduces the risk of missing something important and gives people close to the end markets a fairly direct connection with decision making at the top.

In addition to creating proprietary insight on a scale that smaller companies and market analysts can't match, the FrameworkS dialogues focus the leadership team on the company's sources of advantage and how well it is performing in each of its three cylinders. This focus helps create alignment on the company's granular blueprint and "where to compete" decisions and identifies major opportunities and threats on J&J's equivalent of a growth map. In turn, this results in powerful corporate-level initiatives that shape the way the individual businesses develop their own strategies.

Building an M&A engine

The second type of scale platform we want to discuss here is the M&A engine. With 3 percentage points of the average large company's CAGR coming from M&A (and as much as 6.9 points for the growth giants), it's clear that large companies need to possess strong M&A capabilities and ensure they are properly rewarded for their buying. M&A can help create structural advantages across a variety of markets. We argued earlier that the value created by M&A is higher than is generally understood; however, it is far from guaranteed. That's why the systematic ability to do more and better M&A can create a real scale advantage.

To find out what drives good M&A performance, we looked at some of the largest and most acquisitive US companies of the past ten years.[3] We interviewed twenty of their executives and compared the activities of acquirers with above-market TRS (the "rewarded" companies in Figure 13.1) to the ones with weaker shareholder returns (the "unrewarded").[4]

13.1 Lessons from successful acquirers
Top 33 US inorganic growers, 1999–2004

	Rewarded (outperformed peers on a TRS basis)	Unrewarded (underperformed peers on a TRS basis)
Organization	Often led by CEOs with longer tenure Recruit deal experts from within	Use business development for execution rather than to shape corporate strategy Hire external deal experts
Deal strategy	Use internal and external sources to derive deal ideas Focus on long-term development	Are prone to herd mentality (following industry trends) Use short-term metrics for preliminary evaluation
Due diligence	Use structured processes and procedures Involve business units in evaluation and process	More likely to replace acquired management
Integration	Expected key factor: integration Clear focus on customer retention	Expected key factor: growth Overestimate synergies and ability to capture them

At least one of the things we learned challenges conventional wisdom. When large, busy acquirers struggle to create value, it's not because they have weak or inexperienced M&A teams. Nearly all busy acquirers, whether strong or weak in TRS terms, have a solid mix of world-class lawyers, former investment bankers, and operational or strategy experts.[5] Similarly, senior team members had a strong background in making deals whether they belonged to rewarded or unrewarded acquirers: about half had between five and ten years of experience and the rest had more.

The advantage of volume
We also studied another category of busy acquirers, the private-equity firms. Now that so many buy-outs go to these players, *they* are the real M&A machines, and they gain many advantages from the high volume of their deal pipelines.

Figure 13.2 illustrates the pipeline of a typical private-equity firm. Having started out with as many as 200 acquisition candidates and carried out due diligence on 40 or so, it produces just four deals. Its overall throughput is a sobering 2 percent.

13.2 M&A volume pipeline
Per year for a mid-sized private-equity company

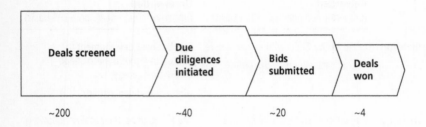

Deals screened	Due diligences initiated	Bids submitted	Deals won
~200	~40	~20	~4

How does the volume of this pipeline create advantage? We believe it does so in three ways. First, if you have 200 candidates to choose from, there is a greater likelihood that one of them will be right for purchase, so you can to some extent avoid the prize bias of the corporate shortlist. Second, you also limit your vulnerability to sample bias because the task of selecting so many potential candidates forces you to look beyond the obvious targets. Third, high volume encourages better pattern recognition: exposure to more potential targets gives the M&A and strategy teams much deeper experience.

High volume is one of the hallmarks of an M&A engine, but there are three other elements that are vital to its success: making sure that deals are a good fit; knowing when and how to integrate acquisitions; and finding the best way to involve business units.

Getting the right fit
Deals need to fit with a company's granular blueprint and originate from its growth direction. If your M&A engine is designed to complement your other scale platforms, you are half way to having the criteria you need to evaluate a deal and identify the non-standard synergies that give rise to sources of advantage. The ability to identify the nature of these synergies is important: without them your company is unlikely to be the natural owner of the company you've targeted.

It's easy to see why some M&A teams fall back on purely financial criteria, such as the target's margins and past growth and whether the deal is accretive (expected to increase earnings per share). In fact, when we asked unrewarded acquirers to rank the key factors that prompted them to proceed with an acquisition, their top answer was "short-term accretion." Rewarded acquirers, on the other hand, nominated "revenue growth potential" or "cost synergy potential." They looked beyond pure financial metrics to identify and evaluate deals with exceptional synergies.

As one executive put it, "Strategic vision *plus* hidden value, not financial footwork, is the secret of creating long-term value. You need deep appreciation of your core skills and vision if your skills are to be transformed into a sustainable competitive advantage." And you have to be selective.

Making smart integration decisions

Nearly all rewarded acquirers agreed that integration is where many if not most acquisitions fall apart. The better acquirers know what to integrate and what to leave alone. When FedEx bought Roadway Package Systems in 1997 to expand its ground business, it knew it was buying many customers with profitable volumes. Clearly that was an asset worth preserving. It was also getting a low-cost contractor and driver network that did all package pick-up and delivery, as well as line haul (inter-city freight transport).

Some observers expected FedEx to integrate RPS's ground network into its own network to increase scale economies and reduce average costs. In the event, though, it decided to keep the RPS network separate and preserve the existing business model, partly because the companies had different unions and labor contracts that would have cancelled out the synergies. It upgraded the quality of the RPS service and rebranded it as FedEx Ground. It also merged RPS's sales forces with its own. These actions reflected the company's view that its brand, sales force, and network operations were the platforms for its growth.

It took two years to complete the integration, but once it was done FedEx Ground took off. Between 1999 and 2004, it achieved average organic growth of 10 percent a year, nearly twice the rate of the small-package market in general.

Involving the business units

According to our interviews with executives, business units generally bear the responsibility for integration. However, that doesn't mean it's their fault when integration goes wrong. As the vice-president of corporate business development at one conglomerate told us, "Our biggest challenge is ensuring that the corporate M&A team and business-unit executives work in concert on an acquisition."

When and how you involve individual business units depends on the type of transaction. Acquisitions designed to transform the company, deals in unfamiliar markets, and deals that don't fall neatly into any one business unit are typically led by the M&A team from start to finish. But if we look at deals destined to be integrated into an existing business unit, the rewarded acquirers we interviewed were twice as likely as the unrewarded to have involved their business units in the acquisitions from the outset, through origination and due diligence to negotiation and integration. As the senior vice-president of corporate strategy at a global media company told us:

> "The individual business units handle joint ventures, partnerships, or acquisitions that are in line with their business and which Corporate considers tactical issues in their growth. For these tactical issues, the business unit drives the acquisition and the M&A team oversees the work and provides support where necessary."

Indeed, while the involvement of the M&A team is essential to ensure that all transactions are consistent in quality and degree of rigor, many rewarded acquirers believe that having the business unit lead the process can yield dramatic improvements in the results of the integration. Rewarded companies involved business units in the due diligence phase, and some set up ad hoc teams comprising high-level business-unit executives, members of the M&A and legal teams, and experts such as tax accountants and environmental specialists. These teams drove the process through to integration and played an active part in identifying and quantifying opportunities and risks, especially during due diligence.

Other scale platforms

We've established that building an insight engine will help you fire on the portfolio momentum cylinder, while building an M&A engine will boost your performance on the inorganic cylinder. We believe there are two other scale platforms that can be just as valuable: a scaling engine and a talent engine. They don't relate to a single cylinder, but can help improve your firing performance across the board.

- **A scaling engine.** *The Alchemy of Growth* argued that the transition from horizon 3 to horizon 2 is the most difficult stage in a company's pipeline of developing businesses.[6] In a recent article, Geoffrey Moore explored the challenges large companies face in making precisely this transition.[7] Drawing on Cisco's experience, he offered six rules of the road that represent compelling advice for any CEO trying to accelerate the growth of major new businesses. We believe that Cisco and a few other companies have managed to create a core competence in moving businesses systematically through the horizons; we call this a scaling engine.

- **A talent engine.** Talent is the fuel that powers most growth strategies. It's common for companies to claim that they see their people as their greatest asset, or to include talent management as one of the four or five planks of their growth strategy. Yet few companies approach this issue in a truly systematic fashion. Those that do manage to build a talent engine that attracts, develops, and retains a pipeline of distinctive people at all levels of the company, thus creating another type of scale advantage.

■ ■ ■

Thinking about your scale platforms in this way can help bring about a change in your definition of what business you are in and thus shape your future growth direction. One client we served described this well: "We ask ourselves provocative questions. Are we really just a payment platform? Are we a processing company? If so, what markets should we think of entering next?" Scale platforms don't only help achieve advantage; they can also bring about renewal.

We've now covered the four key elements of an architecture for growth, but we haven't yet shown how they all come together using the fifth element, management processes. In the next chapter, we describe a model for creating a fully resonating architecture for growth. We call it "cluster-based growth."

NOTES

1 T. A. Stewart, "Growth as a process," *Harvard Business Review,* June 2006, p. 64.

2 For a comprehensive account, see R. Foster and S. Kaplan, *Creative Destruction: Why companies that are built to last underperform the market—and how to successfully transform them* (Currency, New York, 2001), pp. 260–87.

3 This effort was led by our colleagues Rob Palter and Dev Srinivasan. See their article "Habits of the busiest acquirers," *The McKinsey Quarterly,* 2006, number 4, pp. 19–27.

4 The sample here is the same as that used in Figure 10.1. We started with a population that combined the top 75 US companies by market cap with the top 75 by revenues as of June 2005. After accounting for those that appeared in both lists, we were left with 102 companies. From this sample, we identified 33 companies that had accumulated at least 30 percent of their market value through acquisition. The executives most responsible for M&A activity at 20 of these companies agreed to take part in a rigorous 60-minute conversation covering over 100 questions about organization, process, tools, and the metrics used in acquisitions and integration.

5 The only difference we could observe in M&A team composition was that rewarded acquirers were more likely to recruit internal people into the M&A group, while unrewarded acquirers relied more heavily on outside hires. This may help explain why M&A groups are able to work more closely with the business units at rewarded acquirers. That said, we can't necessarily fault the unrewarded for relying on outside hires; we didn't probe deeply enough to know if they had the right talent inside the company.

6 *The Alchemy of Growth,* chapter 5.

7 G. A. Moore, "To succeed in the long term, focus on the middle term," *Harvard Business Review,* July–August 2007, pp. 84–90.

14

Cluster-based growth

"Nothing is particularly hard if you divide it into small jobs."
Henry Ford

- Management processes are critical for aligning the other four elements of the growth architecture

- Cluster-based growth is a model for managing a large organization by treating it as a connected set of small communities

- The strategy for each cluster can be articulated and hardwired into the organization by means of a simplified growth staircase

- The best way to manage the performance of these clusters is to use progressive KPIs rather than the balanced scorecard approach

WHEN WE DISCUSS the leadership of granular growth programs with executives, we hear the same reservations again and again: "I simply don't have the time to give this level of attention to so many units." "Don't I employ managers to look after the business units so that I can concentrate on the big picture?" We agree that all CEOs need breadth of vision, but we believe they also need a clear view down through their organization.

So how do they meet both these demands? The answer isn't to replicate current management practices; adding more detail to more sectors and more businesses just won't work. Anyone who tried it would quickly be overwhelmed by the exponential increase in the demands of the quarterly review process.

What CEOs need is a more elegant solution: a design that adapts current practices so that their control screen shows a larger number of units in sharper focus rather than a fuzzy mass of complexity. This greater clarity will help business units focus on how to fire on more cylinders over time. Scale advantages can be used to pursue granular opportunities; granular opportunities, in turn, define priorities for building new scale advantages.

While there is no sure-fire recipe for success, some companies have found effective ways of redesigning their business processes to reinforce the elements of their growth architecture. We have had success with a new approach that we call the cluster-based growth model, which is based on four simple principles:

- Segmenting the company into granular growth clusters
- Articulating strategies for these clusters
- Hardwiring performance management into them through progressive KPIs
- Actively managing the portfolio at the cluster level

In this chapter we describe how this approach has been applied at one firm, Deloitte Australia. This is a good starting point since it represents a fairly homogenous medium-sized business operating in a single market, and illustrates in a straightforward way how the different elements of architecture can be brought together to drive growth. We then suggest how the model can be extended to more complex industry settings including consumer packaged goods, retail banking, energy, and research.

Accounting for growth

Deloitte is one of the big four global accounting and advisory firms. It operates a federated model that gives regional businesses relatively high autonomy. In some markets, such as the United Kingdom, Deloitte is the clear market leader;

in others it is just one of the pack. Indeed, when Giam Swiegers took over as chief executive in 2003, Deloitte Australia was fourth of the big four.

During the previous CEO's tenure, the firm had lost share, especially at the higher end of the market, and its profitability was in serious decline. Since opportunities for inorganic growth were limited, Swiegers needed to pursue organic growth, and market-share gain in particular. The question was how to go about it.

He began by evaluating the nature of competition in the market at a more granular level than Deloitte usually did. This shed light on the nature of the growth challenge and was instrumental in shaping the firm's new direction. Swiegers found there were few market segments in which Deloitte claimed its fair share as one of the big four firms, and even fewer in which it was the clear market leader.

His aspirations for growth were ambitious: to take the firm from A$515 million to over A$900 million in revenues and to double its profitability by 2009. To

14.1 Deloitte Australia's growth map

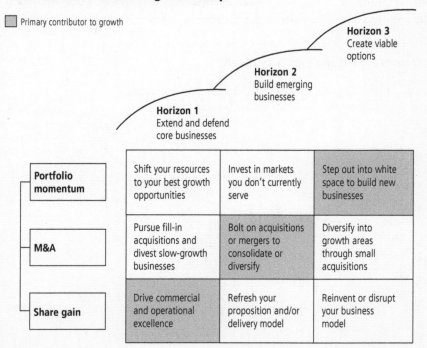

■ Primary contributor to growth

Horizon 3
Create viable
options

Horizon 2
Build emerging
businesses

Horizon 1
Extend and defend
core businesses

	Horizon 1	Horizon 2	Horizon 3
Portfolio momentum	Shift your resources to your best growth opportunities	Invest in markets you don't currently serve	Step out into white space to build new businesses
M&A	Pursue fill-in acquisitions and divest slow-growth businesses	Bolt on acquisitions or mergers to consolidate or diversify	Diversify into growth areas through small acquisitions
Share gain	Drive commercial and operational excellence	Refresh your proposition and/or delivery model	Reinvent or disrupt your business model

bring together the elements of his growth direction, he adopted the three-horizons model. In horizon 1, he emphasized the need to achieve a leading market share of 30 to 40 percent in key market segments defined at a G4 or G5 level. This is where the cluster-based approach proved most helpful. The priority in horizon 2 was to acquire several mid-tier firms that could be integrated and managed through the cluster model. Horizon 3 included organic business-building initiatives that would gradually shift the portfolio into higher-growth arenas. The resulting growth map for Deloitte shown in Figure 14.1 looks very much like the *Alchemy* pattern we examined in chapter 8.

The results have been impressive, with profit growing at 28 percent CAGR over the past three years, compared to about 5 percent for the industry as a whole (Figure 14.2). Let's now look at how the firm implemented the four principles of the cluster-based growth model to drive share gain in horizon 1.

Segmenting the firm into clusters

The challenge for a large professional services firm seeking to gain share is chiefly that of motivating thousands of people and enabling them to contribute to the growth of their organization in a way that makes sense strategically.

Deloitte's granular blueprint was guided by a number of important considerations. The ideal size for a cluster in a knowledge-intensive setting

14.2 Deloitte Australia's growth results

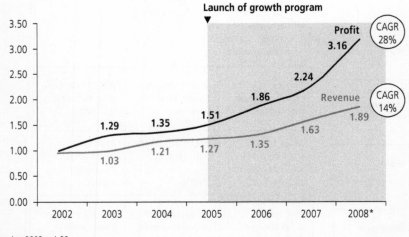

Indexed to 2002 = 1.00
* Projected
Source: Deloitte Australia Financial Management

like accountancy is around 50 to 100 people (in other sectors it might run as high as several hundred). The factors that defined a cluster at Deloitte included a common sense of identity and purpose; similar revenue and cost structures; a critical mass of partners; and, in some cases, a shared location.

Deloitte decided to define its clusters pragmatically and revisit the map after 18 or 24 months. The original 44 clusters were defined largely by geography (Sydney, Melbourne, and so on) and by service line (tax, audit), which produced clusters such as "Corporate tax Sydney" and "Audit for financial services industry Melbourne." Sometimes the commercial nature of the activities was the primary clustering dimension; at other times physical proximity took priority. The relationship between the clusters was then represented on a cluster map that mapped service lines by location (Figure 14.3).

14.3 Deloitte Australia's cluster map

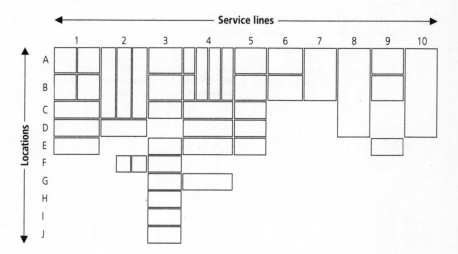

Articulating cluster strategies

How do you ensure that your clusters are on the right track without wading through dozens of business-unit plans? By doing what managers do when product volumes soar—you standardize. The secret of managing a much larger number of units is to create a systematic method for tracking each cluster's progress along a proven growth pathway that leads to a better cylinder-firing pattern. You also need to account for differences in the nature of the challenge at different points in that journey.

To do this, we can draw on an approach that we introduced in *The Alchemy of Growth* and touched on in chapter 5: the growth staircase.[1] The simplified example illustrated in Figure 14.4 shows how a typical cluster moves up a flight of three steps as it builds the capabilities it needs to fire on more cylinders over time. The staircase provides a kind of strategic scaffolding that ensures clusters don't deviate from the proven sequence of capability-building steps (numbered 1A to 3C in the figure).

Step 1 of the staircase involves what we describe as "earning the right to play." Clusters that present a poor cylinder-firing pattern must be focused on building the basic capabilities they need to create an advantage: either a *competitive* advantage in a core area of technical or operational excellence that sets the cluster apart from its rivals, or a *positional* advantage stemming from a unique idea or business model, or even a privileged asset. Before

14.4 Simplified growth staircase

Growth staircase

Building distinctive bundles of capabilities to
pursue or capture a growing set of attractive opportunities

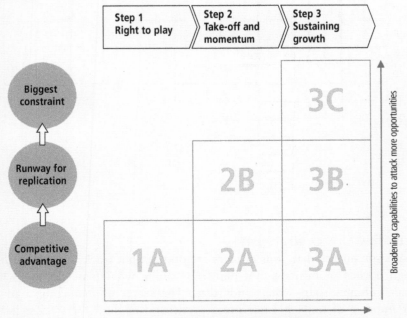

Nature and sequence of steps depends on cluster type and industry

moving to the next step, the company must use external benchmarks to validate its advantage.

Step 2 is about driving top-line growth via a "runway" or replication path in which the proven business model from step 1 is applied repeatedly to more and more market opportunities. At the same time, the underlying capabilities from step 1 are progressively deepened. In other words, step 2 adds the task of generating revenue growth to the step 1 task of building competitive capabilities. We describe this stage as "take-off and momentum"; during it, the cluster should move to a good cylinder-firing pattern.

Step 3 adds the final element: each cluster now needs not only to deepen its advantage and grow its revenues, but also to remove whatever is the biggest constraint to sustaining its growth rate (often leadership capacity). In other words, the challenge is to do whatever is necessary to extend the successful runway built in step 2. Clusters in this stage can move to a great cylinder-firing pattern.

The translation of granular strategies into specific growth staircases is central to the cluster-based growth model. The growth direction that underpins the structure of the staircases must be strategically sound because it will be hardwired into all the clusters.

When Deloitte was constructing its staircase, alternative versions were put forward, debated, and modified. In the end, Swiegers and his team drew on their own recent success stories to bring their staircase to life. Figure 14.5 shows how the generic staircase was adapted to the firm's language and culture (and its look and feel). Experience has taught us that it is vital to adopt the organization's own terminology and style when we are referring to the various elements of the staircase. This maximizes people's buy-in and reduces the risk that they will reject changes.

The first step in Deloitte's staircase is about achieving technical and operational excellence. Each cluster is expected to deliver high-quality services to clients in a profitable way before it can proceed to the next step. The second step is about growth in the client base and in revenues. Because the first step ensures profitability, the revenue growth in the second step drops straight to the bottom line. The third step is about addressing constraints on leadership capacity by growing and hiring more partners to drive cluster growth in new directions. This sequence was consistent with the historical experience of the most successful parts of Deloitte's business.

14.5 Deloitte Australia's staircase

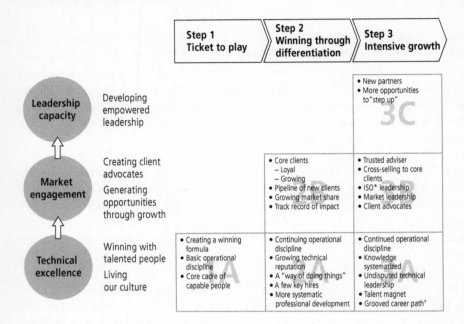

		Step 1 Ticket to play	Step 2 Winning through differentiation	Step 3 Intensive growth
Leadership capacity	Developing empowered leadership			• New partners • More opportunities to "step up"

Market engagement	Creating client advocates
	
	Generating opportunities through growth
			• Core clients
			  – Loyal
			  – Growing
			• Pipeline of new clients
			• Growing market share
			• Track record of impact
				• Trusted adviser
				• Cross-selling to core clients
				• ISO* leadership
				• Market leadership
				• Client advocates

Technical excellence	Winning with talented people Living our culture	• Creating a winning formula • Basic operational discipline • Core cadre of capable people	• Continuing operational discipline • Growing technical reputation • A "way of doing things" • A few key hires • More systematic professional development	• Continued operational discipline • Knowledge systematized • Undisputed technical leadership • Talent magnet • Grooved career path[†]

* Integrated service offerings
[†] Deliberate development pathway

Hardwiring performance management

Once you've specified what each cluster needs to do, you need to ensure that it actually does it. As with bringing up children, it's best to present one new challenge at a time, without abandoning the previous ones. Our cluster-based growth model uses progressive key performance indicators (KPIs) to manage a broad array of clusters at different stages of growth in a systematic way. By defining a standard set of KPIs for each step of the growth staircase, you can monitor the performance of the organization at a granular level with relative ease and watch the clusters fire on more cylinders over time.

You begin by defining a set of KPIs for each step on your staircase, and then select a specific easy-to-measure metric for each KPI. There will typically be more KPIs at the lower levels (say, three to five for step 1, two or three for step 2, and one or two for step 3). For Deloitte, the KPIs for the first step were predominantly operational ones such as utilization, gross margin, working-capital management, and profit per unit. The second step featured growth-oriented KPIs such as revenue growth and customer loyalty. The third step included KPIs on the number of new partners and their engagement with clients.

The staircase approach demands that these KPIs be applied to clusters in an additive fashion for two reasons.

First, in contrast to the balanced scorecard approach that has become popular with some companies, we advocate a *progressive* scorecard for managing cluster growth. Different clusters will be on different steps in the growth staircase, and their performance will need to be managed according to their stage of development. With progressive KPIs, clusters start with a very simple performance framework that becomes more sophisticated over time. It's best to focus step 1 clusters on a few critical things, whereas step 3 clusters can be stretched in several directions.

Second, a progressive approach allows the performance threshold to be raised over time. An advanced cluster should be expected to reach a higher standard of performance than an early-stage cluster. Our experience suggests it is worth building some stretch into the KPIs so that a cluster making the transition from step 1 to 2 must achieve the median level of performance for the relevant cluster population. In this way, the performance of the lower half of the organization is lifted to median levels.

The good news is that this first cluster movement usually generates enough bottom-line improvement to make cluster-based growth a self-funding program. Note that Deloitte's profit CAGR was twice its revenue CAGR. In much the same way, the threshold for the transition from step 2 to 3 should correspond to moving up to the top-quartile mark for the whole population or an appropriate external benchmark of great performance.

By putting these two elements together, we get a systematic way to manage the performance of clusters as they climb the growth staircase. A step 1 cluster is measured only against the KPIs for the bottom step, and only to the median performance threshold.

A step 2 cluster needs to be measured against the KPIs for both the bottom and the middle step, and to the top-quartile performance threshold.

Finally, stage 3 clusters are measured against all KPIs at a stretch performance threshold, which might be defined in a number of different ways: as top-decile performance, perhaps, or in terms of the most ambitious market-based benchmarks.

14.6 Measuring cluster performance

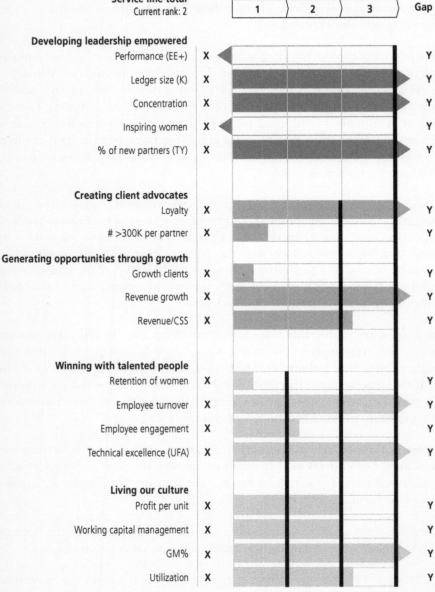

Note: "123" rankings refer to the three stages of cluster development. X and Y represent scorings.
Arrowheads indicate where data is off the chart.

At Deloitte, Swiegers and his team developed a simple yet sophisticated tool for displaying the performance of each cluster in a visual way (Figure 14.6). A quick glance at the chart reveals how far a cluster has travelled on its growth journey and what its most pressing priorities are.

Deloitte chief operating officer Keith Skinner told us that this approach has helped him manage the business by "ensuring clusters stay focused on the right priorities for them, while at the same time giving me as the COO an easy way to manage that level of detail."[2]

We should add a word of caution. Even though progressive KPIs often use the same metrics that appear on monthly reporting dashboards, the two should not be confused. The KPIs are indicators of strategic health and should be reviewed twice a year. For the purpose of managing cluster advancement, the data needs to be annual (perhaps on a rolling 12-month basis), not monthly. The objective is to get a sense of growth over time, not to measure short-term performance swings.

Managing the portfolio
Getting the right number of granular clusters is critical, and so is getting them to perform. Companies that set out on this journey gain an extra advantage: the granular view of opportunity and performance allows for a granular approach to overall portfolio management too.

For Deloitte Australia, the initial cluster classification revealed a preponderance of step 1 and step 2 clusters (Figure 14.7). The firm decided that its first priority was to accelerate the growth of the most advanced clusters. It identified target market segments and launched intensive campaigns to attract them, working to a calendar with three cycles a year. Swiegers focused capacity-building resources on training a cadre of partners to become more proficient at running these campaigns and driving sales. The visibility of their success acted as a beacon for others and strengthened overall support for the growth program.

The next priority was to triage the step 1 clusters. Those whose performance could be improved were supported; those that had become lost causes were either given a shot in the arm or disbanded. Deloitte is now in the process of refining its resource-allocation process and reward system. Cluster leaders will be rewarded at least in part for the rate of advancement of their cluster. Partners' attention is constantly drawn to the status and trajectory of each cluster, which can be seen at a glance on the cluster map (Figure 14.8). At

14.7 Early cluster classification

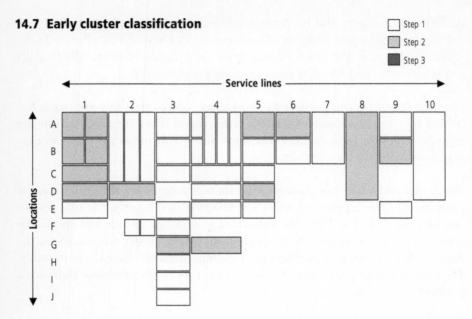

top leadership gatherings, leaders whose clusters have advanced to the next stage of growth are asked to stand so that senior partners can acknowledge their achievement.

Another area where the cluster methodology was very helpful was in the integration of two large acquisitions in Sydney and Melbourne. The new firms were divided into clusters; some were combined with Deloitte's existing clusters and some stayed separate. Progressive KPIs were used to benchmark the growth of the new clusters and to highlight the most pressing priorities for them after the transaction.

In the space of a couple of years, Swiegers and his team have made great progress in their growth journey. By the end of the first year of the program eight of the 44 clusters had already moved to the second step in the staircase; six months later more than half of them had. Swiegers told us: "When people first see what we have done, they think the system is very complicated. But when they get to understand it, and they usually get it very quickly, they understand that nothing could be easier, or more powerful."[3]

It is interesting to note that many partners are defining their own market patches at a more granular level than the clusters—effectively translating the overall growth agenda into a systematic set of granular activities. Swiegers

14.8 Later cluster classification

□ Step 1
▨ Step 2
■ Step 3

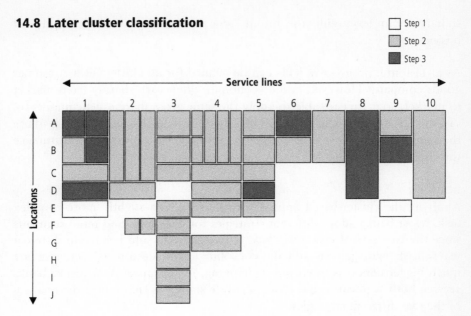

adds that the cluster-based growth approach has had "a huge impact on the culture of the place and the way we speak and think. People are much more granular in terms of the way they manage the business now."

Clusters elsewhere

Introducing a cluster-based growth approach in professional services is a relatively straightforward undertaking because the business activities are fairly homogenous and the best growth strategies are relatively clear. This may not be the case in other settings, though. Let's now look at a few more industries to see how the approach can be modified to match the complexity of different businesses.

Consumer packaged goods

Because large consumer packaged-goods companies such as Procter & Gamble, Unilever, Nestlé, and Kraft are built around brands, their businesses tend already to be managed with a fair degree of granularity. Although a brand like Tide is not positioned, packaged, or priced in the same way all around the world, there is remarkable consistency in the strategies used for *growing* most big consumer brands. The first step of the staircase is usually about maintaining the core of the brand by ensuring the profitability of flagship products; the second step is about extending the brand into adjacent market opportunities through product and channel expansion; and the third step is about leveraging the brand into new markets and even spin-off businesses.

As at Deloitte, progressive KPIs can be defined for all clusters at a consumer goods company. However, brand economics often vary sharply from market to market, so it isn't feasible to apply the same gross margin benchmarks to, say, the US, Argentina, and India. The way to manage this complexity is to use the same staircases and KPIs across the business, but adjust the performance thresholds for different sets of country or regional clusters.

Banking

Applying the cluster-based approach to banking is a slightly more complex task. Most banks adopt different strategies for corporate and retail segments since the two sets of customers have different needs and behave in different ways. Risk management and the consolidation of customers' activities are much bigger concerns in corporate banking, for instance. As a result, banks serving both segments require two separate staircases that reflect the nuances of the two different strategies.

The other main difference between banking and consumer goods has to do with portfolio management. Clearly, linkages and network dependencies between corporate and retail banking will complicate the strategic planning process, but it is still possible to create different portfolios for the two segments and to prioritize clusters within each portfolio.

Retail chains

Large retailers such as Wal-Mart, Target, and Tesco pose an even more complex challenge. Their growth is fueled by mutually reinforcing links between two sets of clusters: stores, which grow through simple geographic roll-out as well as format innovation, and merchandise categories and assortments. As a result, retailers, like retail banks, need two cluster maps and two staircases, each with its own set of KPIs. However, the close interaction between the two sets of clusters means that retailers' portfolio management needs to be even more integrated than it is at retail banks. As with consumer packaged goods, stores may have different performance thresholds in different regions or countries.

Energy utilities

The challenge of applying the cluster-based growth model to this business lies in its asset-intensive nature. What does a cluster mean for an electricity or gas distributor? Remember that the staircase is essentially a model for assembling and building capabilities that are to be deployed to capture growth opportunities. These capabilities are usually skills that reside in people, but there's no reason why they can't be defined in terms of assets.[4]

Consider a large gas distribution network. By dividing the network into local government areas or neighborhoods, you can focus on the growth generated at a more granular level. So clusters can be defined as pieces of the distribution network, and the growth staircase in terms of maximizing the growth generated by each piece. This approach can help to highlight investment priorities across the network, as well as prompting decisions to halt investment. It can also encourage collaboration between previously disconnected groups, such as operations people and marketers. Naturally, decisions need to be taken with network dependencies and their flow-on effects in mind.

Universities and research institutions

Cluster-based growth can even be applied to public-sector enterprises and other non-business settings. Universities, for instance, can improve the quality of their faculty management by taking a more granular view of their research performance and defining clusters at levels below the department or school of studies. In our experience, the same KPIs can be used for all faculties, although science and engineering clusters may need different performance thresholds from those in humanities because of their different financial profiles. Even the largest universities should need no more than three to five staircases.

A similar process can be used for very large research institutes and organizations. In one case, we defined 130 clusters at an organization that was previously managed at the level of 20 divisions. Greater granularity enabled the organization to adopt a much more disciplined approach to shifting resources to high-impact areas.

■ ■ ■

The cluster-based growth model enables you to increase the granularity at which you manage your business without drowning in a sea of reports. The growth staircases offer leaders the simplification and standardization they need, yet without obscuring important differences between the various aspects of their business. Success depends on how well you implement the four key principles we've described here. To find out, you could ask yourself a series of questions:

First, how well have you segmented your company into granular clusters? Does your blueprint match the texture of the marketplace in which you compete? Does your initial cluster definition resemble your existing reporting lines or represent a new departure?

Second, how well have you translated your granular business strategies into growth staircases to improve cylinder firing over time? Did you discuss alternative models? Is your staircase design consistent with your past models of success or are you venturing into new territory? Do you have the right staircases for the different cluster types?

Third, how well have you hardwired your performance management through progressive KPIs that reflect your granular strategies? Have you built sufficient stretch? How far have you varied your performance thresholds for each KPI for different groups of clusters?

Finally, how actively are you managing your portfolio at the cluster level? Are you applying the cluster-based growth model only to your existing business or have you extended it to help you integrate acquisitions? Are you committed to shifting resources across the portfolio to increase your momentum growth rate?

Careful and deliberate work in these four areas should help you manage growth at a granular level without losing the benefits of big-company scale.

NOTES

[1] See chapters 5 to 7 of *The Alchemy of Growth*.

[2] In a private conversation in 2007.

[3] In a private conversation in 2007.

[4] Chapter 6 of *The Alchemy of Growth* offers an extensive definition of capabilities that includes privileged assets and special relationships.

Conclusion: Choosing to lead growth

"Only the paranoid survive."
Andy Grove

WHETHER YOU ARE an incumbent leader with a few years of tenure still to run or a newcomer to your leadership role, we hope that by now you are reflecting on the big choices we've described in this book: your growth ambition, your growth direction, and your growth architecture. All are decisions that leaders need to make for their companies. But there is a fourth big choice: your own personal decision to lead the growth journey.

Leading successful growth brings excitement and satisfaction. But other emotions can all too easily crowd them out. You may feel apprehensive about the hurdles you will face; worried about those quarterly results that lie just around the corner; anxious about the multitude of initiatives already clamoring for your attention.

For most executives, the commitment to lead a growth journey is not to be undertaken lightly. It's often tempting to postpone growth until your second term, or even leave it to your successor. Let's face it, you're bound to encounter opposition, the journey will take a long time, and you'll probably have to make a lot of personal sacrifices. These are all realities that you need to prepare for—and reasons not to undertake your growth journey without long and hard thought.

But try looking at your choice another way: what will happen if you *don't* take action? You ignore growth at your peril. Companies that don't grow run the risk of being toppled before long. On the other hand, if your company succeeds in mapping out a path of profitable growth, the rewards will be great.

So are you still up for it? If you are, you'll discover amazing opportunities for your own personal growth as well as your company's.

Can you take the heat?

When we look back at a successful growth company, we often see that one or two decisions about where its growth was going to come from made a huge difference to its fortunes. In his book *Only the Paranoid Survive*, Intel CEO Andy Grove describes his efforts to shift the company's growth direction from a rapidly declining core business in memory chips to a tailwind business in microprocessors. He endured "a long, torturous struggle" as staff questioned and resisted the change.[1]

When a company adopts a more granular view of its activities, it's as though it is shining a spotlight on areas that senior management has never been able to see before. On the plus side, it will be easy to identify which parts of the organization are performing strongly. On the minus side, all manner of hidden problems are likely to be revealed once patches of weaker performance are no longer obscured by aggregation and consolidation. This change is bound to have a major impact on the organization, its resource allocation, its people, and its politics.

The impact on the top levels of the company may be profound. For successful senior executives, suddenly being confronted with pockets of poor performance for which they are accountable is going to be an uncomfortable experience. It is, of course, the CEO's task to manage the political consequences. Our experience suggests, however, that changes to the top team almost always follow. A would-be growth leader needs to tackle this challenge with eyes wide open.

Do you have the time?

It usually takes at least three years for a growth program to show solid bottom-line impact. Often its true value won't be appreciated for five or ten years; only then does the wisdom of the growth direction come into full view. Given that the average tenure of a chief executive outside Asia is getting shorter by the year, few CEOs can assume they will be in post long enough to lead a far-reaching program to its conclusion.

The CEO's choice isn't easy. Take the path that's safer in the short term but has less long-term potential? Or look to the future and beat a path to real growth? The length of the journey shouldn't deter leaders from setting off in the right direction.

Can you cope with the personal challenges?

Without a doubt, leading a growth program takes its toll on a CEO. From every angle, the demands will be greater and the task tougher. The strategic choices have far-reaching implications; big decisions need to be made more frequently; greater depth means greater involvement. Leading a growth journey requires sacrifices in your personal life: more travel, more thinking time at weekends, more transactions. More . . . more . . . more!

This is no easy path, but if you want to make a strong company into a great one, you can't avoid it. Company performance is now evaluated over longer time periods, and the contribution of leaders is measured well beyond their tenure. There is more to being a CEO than hitting quarterly targets, difficult though that may be.

Some of the most intense demands on a CEO leading a growth journey come during the process of figuring out your direction and building consensus around it. When Kevin Sharer took the helm at Amgen in May 2000, he had spent eight years with the company after earlier stints at GE, MCI, McKinsey, and the US Navy. By this time Amgen was the world's largest biotechnology company, having grown on the back of two products in what was effectively a monopoly environment. But future growth would be much more difficult to generate since new drugs would face stiff competition.

Sharer describes building alignment around Amgen's new growth direction as the single most important thing he did on becoming CEO:

> "When it was announced . . . that I was going to become CEO . . . I asked the top 150 people in the company to meet with me for an hour each—150 hours in total. And I gave each of them the same five questions, which they received in advance: What three things do you want to change? What three things do you want to keep? What are you most worried I might do? What do you want me to do? Is there anything else you want to talk about? And I just listened for an hour. Many of the people came in with stuff written down, and in the case of those who didn't, I took notes. And then I tabulated all the responses, coming up with a pretty accurate and timely picture of what the top 150 leaders in the company wanted to do. I put all of this together and sent a memo to the entire company summarizing my findings. These interviews gave me the mandate to do what I needed to do. It created a shared reality for the company and allowed people to begin aligning around a number of goals."[2]

Once you have chosen your growth direction, you face the huge task of mobilizing your organization. William Zuendt, former president of Wells Fargo, explained to us that he used to tell the company's growth story over and over again to galvanize the bank's executives and managers. "You hear yourself say the same thing twenty, thirty, or forty times, and you're convinced everybody must have heard this story until they're sick, and then they tell you after you've spoken, they've never heard that before."[3]

■ ■ ■

Back in the Introduction, we argued that every company faces an inescapable strategic choice: to grow or go. In the same way, every CEO faces an inescapable personal choice: should I embark on a growth journey, and do I have the resources to see it through? It's a choice that can be made only after deep reflection.

In *The Republic,* Plato describes a similar burden on leaders in the famous allegory of the cave. Those few who leave the darkness of the cave to discover the sunlit world beyond have an unwelcome obligation. They must return to the cave, tell the others what they have seen, overturn all of their ideas about life, and persuade them to walk out of the cave and into the bright new world.

We salute those leaders who take up the challenge of building an enduring enterprise and return to the cave to master the granularity of growth in their companies.

NOTES

[1] A. S. Grove, *Only the Paranoid Survive: How to exploit the crisis points that challenge every company* (HarperCollins, New York, 1997).

[2] For a more detailed account, see the interview by Paul Hemp in *Harvard Business Review,* July–August 2004, pp. 67–74.

[3] From an unpublished interview with Bill Zuendt in 1995.

Appendix 1

Growth and value

"The most powerful force in the universe is compound interest."
Albert Einstein

- Shareholder value creation in large companies has typically been driven by revenue growth, cash distribution to shareholders, and a decline in interest rates

- Each of the four "grow or go" categories exhibits a distinctive value-creation profile

- Companies that grew faster than GDP and expanded their share of the broader economy have delivered 30 percent higher shareholder returns

L EADERS TEND TO ASSUME that growth is a good thing. But is that necessarily so? Put another way, if a company can accelerate its growth trajectory, how confident can it be that it will be rewarded for it?

Finance theory argues that it's not a company's *absolute* growth or profitability that will drive its future stock-price performance, but, rather, the way it performs in relation to the *expectations* that are priced into its stock today. So if investors expect the company to grow at 10 percent a year with a 23 percent profit margin, simply meeting those expectations won't do much for its stock other than delivering a "cost of equity" return.[1]

But what if the company managed to deliver a 12 percent growth rate for a couple of years—2 percentage points above its historic rate? The answer depends on whether investors think the 12 percent is a one-off event or a fundamental change in the company's growth trajectory. If they believe the trajectory is changing, rational investors should be willing to pay significantly more for the new growth rate. Conversely, if they believe this is a one-off event, its impact on value will be more muted.

Investing a million

Imagine that it is 1984, and you have $1 million to invest. You buy shares in our sample of the top US companies described in the Introduction, and you invest in each company in proportion to its market capitalization.[2] How much will you have at the end of twenty years?

Provided that you reinvested your dividends efficiently, your portfolio would have been worth $14.4 million ($13.4 million of returns plus the $1 million initial investment) by the end of 2004. This is a compound annual growth rate of more than 14.2 percent. Clearly this was a good time to be investing in the US stock market![3]

Where did this value come from? First let's compare the shareholder returns for three sets of companies: those that survived, those that got acquired, and those that filed for bankruptcy. Not surprisingly, bankrupt companies generated poor returns (–18 percent a year), but there were only three of them in our sample. The compound annual returns of the acquired and the surviving companies were almost identical (14.0 percent as against 14.3 percent). So on average, sellers and survivors created comparable value for their shareholders.

Where the value comes from

For the survivors, let's go one level deeper and analyze the sources of shareholder return over the twenty-year period. Our methodology takes TRS and breaks it down into three pieces (Figure A1.1):

Cash distributed is cash actually returned to shareholders through dividend payouts and share buybacks, plus net debt repayments.

Change in operating performance includes everything that changes the operations value: revenue growth, differing NOPLAT (net operating profit less allocated tax) margins, and changes in capital turnover.

Change in expectations value includes all financial and investor-related changes such as changes in capital costs[4] as well as changes in investor expectations. It is, in part, calculated as a residual factor.

A1.1 The components of TRS

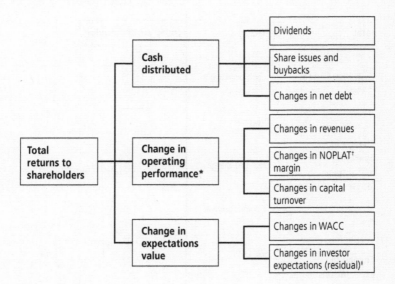

* Calculated based on continuing value formula (CV) with g at GDP growth:
  CV = (revenue (NOPLAT margin − (g/capital turnover))) / (WACC − g)
† Net operating profit less allocated taxes
‡ Change in enterprise value minus the sum of changes in operating levers, disposals, and WACC at GDP growth

Figure A1.2 shows the breakdown of the value generated by the overall sample. The increased value of operational cash flows (consisting of revenue growth, profitability improvement, and improvement of capital turnover) accounted for 45 percent of the value created. A further 33 percent was distributed to shareholders in the form of dividends, share buybacks, and debt repayments. It's interesting that capital turnover improvements, while potentially relevant to value creation for individual companies, didn't contribute to the value creation of the overall sample.[5] The remainder of the value created derived from an overall decrease in the weighted average cost of capital (WACC) due to a drop in prevailing interest rates, plus the residual factor: a reduction in investor expectations.

Now suppose for a minute that back in 1984 we could have had perfect foresight on which quadrant—growth giant, performer, unrewarded, or

A1.2 The sources of TRS for return on $1 million investment

Sum of TRS 1984–2004,* percent

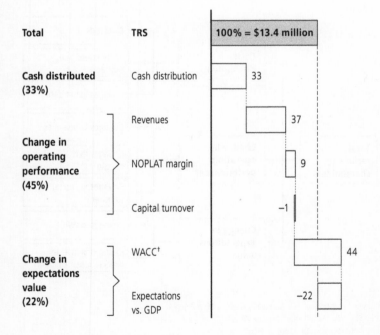

* Top 100 US companies in 1984 minus 13 where data was insufficient, 11 with ROIC<g (rendering CV formula unusable), 3 that went bankrupt before 2004, and 19 that were sold or merged (leaving 54 companies)
† WACC assumed to be the same for all companies (14.7% in 1984 and 7.9% in 2004), with growth at GDP

challenged—each of these companies would belong to twenty years later.[6] What would have become of our investment portfolio then? Obviously we couldn't have done this in real life, but the luxury of perfect hindsight enables us to shine a spotlight on the power of growth as a value generator.

Wisdom with hindsight

If we had sunk our entire $1 million investment into the *growth giants*, we would have ended the period with a portfolio worth $22.2 million ($21.2 million of returns plus the starting portfolio of $1 million). That means a portfolio confined to growth giants would have been worth *more than 50 percent more* than the original portfolio. Put another way, investing in the growth giants resulted in a return more than three times as high than we would have obtained from the average performance of the rest of the companies in our sample.

The average growth giant grew revenue at 9 percent CAGR over 20 years. The increased value of operating performance accounted for 62 percent of the value created, the lion's share of which stemmed from revenue growth. Free cash flow distribution explained 26 percent of the total value created. The remainder derived from an overall decrease in the weighted average cost of capital (Figure A1.3).

If we had placed our bets on the *performers*, the aggregate value after 20 years would have been $18.1 million.[7] Value is accrued differently in this group. Almost three-quarters of its value creation comes from free cash flow distribution: share buybacks, dividends, and debt repayments. Only 15 percent stems from an increase in the value of operating performance. The remaining 12 percent derives from changes in investor expectations and in the weighted average cost of capital.

What of our two below-average segments, the unrewarded and the challenged? (Remember that in the Introduction we defined the unrewarded as companies that grew revenue faster than GDP but lagged in value creation, and the challenged as those that underperformed in both value creation and revenue growth.)

Investing in *unrewarded* companies would have yielded a portfolio worth $8.2 million after twenty years: not terrible, but below the market average for the period. How do the unrewarded differ from the growth giants? Why was it that the growth giants created *nearly three times* as much value while delivering similar top-line growth?

A1.3 How the four groups performed

Sum of TRS 1984–2004,* percent

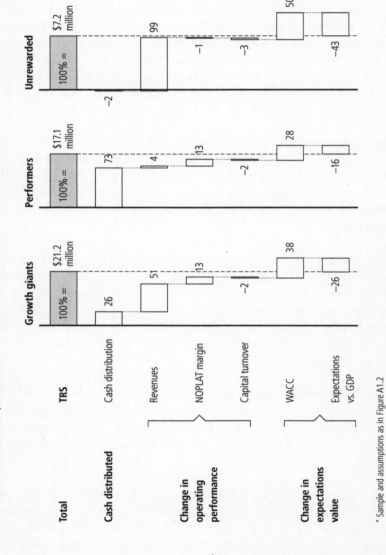

	Growth giants	Performers	Unrewarded	Challenged
Total	$21.2 million	$17.1 million	$7.2 million	$3.7 million
	100% =	100% =	100% =	100% =
TRS				
Cash distributed	**Cash distribution** 26	73	–2	22
Change in operating performance	**Revenues** 51	4	99	20
	NOPLAT margin 13	13	–1	–7
	Capital turnover –2	–2	–3	–1
Change in expectations value	**WACC** 38	28	50	62
	Expectations vs. GDP –26	–16	–43	4

* Sample and assumptions as in Figure A1.2

The answer lies in the fundamentals: nearly all the value of the unrewarded companies came from changes in revenue growth and a decline in the weighted average cost of capital. As a group, the unrewarded didn't make substantial distributions to shareholders during the period; nor did they improve margin. This is important: it reinforces the point that over time, revenue growth alone doesn't generate value; *profitable growth* is what counts.

How about the *challenged* segment? Investing in challenged companies would have yielded a portfolio worth only $4.7 million after twenty years. As a group, these companies achieved limited revenue growth and suffered declining operating performance over the period. What little value they did create appears to have come from cash distribution, revenue, and shifting expectations.

Halcyon days

The twenty-year period from 1984 through 2004 was an extraordinary period for the US capital markets. As interest rates fell from the heights of the early 1980s, company WACCs declined, driving stock valuations (and those of other capital assets) higher. However, large companies varied widely in their performance and in the value they created.

The growth giants delivered outstanding revenue growth at the same time as improving operating performance, and were highly rewarded for it. The performers were highly rewarded for their operating performance and shareholder distributions, but as we saw in the Introduction, this is a recipe for declining returns and possible exit over time. The unrewarded companies derived almost all their value from revenue growth but failed to demonstrate improvement on any of the other operating dimensions. Finally, the challenged companies lagged on all dimensions, demonstrating modest growth and cash distribution in addition to deteriorating margin performance over the period.

■ ■ ■

Both growth and profitability drive value. Our twenty-year look at TRS patterns in large companies shows that revenue growth and improved profitability are the key to the growth giants' performance, and that cash flow distribution and profit improvement drive the performers' results. For lower-growth companies, cash flow distribution becomes increasingly important as a value driver.

Appendix 1 has focused on understanding companies' performance by comparing the sources of value. Appendix 2 seeks to gain more insight into growth, profitability, and their relation to value creation by asking how much is enough: what does it take, in either growth or profit improvement, to outperform the market over time?

NOTES

[1] A detailed discussion of the drivers of corporate value can be found in T. Koller, M. Goedhart, and D. Wessels, *Valuation: Measuring and managing the value of companies* (Wiley, New York, 2005).

[2] In effect, you are building a "large company" index fund that is not rebalanced during the period.

[3] The S&P's return for the period was slightly higher, at 14.7 percent.

[4] Measured as WACC (weighted average cost of capital), considering equity and debt cost.

[5] This isn't to say that capital turnover improvements don't create value, but, rather, that they weren't a significant contributor to total TRS over the period for our large-company sample. In fact, on average they reduced value.

[6] In this analysis the classification is based on companies' performance across the full twenty-year period, as distinct from the cycle-by-cycle analysis in the Introduction.

[7] As before, $17.1 million from returns, plus the initial $1 million starting portfolio. It's interesting to note that in our twenty-year analysis the performers delivered less value than the growth giants, although they still outperformed the market. This wasn't true of our cycle-specific analyses in the Introduction, where the two groups delivered similar returns. We believe the lower returns from performers in the twenty-year period reflect the long-term problems of slow growth.

Appendix 2

Two ways to grow, two ways to go

"If you see a fork in the road, take it."
Yogi Berra

- Companies that outperform the market are likely to follow either a "grow" path or a "go" path

- There are two ways to grow: rapid growth with stable margins or moderate growth with improving margins

- There are two ways to go: significant ongoing return of cash to shareholders or an attractive exit

- There is no middle way: all other performance patterns are highly likely to underperform the market

APPENDIX 1 ESTABLISHED that growth is good, but it's not everything. Profit and operating performance matter a lot. So how do you balance the two? Surely going for revenue growth is not the answer for every company? Is there a value-creation strategy that is sustainable *without* revenue growth? What's the right way to balance growth in revenues with growth in profits? How do you decide how much growth is appropriate?

To tackle these questions, let's take a closer look at the performance trajectories of individual companies. Our objective here is to develop a set of meaningful performance patterns that correlate with shareholder value. What we're shooting for is an answer to a question that every CEO and management team asks again and again: what levels of growth and/or operating performance will create the most value for us?

As before, we're focusing on large companies and taking a twenty-year view in order to pick up long-term trends in shareholder value creation. Our next step parallels what companies routinely do when they look at their customers: we conduct a "market segmentation" of our sample of the top 100 US companies.

Segmenting the sample

When companies segment their markets, they take a sample of customers, profile their attitudes, behaviors, or needs, and then use statistics to derive groups of similar customers, or segments. In our case, the "customers" were individual companies, and instead of using attitudes, behaviors, or needs to segment them, we used financial performance metrics.

To drive the statistical analysis, we establish two thresholds: an "outperformance" threshold and an "underperformance" threshold. The segmentation seeks combinations of characteristics (including revenue growth, profitability, and return on invested capital) that are associated with a 70 percent or greater probability of exceeding market returns for the outperformers, or, conversely, of delivering returns below the broad market index for the underperformers.[1]

Our segmentation yields seven groups of companies with different performance profiles, or "value segments" (Figure A2.1). Note that *we* didn't select these segments or the criteria for belonging to them; that was done by the segmentation algorithm. There are three segments that outperformed the broad market index in value creation (1, 2, and 6), one that is just shy of our threshold (7), and three that underperformed (3, 4, and 5). Three other companies went bankrupt and were excluded from the segmentation.

We'll get to the specific segments shortly, but first let's look at a key finding on the link between growth and value. As we've said before, over the long term, the market rewards profitable growth. The companies that managed to sustain top-line growth above 8.5 percent a year without sacrificing profitability did very well for their shareholders.

Slower growth (between the inflation rate and 8.5 percent) was also rewarded, *if* companies also improved profitability during the period.

Finally, there is a group of low-growth companies that sustained outstanding performance over this period. These companies grew more slowly than inflation, but followed a path of aggressive capital disposal. Through a combination of share buybacks, dividends, and divestitures, these slow growers were outstanding value creators.[2]

Conversely, high growth without at least stable profitability, moderate growth without strengthening profitability, and low growth without capital disposal were all statistically likely to underperform the market index.

Let's now take a closer look at the segments. We'll see that there are two ways to grow, two ways to go, and no middle way.

Two ways to grow
In Figure A2.1, segments 1 and 2 illustrate the ways to grow.

Sustain rapid growth and maintain margins
If you're a large company with a high-growth business model, what does it take to outperform the market? Our high-growth threshold for the period, determined by the segmentation algorithm, was top-line growth of more than 8.5 percent a year. For a company to have a high probability of outperformance, its margins at the end of the period had to be no more than 2 percent below those at the beginning.

Segment 1 companies delivered high revenue growth throughout the period while maintaining stable profit margins. They included Johnson & Johnson, Merck, Wal-Mart, Altria, Target, Pfizer, and Abbott Laboratories. Every company in this segment outperformed the market average across the period. High and steady revenue growth, for longer than the market expected, led to these outsize returns.

The median company in this segment generated compound annual revenue growth of 9.7 percent, well above nominal GDP. Several outliers, including

A2.1 Segmentation by value creation pattern

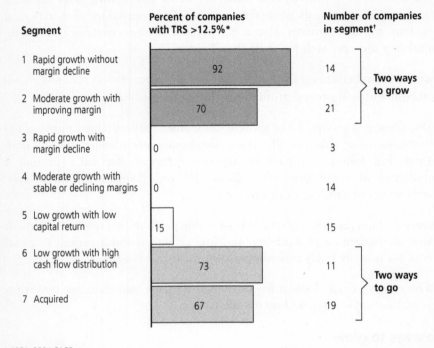

Segment	Percent of companies with TRS >12.5%*	Number of companies in segment†	
1 Rapid growth without margin decline	92	14	} Two ways to grow
2 Moderate growth with improving margin	70	21	
3 Rapid growth with margin decline	0	3	
4 Moderate growth with stable or declining margins	0	14	
5 Low growth with low capital return	15	15	
6 Low growth with high cash flow distribution	73	11	} Two ways to go
7 Acquired	67	19	

* 1984–2004 CAGR
† Total sample comprises top 100 US companies as of end 1984 that survived to 1994 (i.e., minus 3 bankruptcies). To obtain this list, we merged the top 70 survivors based on revenues and the top 70 based on market capitalization. From this list, 5 companies were excluded because data was insufficient

Wal-Mart and Intel, grew considerably faster but still maintained the integrity of their economic performance. Operating margins remained steady for all the companies in this segment; none saw their NOPLAT decline by more than 2 percent. Many of them, including Wal-Mart, Target, and several pharmaceutical companies, were driving core businesses in expansionary phases.

One example was Altria Group, which began the period as Philip Morris. Altria drove compound annual growth in revenues of 10 percent a year over the period, while delivering TRS of 20 percent. It achieved this in the face of a core business—tobacco—that was growing far more slowly. As well as expanding its tobacco business internationally and through acquisitions, the company also diversified into food through M&A, paying $5.6 billion for General Foods in 1985, $12.9 billion for Kraft in 1988, and $18.9 billion for

Nabisco Holdings in 2000. These purchases built Altria a major second business that by 2005 represented 35 percent of its total net revenues.

For a company in a sector disposed to slow growth, the best hope may be to acquire and diversify, but without ever letting up on operational efficiency in the core business.

Achieve moderate growth and improve margin

For a large company to sustain 8.5 percent growth over 20 years is no mean feat. What if your business simply isn't up to it? Our second segment comprised moderate growers. Again, our segmentation algorithm chose the performance thresholds and the individual companies. The growth threshold was set between inflation (which averaged 3.0 percent a year over the twenty-year period)[3] and 8.5 percent.

Notably, all the companies in this segment improved their margins by more than 1.2 percent during the period. The median company achieved revenue growth of 5.9 percent, close to GDP, and showed margin improvement of 4.4 percent during the period. Companies in this segment included Southern Company, Weyerhaeuser, Ford, Dow, Norfolk Southern, 3M, and Caterpillar.

Leading within this segment in terms of margin improvement are such household names as Coca-Cola (from a NOPLAT margin of 8 percent in 1982–84 to 21 percent in 2002–04), PepsiCo (from 5 to 14 percent), and Bristol-Myers Squibb (from 10 to 18 percent). Coke and PepsiCo steadily improved the margins of their core products, in part by selling their bottling businesses.

Caterpillar is the only restructuring case in this segment. In the early 1980s, its NOPLAT margin was running at –3 percent. The worldwide recession cost the company the equivalent of $1 million a day, forcing it to reduce employment dramatically. It has recovered to a NOPLAT margin of 7 percent today. More recently, Caterpillar's story has been one of stunning growth. The company has almost doubled in size over the past three years by profiting from a stronger global economy. It was and is well placed to benefit from rising commodity prices as well as increases in global investment in natural-resource development and global infrastructure.[4]

The moderate-growth segment sheds some light on the question, "How much growth is enough to drive value?" If operating performance can be strengthened significantly, then growth that exceeds the inflation rate is a good bet for above-average value creation.

Two ways to go
In Figure A2.1, segments 6 and 7 illustrate the ways to go.

Grow slowly and dispose of capital
Segment 6 comprises companies that managed to outperform in value creation for twenty years without any real growth in revenue. To do this, they took a different path: massive distribution of cash to shareholders. Sears, DuPont, ITT, Rockwell Automation, and Fortune Brands all followed this route.

Though these companies grew at a rate below inflation, they delivered value to their shareholders through a combination of dividends, share buybacks, and divestments. To put this in perspective, the average company in the segment returned capital at *twelve times* the rate of the overall sample.

Though they began the period with market capitalizations similar to those of the overall sample, their market caps grew much more slowly, at one-fifth the rate of the other companies. This was because these companies were literally "giving it back": the threshold level was capital disposal greater than *six and a half times* the 1984 market cap! Further analysis revealed that most of their outperformance appeared to result from buybacks.

Buybacks are popular: by reducing the number of shares outstanding, they boost earnings per share, thus delivering value to shareholders.[5] Moreover, the ompanies in this segment were all active asset traders and divestors, resulting in high capital payout but only a limited increase in market cap or enterprise value.

Exit by being acquired
Segment 7 comprises the companies in our sample that no longer exist as independent entities, having been acquired. These companies were as likely to outperform as the moderate growers (segment 2). They act as a reminder that selling can be a viable path to value creation for some companies.

In the Introduction, we described sustained performance as a "grow or go" imperative. Selling is one way to go; slow revenue growth with high capital disposal is another. For a company with a mature business that generates significant cash flow, either option could create value for shareholders.

No middle way

What about the three segments that underperformed? The segments that lagged the market index mirrored those that outperformed it on the growth dimension, but fell short in operating performance (or, in the case of segment 5, free cash distribution).

Segment 3 combined rapid growth of more than 8.5 percent CAGR with margin decline of more than 2.0 percent.

Segment 4 combined moderate growth (between the inflation rate and 8.5 percent) with stable or declining margins (less than 1.2 percent decline).

Segment 5 combined growth below the inflation rate with free cash distribution of less than 6.5 times the company's initial market capitalization.

By definition, the companies in these segments had a low probability of creating value above the market benchmark. The lesson we can take from this analysis—one that reinforces the value-generation analysis in Appendix 1—is that the stock market doesn't value revenue growth when it is accompanied by deteriorating economics in a company's business model.

Implications for management

You might want to ask whether these patterns depended on the strategies adopted by the companies. For example, were the companies that achieved growth through consolidation less likely to generate value than those that grew organically? Our analysis found no such correlation; the amount of acquisition activity was immaterial. Broadly, the analysis described in this appendix suggests two implications for management teams:

First, the quality of your growth path matters, and so does the underlying health of your business. Though we insist that top-line growth is important, we don't argue that companies should favor growth over profitability. In fact, the key differentiator between segments 1 and 2 on the one hand and segments 3 and 4 on the other has to do with how margins develop over time, not their differing growth rates.

Second, creating value through growth requires commensurate performance on profit. Sustained revenue growth accompanied by relatively stable or increasing margins is highly likely to outperform the market at delivering value; sustained revenue growth accompanied by declining profitability is highly likely to underperform it. But the lower your growth rate, the higher the bar on strengthening operating performance and free cash delivery in order to create real value.

■ ■ ■

The value segments show that outperformance is highly likely when companies follow either a successful "growth" path (defined as either rapid growth with stable margins or moderate growth with improving margins), or a successful "go" path (defined as either low growth coupled with significant return of cash or the outright sale of the company). Middle paths—low growth with low performance, for example—are highly unlikely to outperform. Of course, these are long-term trajectories, but then growth strategy is a long-term consideration. By identifying what it took to succeed in the past, the value segments offer useful pointers as to how companies might plan to succeed in the future.

NOTES

1   As with the first "grow or go" analysis, this analysis reflects what companies *actually achieved*, and not what they might have set out to do.

2   ROIC did not turn out to be a significant factor, perhaps because most changes in ROIC are already reflected in changes in NOPLAT margin and revenue.

3   Inflation declined from 4.4 percent in 1984 to 2.7 percent in 2004.

4   I. Brat and B. Gruley, "Global trade galvanizes Caterpillar: Maker of heavy equipment thrives under CEO Owens," *Wall Street Journal*, 26 February 2007.

5   Many academic studies have examined how share buybacks create value. See, for instance, M. Goddard, "Share buybacks," *Financial Management*, October 2005, volume 24, number 2.

Bibliography

C. Anderson, *The Long Tail: How endless choice is creating unlimited demand* (Random House, London, 2006)

J. C. Anderson and J. A. Narus, "Capturing the value of supplementary services," *Harvard Business Review on Strategies for Growth* (Harvard Business School Press, Boston, Mass., 1995), pp. 75–83

P. L. Anslinger and T. E. Copeland, "Growth through acquisitions: A fresh look," *Harvard Business Review,* January–February 1996, pp. 126–35

S. D. Anthony and C. M. Christensen, "Forging innovation from disruption," *Optimize Magazine,* August 2004, pp. 53–7

S. D. Anthony and C. M. Christensen, "How you can benefit by predicting change," *Financial Executive,* 2005, volume 21, number 2, pp. 36–41

R. N. Ashkenas, L. J. Demonaco, and S. C. Francis, "Making the deal real," *Harvard Business Review on Strategies for Growth* (Harvard Business School Press, Boston, Mass., 1998), pp. 165–78

J. E. Ashton, F. X. Cook, and P. Schmitz, "Uncovering hidden value in a midsize manufacturing company," *Harvard Business Review,* 2003, volume 81, number 6, pp. 11–19

M. A. Baghai, S. C. Coley, R. H. Farmer, and H. Sarrazin, "The growth philosophy of Bombardier," *The McKinsey Quarterly,* 1997, number 2, pp. 4–29

M. A. Baghai, S. C. Coley, and D. White, *The Alchemy of Growth* (Orion Business, London, 1999)

M. A. Baghai, S. C. Coley, and D. White, "Staircases to growth," *The McKinsey Quarterly,* 1996, number 4, pp. 38–61

M. A. Baghai, S. C. Coley, and D. White, "Turning capabilities to advantages," *The McKinsey Quarterly,* 1999, number 1, pp. 100–109

M. A. Baghai, S. Smit, and S. P. Viguerie, "The granularity of growth," *The McKinsey Quarterly,* 2007, number 2, pp. 41–51

J. Bain, *Barriers to New Competition* (Harvard University Press, Cambridge, Mass., 1956)

J. Baptista,"Viewpoint: Growing to greatness," *International Journal of Retail & Distribution Management,* 1996, volume 24, number 10, p. II

E. Bär, K. T. Chye, C. Clarke, N. D'Aquino, J. Haritz, B. Harrison, A. Livis, D. Rams, T. Shin, D. Tunnel, and A. Vizjak, *Sustaining Corporate Growth* (St Lucie Press, Boca Raton, Florida, 2000)

D. Bardolet, D. Lovallo, and R. Rumelt, "The hand of management: Differences in capital investment behavior between multi-business and single-business firms," UCLA working paper, 2006

M. H. Bazerman and D. Chugh, "Decisions without blinders," *Harvard Business Review,* January 2006, pp. 88–97

Eric Beinhocker, *The Origin of Wealth: Evolution, complexity, and the radical remaking of economics* (Harvard Business School Press, Boston, Mass., 2006)

W. Bennis, *Managing the Dream: Reflections on leadership and change* (Perseus Publishing, Cambridge, Mass., 2000)

D. Berry, "Strategic processes for organic growth: What we need versus what we've got," *Strategy & Leadership,* 1996, volume 24, number 5, p. 42

A. Bhide, "How entrepreneurs craft strategies that work," *Harvard Business Review,* March–April 1994, pp. 150–61

A. Bhide, "The questions every entrepreneur must answer," *Harvard Business Review,* November–December 1996, pp. 120–30

R. E. S. Boulton, B. D. Libert, and S. M. Samek, *Cracking the Value Code: How successful businesses are creating wealth in the new economy* (HarperBusiness, New York, 2000)

M. Bower, *The Will to Lead: Running a business with a network of leaders* (Harvard Business School Press, Boston, Mass., 1997)

M. Bower, *The Will to Manage: Corporate success through programmed management* (McGraw-Hill, New York, 1966)

O. Brafman and R. A. Beckstrom, *The Starfish and the Spider: The unstoppable power of leaderless organizations* (Portfolio, New York, 2006)

J. P. Brandimarte, W. C. Fallon, and R. S. McNish, "Trading the corporate portfolio," *McKinsey on Finance,* autumn 2001, number 2, pp. 1–5

I. Brat and B. Gruley, "Global trade galvanizes Caterpillar: Maker of heavy equipment thrives under CEO Owens," *Wall Street Journal,* 26 February 2007

A. Campbell and M. Alexander, "What's wrong with strategy?" *Harvard Business Review,* November–December 1997, pp. 42–51

A. Campbell and R. Park, "Stop kissing frogs," *Harvard Business Review,* July–August 2004, pp. 27–8

J. Canals, "How to think about corporate growth," *European Management Journal,* 2001, volume 19, number 6, pp. 587–98

J. Canals, *Managing Corporate Growth* (Oxford University Press, Oxford, 2000)

S. Carl and V. Hal, *Information Rules: A strategic guide to the network economy* (Harvard Business School Press, Boston, Mass., 1999)

R. E. Caves, "Industrial organizations and new findings on the turnover and mobility of firms," *Journal of Economic Literature,* 1998, volume 36, number 4, pp. 1947–82

R. Charan, "Profitable growth," *Executive Excellence,* volume 21, number 3, p. 15

R. Charan, *Profitable Growth is Everyone's Business: 10 tools you can use Monday morning* (Crown Business, New York, 2004)

R. Charan, S. Drotter, and J. Noel, *The Leadership Pipeline: How to build the leadership-powered company* (Jossey-Bass, San Francisco, California, 2001)

H. Chesbrough, *Open Innovation: The new imperative for creating and profiting from technology* (Harvard Business School Press, Boston, Mass., 2003)

H. W. Chesbrough and D. J. Teece, "When is virtual virtuous? Organizing for innovation," *Harvard Business Review,* January–February 1996, pp. 65–73

C. M. Christensen, *The Innovator's Dilemma: When new technologies cause great firms to fail* (Harvard Business School Press, Boston, Mass., 1997)

C. M. Christensen and S. D. Anthony, "Building your internal growth engine," *Strategy & Innovation,* 2005, volume 3, number 1, pp. 2–15

C. M. Christensen and S. D. Anthony, "New avenues to growth," *Strategy & Innovation,* 2004, volume 2, number 6, pp. 1–5

C. M. Christensen, M. Johnson, and J. Dann, "Disrupt and prosper," *Optimize,* November 2002, pp. 41–8

C. M. Christensen, M. Marx, and H. H. Stevenson, "The tools of cooperation and change," *Harvard Business Review,* October 2006, pp. 73–80

C. M. Christensen and M. E. Raynor, *The Innovator's Solution: Creating and sustaining successful growth* (Harvard Business School Press, Boston, Mass., 2003)

C. M. Christensen, M. E. Raynor, and S. D. Anthony, "Six keys to creating new growth businesses," *Harvard Management Update,* January 2003, pp. 1–6

J. C. Collins, *Good to Great: Why some companies make the leap and others don't* (HarperCollins, New York, 2001)

J. C. Collins and J. I. Porras, *Built to Last: Successful habits of visionary companies* (Century, London, 1994)

D. Collis, "Corporate advantage: Identifying and exploiting resources," Harvard Business School, Notes 6/10/91, pp. 1–12

D. J. Collis and C. A. Montgomery, "Competing on resources: Strategy in the 1990s," *Harvard Business Review,* July–August 1995, pp. 118–28

A. Corbett, H. L. Simon, and G. Williams, "Has your company sprung a revenue leak?" *Harvard Management Update,* 2005, volume 10, number 6, pp. 3–4

K. Coyne, S. Hall, and P. Clifford, "Is your core competence a mirage?" *The McKinsey Quarterly,* 1997, number 1, pp. 40–54

F. Crawford and R. Mathews, *The Myth of Excellence: Why great companies never try to be the best at everything* (Crown Business, New York, 2001)

T. H. Davenport, "Competing on analytics," *Harvard Business Review,* January 2006, pp. 99–107

G. S. Day, "Which way should you grow?" *Harvard Business Review,* 2004, volume 82, number 7/8, pp. 24–6

A. De Geus, *The Living Company: Growth, learning and longevity in business* (Nicholas Brealey, London, 1997)

M. Dell and C. Fredman, *Direct from Dell: Strategies that revolutionized an industry* (HarperCollins, New York, 1999)

M. De Pree, *Leadership is an Art* (Dell, New York, 1989)

P. F. Drucker, *The Frontiers of Management: Where tomorrow's decisions are being shaped today* (Perennial Library, New York, 1986)

R. S. Edwards and H. Townsend, *Business Enterprise: Its growth and organisation* (Macmillan, London, 1965), pp. 32–62

K. M. Eisenhardt and S. L. Brown, *Competing on the Edge: Strategy as structured chaos* (Harvard Business School Press, Boston, Mass., 1998)

K. M. Eisenhardt and S. L. Brown, "Time pacing: Competing in markets that won't stand still," *Harvard Business Review*, March 1998, pp. 59–71

T. C. Fishman, *China Inc.: How the rise of the next superpower challenges America and the world* (Scribner, New York, 2005)

T. C. Fishman, "The Wal-Mart Effect: How the world's most powerful company really works—and how it's transforming the American economy" (Penguin, New York, 2006)

R. Foster, *Innovation: The attacker's advantage* (Summit Books, New York, 1986)

R. Foster and S. Kaplan, "Creative destruction," *The McKinsey Quarterly*, 2001, number 3, pp. 40–51

R. Foster and S. Kaplan, *Creative Destruction: Why companies that are built to last underperform the market—and how to successfully transform them* (Currency, New York, 2001)

R. Frank, D. Gertz, and J. Porter, "Leadership for growth," *Strategy & Leadership*, 1996, volume 24, number 5, pp. 6–11

J. R. Galbraith, *Designing Organizations: An executive guide to strategy, structure, and process* (Jossey-Bass, San Francisco, California, 2002)

R. P. Gandossy and M. Treacy, "Do you have the disciplines to grow?" *Chief Executive*, 2004, issue 202, pp. 22–3

D. A. Garvin, "What every CEO should know about creating new businesses," *Harvard Business Review*, July–August 2004

P. A. Geroski and S. Machin, "The dynamics of corporate growth," Working Paper, London Business School, 1992

L. V. Gerstner, Jr., *Who Says Elephants Can't Dance? Inside IBM's historic turnaround* (HarperBusiness, Sydney, 2002)

D. Gertz, "The dynamics of corporate growth," *Management Review*, 1995, volume 84, number 1, pp. 46–8

D. Gertz and J. Baptista, *Grow to be Great: Breaking the downsizing cycle* (The Free Press, New York, 1995)

P. Ghemawat, *Commitment: The dynamics of strategy* (Free Press, New York, 1991)

P. Ghemawat, "The growth boosters," *Harvard Business Review*, July 2004, pp. 35–40

S. Ghosal and C. A. Bartlett, *The Individualized Corporation: A fundamentally new approach to management* (HarperBusiness, New York, 1997)

S. Ghoshal, M. Hahn, and P. Moran, "Management competence, firm growth and economic progress," *Contributions to Political Economy*, 1999, volume 18, number 1, p. 121

S. Ghosal and H. Mintzberg, "Diversification and diversifact," *California Management Review*, fall 1994, volume 37, number 1, pp. 8–27

M. Gladwell, *The Tipping Point: How little things can make a big difference* (Abacus, London, 2001)

M. Goddard, "Share buybacks," *Financial Management,* October 2005, volume 24, number 2

A. Gore, *The Assault on Reason* (Penguin, New York, 2007)

R. M. Grant, "The resource-based theory of competitive advantage: Implications for strategy formulations," *California Management Review,* spring 1991, volume 33, number 3, pp. 114–34

A. S. Grove, *Only the Paranoid Survive: How to exploit the crisis points that challenge every company* (HarperCollins, New York, 1997)

G. Hamel, "Innovation now! (It's the only way to win today)," *Fast Company,* December 2002, pp. 114–23

G. Hamel, *Leading the revolution* (Plume, New York, 2002)

G. Hamel and G. Getz, "Funding growth in an age of austerity," *Harvard Business Review,* 2004, volume 82, number 7/8, pp. 76–84

G. Hamel and R. B. Lieber, "Killer strategies that make shareholders rich," *Fortune,* 23 June 1997

G. Hamel and C. K. Prahalad, *Competing for the Future: Breakthrough strategies for seizing control of your industry and creating the markets of tomorrow* (Harvard Business School Press, Boston, Mass., 1994)

G. Hamel and C. K. Prahalad, "Core competence of the corporation," *Harvard Business Review,* May–June 1990, pp. 79–91

G. Hamel and C. K. Prahalad, "Strategy as stretch and leverage," *Harvard Business Review,* March–April 1993, pp. 75–84

G. Hamel and P. Sarzynski, "Innovation: The new route to wealth," *Journal of Accountancy,* 2001, volume 192, number 5, pp. 65–8

M. Hammer, "Deep change: How operational innovation can transform your company," *Harvard Business Review,* 2004, volume 82, number 4, pp. 84–93

M. Hammer, "The superefficient company," *Harvard Business Review,* 2001, volume 79, number 8, pp. 82–9

J. S. Hammond, R. L. Keeney, and H. Raiffa, "The hidden traps in decision making," *Harvard Business Review,* January 2006, pp. 118–26

N. W. C. Harper and S. P. Viguerie, "Are you too focused?" *The McKinsey Quarterly,* August 2002, special edition, *Risk and Resilience,* pp. 29–37

J. Harrison, "Mixing M&A and R&D for the best results," *Mergers and Acquisitions,* 2005, volume 40, number 10, p. 24

P. Hemp, "A time for growth: An interview with Amgen CEO Kevin Sharer," *Harvard Business Review,* July–August 2004, p. 73

F. Hesselbein, M. Goldsmith, and R. Beckhard (eds.), *The Organization of the Future* (Jossey-Bass, San Francisco, California, 1997)

F. G. Hilmer and L. Donaldson, *Management Redeemed: Debunking the fads that undermine corporate performance* (Free Press, New York 1996)

A. O. Hirschman, *Exit, Voice, and Loyalty: Responses to decline in firms, organizations, and states* (Harvard University Press, Cambridge, Mass., 1970)

J. Horn, D. Lovallo, P. Viguerie, "Beating the odds in market entry," *The McKinsey Quarterly,* 2005, number 4, pp. 34–5

J. Horn, D. Lovallo, P. Viguerie, "Learning to let go," *The McKinsey Quarterly,* 2006, number 2, pp. 2–8

R. A. Howell, "Turn your budgeting process upside down," *Harvard Business Review,* 2004, volume 82, number 7/8, pp. 21–2

P. Hsieh, T. Koller, and S. R. Rajan, "The misguided practice of earnings guidance," *McKinsey on Finance,* 2006, pp. 1–5

L. Huston and N. Sakkab, "Connect and Develop: Inside Procter & Gamble's new model for innovation," *Harvard Business Review,* March 2006, pp. 58–66

W. I. Huyett and S. P. Viguerie, "Extreme competition," *The McKinsey Quarterly,* 2005, number 1, pp. 47–57

K. Inamori, *A Passion for Success: Practical, inspirational, and spiritual insights from Japan's leading entrepreneur* (McGraw-Hill, New York, 1995)

E. Jaques, *Requisite Organization: The CEO's guide to creative structure and leadership* (Cason Hall, Arlington, Virginia, 1989)

M. Jenkins and D. Meer, "Organic growth: Profiting from the union of finance and marketing," *Financial Executive,* 2002, volume 1, number 8, pp. 39–44

R. M. Kanter, "Innovation: The classic traps," *Harvard Business Review,* November 2006, pp. 73–83

R. S. Kaplan and D. P. Norton, *Alignment: Using the balanced scorecard to create corporate synergies* (Harvard Business School Press, Boston, Mass., 2006)

R. S. Kaplan and D. P. Norton, *The Balanced Scorecard* (Harvard Business School Press, Boston, Mass., 1996)

J. Katzenbach, *Teams at the Top: Unleashing the potential of both teams and individual leaders* (Harvard Business School Press, Boston, Mass., 1997)

J. Katzenbach et al., *Real Change Leaders: How you can create growth and high performance at your company* (Times Business, New York, 1995)

J. Kay, *Foundations of Corporate Success: How business strategies add value* (Oxford University Press, Oxford, 1993)

C. W. Kim and R. Mauborgne, *Blue Ocean Strategy* (Harvard Business School Press, Boston, Mass., 2005)

C. W. Kim and R. Mauborgne, "Value innovation, the strategic logic of high growth," *Harvard Business Review on Strategies for Growth,* (Harvard Business School Press, Boston, Mass., 1997), pp. 25–53

T. Koller, M. Goedhart, and D. Wessels, *Valuation: Measuring and managing the value of companies* (Wiley, New York, 2005)

P. Kontes, "A new look for the corporate center: Reorganizing to maximize value," *Journal of Business Strategy,* 2004, volume 25, number 4, pp. 18–24

R. Leifer, C. M. McDermott, G. Colarelli O'Connor, L. S. Peters, M. Rice, and R. W. Veryzer, *Radical Innovation* (Harvard Business School Press, Boston, Mass., 2000)

S. D. Levitt and S. J. Dubner, *Freakonomics: A rogue economist explores the hidden side of everything* (Allen Lane, London, 2005)

T. Levitt, *Marketing for Business Growth* (McGraw-Hill, New York, 1974)

T. Levitt, "Marketing myopia," *Harvard Business Review,* July–August 1960, pp. 45–60

R. L. Lippert, D. M. Scheiger, and A. I. Scheiger, "Strategic growth initiatives: Taking a fresh look," *Business and Economic Review,* 2005, volume 51, number 4, pp. 13–17

J. Mackey and L. Välikangas, "The myth of unbounded growth," *MIT Sloan Management Review,* 2004, volume 45, number 2, pp. 89–92

I. C. MacMillan and R. G. McGrath, *MarketBusters: 40 strategic moves that drive exceptional business growth* (Harvard Business School Press, Boston, Mass., 2005)

I. C. MacMillan and R. G. McGrath, "MarketBusting: Strategies for exceptional business growth," *Harvard Business Review,* March 2005, pp. 81–9

C. Markides, "To diversify or not to diversify," *Harvard Business Review on Strategies for Growth* (Harvard Business School Press, Boston, Mass., 1997), pp. 79–97

N. J. Mass, "The relative value of growth," *Harvard Business Review,* 2005, volume 83, number 4, pp. 102–12

A. McGahan, *How industries evolve: Principles for achieving and sustaining superior performance* (Harvard Business School Press, Boston, Mass., 2004)

A. McGahan and M. E. Porter, "How much does industry matter, really?" *Strategic Management Journal,* 1997, volume 18, pp. 15–30

D. Meer, "Enter the 'Chief Growth Officer': Searching for organic growth," *Journal of Business Strategy,* 2005, volume 26, number 1, pp. 13–17

M. S. Mentzer, "The innovator's solution: Creating and sustaining successful growth," *Academy of Management Executive,* 2004, volume 18, number 1, pp. 132–3

H. Mintzberg, *The Rise and Fall of Strategic Planning: Reconceiving roles for planning, plans, planners* (Free Press, New York, 1994)

C. A. Montgomery (ed.), *Resource-Based and Evolutionary Theories of the Firm: Towards a synthesis* (Kluwer, Norwell, Mass., 1995)

G. A. Moore, "Darwin and the demon: Innovating within established enterprises," *Harvard Business Review,* July–August 2004, pp. 86–92

G. A. Moore, "To succeed in the long term, focus on the middle term," *Harvard Business Review,* July–August 2007, pp. 84–90

J. F. Moore, *The Death of Competition: Leadership and strategy in the age of business ecosystems* (HarperBusiness, New York, 1996)

I. Morrison, *The Second Curve: Managing the velocity of change* (Ballantine Books, New York, 1996)

C. G. Mortimer, *The Purposeful Pursuit of Profits and Growth in Business* (McGraw-Hill, New York, 1965)

M. Olson, *The Logic of Collective Action: Public goods and the theory of groups* (Harvard University Press, Cambridge, Mass., 1965)

R. N. Palter and D. Srinivasan, "Habits of the busiest acquirers," *The McKinsey Quarterly,* 2006, number 4, pp. 19–27

M. A. Peteraf, "The cornerstones of competitive advantage: A resource-based view," *Strategic Management Journal,* March 1993, number 14, pp. 179–91

T. J. Peters and R. H. Waterman, Jr., *In Search of Excellence: Lessons from America's best-run companies* (HarperCollins, Sydney, 1994)

E. Philip and S. W. Thomas, *Blown to Bits: How the new economics of information transforms strategy* (Harvard Business School Press, Boston, Mass., 1999)

C. Pitelis, *The Growth of the Firm: The legacy of Edith Penrose* (Oxford University Press, New York, 2002)

M. Porter, *Competitive Strategy: Techniques for analyzing industries and competitors* (Free Press, New York, 1980)

M. Porter, "What is strategy?" *Harvard Business Review*, November–December 1996, pp. 61–78

E. J. Poza, *Smart Growth: Critical choices for business continuity and prosperity* (Jossey-Bass, San Francisco, California, 1989)

C. Prestowitz, *Three Billion New Capitalists: The great shift of wealth and power to the east* (Basic Books, New York, 2005)

E. T. Prince, *The Three Financial Styles of Very Successful Leaders: Strategic approaches to identifying the growth drivers of every company* (McGraw-Hill, New York 2005)

F. F. Reichheld, "The one number you need to grow," *Harvard Business Review*, 2003, volume 81, number 12, pp. 46–54

J. Ridderstrale and K.A. Nordstrom, *Karaoke Capitalism: Daring to be different in a copycat world* (Praeger, Stockholm, 2005)

G. Rita and I. MacMillan, *Entrepreneurial Mindset: Strategies for continuously creating opportunity in an age of uncertainty* (Harvard Business School Press, Boston, Mass., 2000)

J. Roberts, *The Modern Firm: Organizational design for performance and growth* (Oxford University Press, New York, 2004)

P. Rogers and M. Blenko, "Who has the D? How clear decision roles enhance organizational performance," *Harvard Business Review*, January 2006, pp. 53–61

G. Rommel et al., *Simplicity Wins: How Germany's mid-sized industrial companies succeed* (Harvard Business School Press, Boston, Mass., 1995)

P. Rosenzweig, *The Halo Effect: . . . And the eight other business delusions that deceive managers* (Free Press, New York, 2007)

C. Roxburgh, "Hidden flaws in strategy," *The McKinsey Quarterly*, 2003, number 2, pp. 26–39

R. P. Rumelt, "How much does industry matter?" *Strategic Management Journal*, 1991, volume 12, pp. 167–85

R. P. Rumelt, D. E. Schendel, and D. J. Teece (eds.), *Fundamental Issues in Strategy: A research agenda* (Harvard Business School Press, Boston, Mass., 1994)

T. C. Schelling, *Micromotives and Macrobehavior* (W. W. Norton, New York, 1978)

R. Schmalensee, "Do markets differ much?" *American Economic Review*, 1985, volume 75, number 3, pp. 341–51

R. Schoenberg, "An integrated approach to strategy innovation," *European Business Journal*, 2003, volume 15, number 3, pp. 99–103

H. Schultz and D. J. Yang, *Pour Your Heart into It: How Starbucks built a company one cup at a time* (Hyperion, New York, 1997)

J. Seely Brown (ed.), *Seeing Differently: Insights on innovation* (Harvard Business School Press, Boston, Mass., 1997)

A. J. Slywotsky, *Value Migration: How to think several moves ahead of the competition* (Harvard Business School Press, Boston, Mass., 1996)

A. J. Slywotsky and D. J. Morrison, *The Profit Zone: How strategic business design will lead you to tomorrow's profits* (Harvard Business School Press, Boston, Mass., 1997)

A. J. Slywotzky and R. Wise, "The growth crisis—and how to escape it," *Harvard Business Review On Point*, 2002, pp. 16–28

A. J. Slywotzky, R. Wise, and K. Weber, *How to Grow When Markets Don't* (Warner Business Books, New York, 2003)

S. Smit, C. M. Thompson, and S. P. Viguerie, "The do-or-die struggle for growth," *The McKinsey Quarterly*, 2005, number 3, pp. 35–45

G. Soros with B. Wein and K. Koenen, *Soros on Soros: Staying ahead of the curve* (Wiley, New York, 1995)

G. Stalk, Jr., P. Evans, and L. E. Schulman, "Competing on capabilities," *Harvard Business Review*, March–April 1992, pp. 57–69

G. Stalk, Jr., D. K. Pecaut, and B. Burnett, "Breaking compromises, breakaway growth," *Harvard Business Review*, September–October 1996, pp. 131–9

T. A. Stewart, "Growth as a process," *Harvard Business Review*, June 2006, pp. 60–70

J. Stuckey and D. White, "When and when not to vertically integrate," *Sloan Management Review*, spring 1993, volume 34, number 3, pp. 71–83

D. Teece and G. Pisaro, "The dynamic capabilities of firms: An introduction," *Industrial and Corporate Change*, 1994, volume 3, number 3, pp. 537–56

D. Teece, G. Pisaro, and A. Shuler, "Dynamic capabilities and strategic management," CCC Working Paper No. 94–9, University of California, Berkeley, August 1994

N. M. Tichy with E. Cohen, *The Leadership Engine: How winning companies build leaders at every level* (HarperBusiness, New York, 1997)

N. M. Tichy and S. Sherman, *Control Your Destiny or Someone Else Will* (Currency/Doubleday, New York, 1993)

M. Treacy, *Double-digit Growth: How great companies achieve it—No matter what* (Penguin, New York, 2003)

M. Treacy, "Innovation as a last resort," *Harvard Business Review*, July–August 2004, pp. 29–30

M. Treacy and J. Sims, "Take command of your growth," *Harvard Business Review*, April 2004, pp. 1–9

M. Treacy and F. Wiersma, *The Discipline of Market Leaders: Choose your customers, narrow your focus, and dominate your market* (Addison-Wesley, Reading, 1995)

M. L. Tushman and C. A. O'Reilly III, "Ambidextrous organizations: Managing evolutionary and revolutionary change," *California Management Review*, summer 1996, volume 38, number 4, pp. 8–30

F. Vermeulen, "How acquisitions can revitalize companies," *MIT Sloan Management Review*, 2005, volume 46, number 4, pp. 45–51

A. A. Vicere and R. M. Fulmer, *Leadership by Design: How benchmark companies sustain success through investment in continuous learning* (Harvard Business School Press, Boston, Mass., 1997)

E. von Hippel, *Democratizing Innovation* (MIT Press, Cambridge, Mass., 2005)

G. Von Krogh and M. A. Cusumano, "Three strategies for managing fast growth," *MIT Sloan Management Review,* 2001, volume 42, number 2, pp. 53–61

M. M. Waldrop, *Complexity: The emerging science at the edge of order and chaos* (Simon & Schuster, New York, 1992)

J. A. Weber, *Growth Opportunity Analysis* (Reston, Virginia, 1976)

B. Wernerfelt, "A resource-based view of the firm," *Strategic Management Journal,* September–October 1984, volume 5, pp. 171–80

P. Williamson and M. Hay, "Strategic staircases," *Long Range Planning,* 1991, volume 24, number 4, pp. 36–43

R. R. Wiggins and T. W. Ruefli, "Schumpeter's ghost: Is hypercompetition making the best of times shorter?" *Strategic Management Journal,* 2005, volume 26, pp. 887–911

R. R. Wiggins and T. W. Ruefli, "Sustained competitive advantage: Temporal dynamics and the incidence and persistence of superior economic performance," *Organization Science,* 2002, volume 13, number 1, pp. 81–105

Y. Wind, "Marketing as an engine of business growth: A cross-functional perspective," *Journal of Business Research,* 2005, volume 58, number 7, pp. 863–73

J. P. Womack, D. T. Jones, and D. Roos, *The Machine That Changed the World: The story of lean production* (Rawson Associates, New York, 1990)

C. Zook, *Beyond the Core: Expand your market without abandoning your roots* (Harvard Business School Press, Boston, Mass., 2004)

C. Zook, *Unstoppable: Finding hidden assets to renew the core and fuel profitable growth* (Harvard Business School Press, Boston, Mass., 2007)

C. Zook and J. Allen, "Growth outside the core," *Harvard Business Review,* 2003, volume 81, number 12, pp. 66–73

C. Zook and J. Allen, *Profit from the Core: Growth strategy in an era of turbulences* (Harvard Business School Press, Boston, Mass., 2001)